IMPERIAL CRUSADES
Iraq, Afghanistan and Yugoslavia

IMPERIAL CRUSADES
Iraq, Afghanistan and Yugoslavia

---◆---

A Diary of Three Wars

by ALEXANDER COCKBURN
and JEFFREY ST. CLAIR,
the editors of *CounterPunch*

VERSO

London • New York

First published by Verso 2004

1 3 5 7 9 10 8 6 4 2

Verso
UK: 6 Meard Street, London W1F 0EG
USA: 180 Varick Street, New York, NY 10014-4606
www.versobooks.com

Verso is the imprint of New Left Books

ISBN 1-84467-506-8

British Library Cataloguing in Publication Data
Imperial crusades: Iraq, Afghanistan and Yugoslavia: a diary of three wars
1. Iraq War, 2003 2. Yugoslav War, 1991–1995 3. Afghanistan –
History – 2001– 4. United States – Politics and government – 2001–
I. CounterPunch
973.9'31
ISBN 1844675068

Library of Congress Cataloging-in-Publication Data
Cockburn, Alexander
St. Clair, Jeffrey
  Imperial Crusades: Iraq, Afghanistan and Yugoslavia: a diary of three wars/
  edited by Alexander Cockburn & Jeffrey St. Clair
    p.cm
  Includes index
  ISBN 1844675068
  1. Iraq War, 2003 2. Yugoslav War, 1991–1995 3. Afghanistan –
  History – 2001 4. United States – Politics and government – 1993–2001
  5. United States – Politics and government – 2001–
  DS79.76.146 2004-03-16
  973.931 22

Typeset in Bembo
Printed in the USA by R. R. Donnelley & Sons

CONTENTS

PART ONE

THE LAPTOP BOMBARDIERS AND THE YUGOSLAV CAMPAIGN

March 6, 1999

THE LAPTOP BOMBARDIERS
by Alexander Cockburn

Strange are the ways of men! It feels like only yesterday that the *New York Times* was denouncing President Bill as a moral midget, deserving of the harshest reprobation for fondling Monica Lewinsky's breasts. And today here's the *New York Times* doling out measured praise to the same president for blowing little children to pieces. The *Times* last Thursday had pictures of those dead refugees on its cover, bombed by one of NATO's aviators. Editorial page editor Howell Raines staked out the *Times* official view that 'For now, NATO must sustain and intensify the bombing.' What a weird guy Raines must be. Kiss Monica's tits and he goes crazy. Bomb peasants and he shouts for more.

Maybe some corner of Clinton's brain reckons that bombs on Serbia will extinguish Monica Lewinksy from popular memory. But what man of mature judgement and compassion would not prefer to be remembered by the Starr report than by bomb craters and dead bodies? Many people thought Clinton would be the first president who would somehow prefer Starr's volume as his epitaph, however embarrassing. But no. Like all the others he wants craters and corpses as his requiem.

Being a peacenik is definitely passé. Liberals are learning once again – did they ever truly forget? – it's fun to be a warmonger and cheer the high explosive as it falls. After suffering indigestion towards the end of the Vietnam affair, they got the taste for war again in the mid-1990s, with Bosnia. They became the 'laptop bombardiers,' a phrase coined by Simon Jenkins in the *Spectator* in 1995.

Back then, there wasn't a week, for months on end, that Anthony Lewis didn't call for the bombardment of Serbia. The Serbs became demons, monsters, and Milosevic the most demonic of all. Last week I ran across an interesting piece by an Indian, Lt. General Satish Nambiar, who had been First Force Commissioner and Head of Mission of the United Nations force deployed in the former Yugoslavia from March 1992 to March 1993. He was writing in an Indian journal. 'Portraying the Serbs as evil and everybody else as good was not only counterproductive but dishonest,' the general writes. 'According to my experience all sides were guilty but only the Serbs would admit that they were no angels while the others would insist that they were.'

Nambiar says accurately that there were plenty of chances for agreement on a Bosnian settlement in the mid-1990s but the Americans always nixed them. There was the Lisbon plan and then the Vance–Owen plan, both not so different – after thousands of deaths – from the final Dayton plan. But the trouble was that the US, amid the furious screams of the liberals, refused to admit the Serbs had legitimate grievances and rights.

In Britain in 1995 there was a coalition running from Margaret Thatcher to the Labourite *New Statesman* in favor of bombing the Serbs. Ken Livingstone, the pinko firebrand of London, bellowed for bombs. So did Michael Ignatieff. In the US the laptop bombardiers crossed from the *Wall Street Journal* editorial page, which likes to bomb anything (though most of all, Little Rock), to William Safire, to Anthony Lewis, to the Democratic Socialists of America.

The worst offender was the press, which carefully ignored detailed accounts of how the Bosnian Muslims were manipulating Western opinion, most notoriously by almost certainly lobbing a missile into a marketplace filled with their own people. When the Croats ethnically cleansed the Krajina of hundreds of thousands of Serbs – the biggest such cleansing in the Balkans since World War Two – with direction from US military and CIA officers, reporters and commentators mostly looked the other way or actually cheered. 'The Serbs Asked For It,' exulted the headline on a piece in the *Los Angeles Times* by pundit William Pfaff. Monitors for the European Union prepared a report on the Croat atrocities and, though it was confidential, Robert Fisk of the London *Independent* was able to get a copy:

> Evidence of atrocities, an average of six corpses a day, continues to emerge … the corpses – some fresh, some decomposed – are mainly of old men. Many have been shot in the back of the head or had throats slit, others have been mutilated … Serbian homes and lands continue to be looted. The crimes have been perpetrated by the HV (Croatian Army), the CR (Croatian Police) and CR civilians. There have been no observed attempts to stop it and the indications point to a scorched earth policy.

If American journalists had bothered to report this, then perhaps public opinion would have been prepared for the notion that there are no innocent political players in the Balkans. The better-informed the people are, the harder it is to demagogue them with the idea that the best way forward now is – to get back to Howell Raines and that *New York Times* editorial – to 'sustain and intensify the bombing.'

But Bosnia, back in the middle 1990s, rode on a hysteria that was never properly confronted, and now the price is being paid, with contemptible opportunists like Senator John McCain shouting for 'lights out in Belgrade' (why doesn't McCain have the guts to emulate John Glenn's *temps retrouvé*, and get assigned to a bombing crew and go strafe refugees in Kosovo?). But McCain is more than matched by Democrats like Senator Carl Levin, or by that brass-lunged fraud from Vermont Bernard Sanders, 'socialist progressive,' who has endorsed Clinton's bombs.

Well over 80 per cent of the Democrats in the House are cheering the bombs, and senatorial liberals like Barbara Boxer are discovering the joys of war. 'I never believed I'd go back and vote on air strikes,' she marveled in an article in the *Boston Globe* for March 31.

These days, to get a dose of common sense you have to go over the Republican side of the aisle and listen to people like Rep. Curt Weldon of Pennsylvania, who made a fine speech in Congress on April 12, reporting on his contacts with members of the Russian Duma (where Weldon has many friends), endorsing their idea that Russia should pledge that Milosevic will abide by the Rambouillet accords on condition that an international peacekeeping force moves into Kosovo, devoid of any personnel from nations now bombing Serbia.

Follow this carefully, because the exact nature of such a force is what's causing bombs to fall on civilians in Belgrade and Kosovo. Remember that Milosevic agreed to virtually everything on the table at the Rambouillet meeting, with two exceptions. For him the status of Kosovo as part of Serbia was non-negotiable, and he wouldn't agree to the stationing of NATO forces on Yugoslav soil, which does after all include Kosovo. But it's clear enough that a solution could have been found.

It's plain too that the US and its NATO subordinates wanted a confrontation and ultimately forced it. It's also clear that increasingly vocal and explicit charges by the Russians that the Kosovo Liberation Army (KLA) was supplied by the Germans and the CIA have merit. The KLA itself was roundly denounced – before the bombings – in the London *Times* as a Maoist gang fueled by heroin-trafficking. (This is standard operating procedure for a CIA operation, as any scrutiny of recent histories of Afghanistan or Southeast Asia will attest.)

So the NATO bombs began to fall and, exactly as could have been predicted, the Serbian brutalities in Kosovo escalated and the tidal wave of refugees began. Everything has gone according to the script. NATO bombs destroying Serbian civilian infrastructure: power plants, sewage treatment, electricity, gas, oil supplies. Everything that's hit is hastily described by NATO spokesmen as 'dual-purpose' (i.e., possibly also for Serb military use) unless it's obvious to all that only peasants, with no conceivable 'dual purposes,' have been blasted to bits. Wednesday last saw the NATO supreme commander, Wesley Clark, utter his most deliberate and obvious lie to date, when he said that 'There was a military convoy and a refugee convoy. We struck the Serb convoy and we have very strong evidence that the Serbs then retaliated by attacking the column of refugees.' By the next day it became clear that there was no 'Serb convoy,' no 'very strong evidence,' and that a column of Albanian refugees on tractors had been killed by NATO bombers.

March 10, 1999

SIEG HEIL!
by Alexander Cockburn

It's bracing to see the Germans taking part in NATO's bombing. It lends moral tone to an operation to have the grandsons of the Third Reich willing, able and eager to drop high explosive again, in this instance on the Serbs. To add symmetry to the affair, the last time Serbs in Belgrade had high explosive dropped on them was in 1941 by the sons of the Third Reich. To bring even deeper symmetry, the German political party whose leader, Schroeder, ordered German participation in the bombing is that of the Social Democrats, whose great-grandfathers enthusiastically voted credits to wage war in 1914. Whether in Germany or England or France, all social democratic parties in 1914 tossed aside previous pledges against war, thus helping produce the first great bloodletting of our century. Today, with social democrats leading governments across Europe – Schroeder, Blair, Jospin, Prodi – all fall in behind Clinton. This is, largely, a war most earnestly supported by liberals and many so-called leftists. Bernie Sanders has voted Aye, and in London Vanessa Redgrave cheers on the NATO bombers.

There's been some patronizing talk here about the Serbs' deep sense of 'grievance' at the way history has treated them, with the implication that the Serbs are irrational in this regard. But it's scarcely irrational to remember that Nazi Germany bombed Belgrade in World War Two, or that Germany's prime ally in the region, Croatia, ran a concentration camp at Jasenovac where tens of thousands of Serbs – along with Jews and Gypsies – were liquidated. Nor is it irrational to recall that Germany in more recent years has been an unrelenting assailant of the former Yugoslav federation, encouraging Slovenia to secede and lending determined support to Croatia, in gratitude for which Croatia adopted, on independence in 1991, the German hymn, 'Danke Deutschland.'

So much for Serb feelings about Germany. Serbia has some reason to feel similar resentment towards the United States. The biggest single ethnic cleansing of the mid-1990s in the former Yugoslavia was conducted by Croatia under the supervision of the United States, whose military generals and CIA officers issued targeting instructions to Croatian artillery for the ethnic clearing. The targets were Serbs, living in Serbian territory, in the Krajina. Heading the Croatian cleansers was President Franjo Tudjman, who has rehabbed Nazi war criminals. Yet somehow it is Serbia's Milosevic who is demonized here as Hitler.

Now the Serbs are being asked to give the Albanians living in a southern province of Serbia – Kosovo – autonomy for three years, at the end of which time NATO would probably have issued a peremptory command for Kosovo's independence. Even so, the Serbs balked only at NATO's insistence that a Serbian province, Kosovo, should accept a Western garrison force, and this doubtless could have been negotiated peacefully, but as Mikhail Gorbachev has been saying in Europe, the US apparently wanted to rush into war, on an obviously illegal pretext. The Serbs feel as outraged as would India if the United States started bombing New Delhi, Bombay and other towns and cities until India surrendered to the Kashmiris' and Tamils' demands. You can make the same parallel about China and Tibet or Spain and the Basques, or the Turks and the Kurds, or the Israelis and the Palestinians. Would we ever bomb Istanbul or Tel Aviv? Of course not.

It's remarkable how America's gangsterism has grown more shameless even since the days of George Bush. In 1991 Bush devoted months of diplomatic effort towards getting supportive votes in the United Nations for the expedition to free Kuwait. In 1999 Bill Clinton more or less left the UN's secretary-general, Kofi Annan, to find out from CNN about NATO's decision to bomb. Appropriately enough, last week brought news that unless the United States pays some of its back dues, it won't be entitled to vote in the UN anyway. But would it bother? The US game, abetted chiefly by Blair's UK, is to make NATO the arbiter of Europe's borders and 'security.' Without doubt it's disgusting that Serb police, paramilitary and army units have been killing Albanians in Kosovo – 2,000 or so before the bombing began. It was disgusting that Russians killed Chechens, that Indonesians killed East Timorese, that US cavalry killed the Sioux, that … You get the idea.

The Hutus killed around a million Tutsis in Rwanda and Clinton didn't lift a finger. He refused to call it genocide, a significant decision since it meant UN forces weren't compelled to intervene under the Genocide Treaty. If the US decides in the waning hours of the millennium that it can bomb anyone it wants to, regardless of legality, solemn treaty and obligation, so be it. But do not pretend that cause is just or even humane.

May 4, 1999

MAY DAY MISSILES

by Alexander Cockburn and Jeffrey St. Clair

The same weekend NATO planes celebrated May Day by blowing in pieces a busload of forty-nine Serbs, men women and children, *CounterPunch* was relayed this confidential assessment from a senior member of the US military at NATO HQ in Mons, Belgium.

'The White House,' said the officer, 'is in a complete panic over this. They're desperate to get out.'

Bill Clinton knows how to read polls. All agree on that. In the last days of April he saw the trend lines pointing down. Even General Wesley Clark admitted the air war had done nothing towards its proclaimed objective: grinding down the Serb forces in Kosovo. Support for a ground war was melting away. In an amazing vote, radical Democrats lined up the Republicans and forced a 213–213 tie vote, thus withholding congressional support for the war.

Hence the back-channel overture to Milosevic via the Reverend Jesse Jackson, with a desperate appeal to the Beast of Serbia that he give Clinton cover for the big climb-down, said cover being maybe that Serbia will allow a small NATO contingent in the international force assigned to Kosovo to supervise partition, when the bombing stops. The other function of Jackson's mission was to head off any unpalatable negotiating with Milosevic by Rep. Curt Weldon, the Pennsylvania Republican, who was in Vienna after conferring in Moscow with members of the Russian Duma on terms for a deal.

The end is in sight. NATO has achieved none of its objectives. The hunt is on for a brokered solution, not too far removed from the deal that could have been struck with Milosevic before the bombing started. This does not mean the bombing will stop. The day after Milosevic released the three American POWs, NATO intensified its raids and readied B-52s for carpet bombing in a reprise of the Arclight sorties over Vietnam when hundreds of square miles of countryside were saturated with 500-lb iron bombs.

Even though NATO has destroyed a lot of Serbia, it has achieved no other objective. The White House wants out. Hence Jesse Jackson's mission to ask Milosevic to give Clinton some cover. The war emptied Kosovo of most Albanians and failed to cow the Serbs.

It is also beginning to have a seismic effect on the political landscape of Western Europe, where almost all the ruling warmongering parties are social democrats. Even here its tremors can be felt, not just in Columbine High but also in Washington DC.

Here in the US we're having to redraw the political maps. Leftist opponents of the war now march shoulder to shoulder with Chuck Colson, Barry Farber, Don Feder, Bob Grant, Bob Novak, Arianna Huffington, A. M. Rosenthal, Charles Krauthammer, Edward Luttwak, Oliver North, Joe Sobran and the Pope.

Support for a ground assault is fading. There were the dead refugees and broadcasters in Serbia. There were the killings in Columbine High, which rubbed people's noses in death in the most familiar and universal of contexts (Johnny isn't coming home from school today), and the House vote. In the Vietnam era it took years for resistance in the House even to approach that level. It's been the Progressives' War, even the First Progressives' War, if you read Tony Blair's excited communiqué in *Newsweek*. In the eyes of those waging them many a war has been progressive, in the imperial sense of imposing progress upon those in the cross-hairs. Teddy Roosevelt undoubtedly thought the wars on America's natives were progressive. If history is progress, then wars have often been fuel for the onward march. The Democrats – about 80 per cent of them in a congressional vote – have affirmed their confidence in the just cause of bombing Serbia.

The Republicans are more deeply divided, many of them saying the United States has no business fighting a war in the Balkans. This stance excites the derision of liberal Democrats. Listen to Joe Conason, writing in *Salon*: 'Action against Milosevic was necessary for reasons that go well beyond humanitarian interest in the fate of Kosovo. The Western allies needed to draw a line against a destabilizing force in Central Europe and to demonstrate to tyrants and demagogues elsewhere that their ambitions too may encounter fierce resistance.' This repellent passage offers both the human-itarian rationale and the true motives of the United States and its accomplices: to wit, that no one had better mess with Uncle Sam. The liberals are on a crusade, historically the most merciless of all forms of bellicose engagement, albeit the one most suffused with self-serving illusions. 'If there is such a thing as progressive war-making,' Conason writes, 'it must be preceded by every possible diplomatic approach to the avoidance of war. It must be accomp-anied by the informed consent of the nations whose children and resources may be lost. It must be conducted with the maximum feasible regard for sparing innocent lives.'

Let's take those Protocols of the Liberals of *Salon* in reverse order. Maximum feasible regard. We are now at the point at which Gen. Wesley Clark and his war planners are reaching the conclusion that air wars don't work. Also, their vaunted arsenal of million-dollar missiles is dwindling rapidly. The answer will be ever-increasing recourse to cluster bombs, which are cheap. Cluster bombs tend to kill civilians, not soldiers. About 25 per cent of them fail to detonate, thus littering the terrain as landmines for years to come. This is what lies in store for Kosovo and large swaths of Serbia at the progressive hands of NATO. There won't be fancy camera shots of those cluster bombs blowing up peasants and children. And the Pentagon will not, on past evidence, be helping the cluster-bomb clearing crews. Back in the Sixties the United States, with the most progressive of intentions, showered the Plain of Jars in Laos with millions of these cluster bombs and today refuses to contribute its expertise to the clearing crews. So much for maximum feasible regard.

As for the informed consent of the nations whose children and resources may be lost, those people on the streets of Belgrade are scarcely sending up cries of welcome. Perhaps the only consent of relevance here is that of the KLA, which of course requires

catastrophe sufficient to inflame Western passions. So what about
Conason's protocol of progressive warmaking, that every diplomatic
avenue has to be exhausted? Wesley Clark and Madeleine Albright,
as surrogates for Clinton, had no interest in peaceful diplomatic
resolution; otherwise, they would have parleyed further with
Milosevic on the Serbs' final offer to countenance peacekeepers in
Kosovo if the latter were under the auspices of the UN. The Serbs
would not accept NATO troops, which seems entirely reasonable.
Nor would they yield on the matter of Kosovo being part of Serbia's
sovereign territory, which is also understandable.

The Serbian military in Kosovo was certainly behaving in a
disgustingly brutal fashion. What army doesn't, when under attack
by a rebel army, this one almost certainly supplied by NATO
powers, in breach of the UN Security Council's embargo on arms
imports into the territory of the former Yugoslavia? Listen to Dr
Jan Oberg, director of the Transnational Foundation's conflict-
mitigation team to the Balkans and Georgia, who wrote in mid-
April: 'The truth is there [were] no mass killings, no systematic
ethnic cleansing, no genocide.' Oberg states readily enough that
Kosovo has been a police state. 'Many Albanians left because of the
repression but also because of the misery, the utter poverty and lack
of future opportunities for themselves and their children. Serbs, too,
left for such reasons and not – as they sometimes claim – because
they were victims of an Albanian genocide plan.' NATO's bombs
have turned the flow of refugees into a torrent. But before the
bombs came the guided missiles of the IMF, which ravaged the
Yugoslav economy throughout the Eighties.

The KLA wanted confrontation, which has been US strategy
with Serbia for close to a decade: the dismemberment of the
former Yugoslavia, the heightening of ethnic tensions, economic
siege and the supply of a client armed force (the KLA). Seen that

scenario before? In Sarajevo the Bosnian Muslims kept Western sympathies aflame with contrived incidents, culminating in the lobbing of that shell into the marketplace. The KLA and its Western advisers would not have forgotten the lesson. Milosevic is a monstrous fellow, though a midget in thuggery when his deeds are compared with the records of those now bombing his country. But Serbs, many of whom detest him and have worked for his downfall, have rallied to the national flag; and who – looking at their analysis and those of the progressive warmakers of the West – cannot but agree with them? For years they awaited invasion from the East. What a shock to get it in the neck, be reduced to rubble, by those liberals who spent so much time hailing Yugoslav exceptionalism.

May 11, 1999

YES, PEACE IS AT HAND
by Alexander Cockburn and Jeffrey St. Clair

As so often when peace is supposedly at hand, the US bombs are raining down on Serbia more heavily than ever! Shrapnel in the marketplace; high explosives on a hospital; and, for good measure, NATO bombed Chinese sovereign territory in the form of its embassy in Belgrade. On the latter blunder, NATO flacks at first tried to argue that this embassy was inconveniently located amid 'targets' in downtown Belgrade and it was all an understandable error. But the embassy's actual location was in a residential neighborhood and, as someone said, the 'mistargeting' was like aiming for Newark and hitting Queens.

Exactly as happened in the Vietnam era, the liberal hawks are doubling up the ferocity of their war bluster in step with every mile they forge farther into the quagmire. Back in 1982 when the Israelis were shelling Beirut, Tom Friedman, at that time the *New York Times* correspondent there, wrote a famous internal memo to his editors complaining that they had softened his unsparing description of the indiscriminate Israeli shelling of west Beirut. (The *Times* refused to use the word 'indiscriminate.') It was eloquent, quickly made public and, for a while, did nothing to advance Friedman's career. These days Friedman is the mad dog of the journalistic claque for war, urging that if necessary the Serbs be bombed back to the fourteenth century.

There are plenty of history's little ironies here. Tom Hayden and Jane Fonda flew out to Israel in 1982, were escorted north by Gen. Sharon to the Israeli gun batteries denounced by Friedman, and the two erstwhile protesters of the Vietnam War cheered on the Israeli assault on Arab civilians. Last week, in the May 5 *Los Angeles Times*, Hayden issued a ringing denunciation of the present NATO bombardment. The cluster bombs used by the Israelis didn't prompt his outrage seventeen years ago, but now – quite rightly – they do.

> What then of the intentional indiscriminate infliction of shrapnel wounds on children? Unexploded cluster-bomb units are turning whole areas of Yugoslavia into a 'no man's land,' wounding large numbers of children in the process. According to the *Los Angeles Times*, the director of Pristina's hospital says he has never done so many amputations as he has since victims of the weapons started coming in.
>
> I keep an early model of the cluster bombs used in Vietnam on my shelf as a reminder of the evil done in the name of good intentions. The bombs are dropped over a broad landscape, where they explode via timers or the simple vibration of a passerby. The blast causes up to

300 pieces of deadly shrapnel to scatter in all directions. The shrapnel
is very difficult to remove because of its deliberately jagged design.

The right-wing peaceniks continue to put out magnificent
specimens of antiwar prose. On May 6 Robert Novak wrote a
column essentially accusing Gen. Wesley Clark of war crimes: 'The
Pentagon has announced NATO "area bombing" with "dumb"
bombs carried by B-52s – clearly an anti-population tactic. In a
highly limited war, Clark is using the methods of total war.'

As NATO descends rapidly into straightforward terror bombing,
we cannot detect too many signs of revulsion across the country.
Amid the repulsive cheerleading for the war, on National Public
Radio I heard one morning the voice of some young woman at a
college in Pomona disparaging the notion that the bombing is
stimulated by compassion for the Albanians in Kosovo. She said she
was always cynical about such claims by her government, but added
that she was indeed in favor of the bombing. A lot of her friends,
she said, already had jobs with big companies, doing international
marketing, and she herself was planning to go into this line of
business. She seemed to think the bombing would ensure tranquil
markets in the Balkans. At least she was honest.

What will it take to stir public emotion in this virtually risk-free
war for Americans, where the verbal currency for discussing war has
become so debased that Jesse Jackson could tell three US POWs that
they were 'heroes'? Why are they heroes? Jackson supplied the answer.
They were heroes because they were known around the world.

We've seen those endlessly repeated snippets of footage of bomb
explosions lighting up the night sky over Belgrade. We've even seen
pictures of that burned train at the Grdelica gorge where fifty-five
Serb passengers were blown to bits or burned alive and another
sixteen wounded. There was the carnage amid the refugee column.

But these snapshots don't give a proper sense of what is happening to Serbia.

The Yugoslav foreign minister has been putting out a running bulletin of what has been hit. It seems pretty credible. The best way to assess the cumulative effect of the list of targets is to think of it in terms of a county or a state here. Want to go to work? Railways gone. Bridges gone. Factories destroyed or damaged. Want to take the kids to school? More than 200 schools damaged or destroyed. Want to stay warm next winter? Power plants bombed out. Got a sick grandma? No gas for the car, road cut, phones out and a good chance the hospital itself has been bombed. The day after Jackson told those three POWs released by the Serbs that they were heroes, NATO intensified its attacks, inching the body count up from the 1,000 or so dead and 4,500 seriously injured in the first month of bombing.

The Serbs say that after the demolition of the Petrovaradin bridge, water supplies to Novi Sad and Petrovaradin were cut, leaving a million people short of water. The bombing has put about 500,000 people out of work; the Serbs reckon that around 2 million citizens are therefore destitute. Think of it all in the context of where you live and, amid all the talk about putting Milosevic on trial as a war criminal, remember that under the Protocols of the Geneva Convention of 1949, if there is any likelihood that the target has a civilian function, bombing is prohibited.

Back in the years of the Vietnam War one would meet Vietnamese who would never fail to make an absolute distinction between the American government and the American people. They would stress that the American people were not responsible for their government's action. But could one ask for the indulgence of that distinction from a Serb today amid the falling bombs? After all, the Vietnamese knew there was real resistance here to the war. That distinction has to be earned.

The relentless devaluation of history continues. The hawks nesting in the editorial page bomb pod at the *Wall Street Journal* reverently quoted George Will as saying that Milosevic's depredations represent the greatest crimes against humanity since World War Two. Greater than the US's wipeout in Vietnam? Pol Pot's massacres? The US-backed Guatemalan junta's rampages that lasted twenty years? Rwanda?

May 16, 1999

'A VAIN, POMPOUS BROWN-NOSER'
by Andrew Cockburn

Anyone seeking to understand the bloody fiasco of war on the Serbs need hardly look further than the person of the beribboned Supreme Allied Commander, General Wesley K. Clark. Politicians and journalists are generally according him a respectful hearing as he discourses on the 'schedule' for the destruction of Serbia, embracing words favored by military bureaucrats such as 'systematic' and 'methodical.'

The reaction from former army subordinates is very different. 'The poster child for everything that is wrong with the GO [general officer] corps,' exclaims one colonel, who has had occasion to observe Clark in action, citing, among other examples, his command of the 1st Cavalry Division at Fort Hood from 1992 to 1994. While Clark's official Pentagon biography proclaims his triumph in 'transitioning the Division into a rapidly deployable force' this officer describes the '1st Horse Division' as 'easily the worst division I have ever seen in 25 years of doing this stuff.'

Such strong reactions are common. A major in the 3rd Brigade of the 4th Infantry Division at Fort Carson, Colorado, when Clark was in command there in the early 1980s described him as a man who 'regards each and every one of his subordinates as a potential threat to his career.' While he regards his junior officers with watchful suspicion, he customarily accords the lower ranks little more than arrogant contempt. A veteran of Clark's tenure at Fort Hood recalls the general's 'massive tantrum because the privates and sergeants and wives in the crowded [canteen] checkout lines didn't jump out of the way fast enough to let him through.'

Clark's demeanor to those above is, of course, very different, a mode of behavior that has earned him rich dividends over the years. Thus, early in 1994 he was a candidate for promotion from two- to three-star general. Only one hurdle remained – a war-game exercise known as the Battle Command Training Program in which Clark would have to maneuver his division against an opposing force. The commander of the opposing force, or 'OPFOR,' was known for the military skill with which he routinely demolished opponents.

But Clark's patrons on high were determined that no such humiliation should be visited on their favorite. Prior to the exercise, therefore, strict orders came down that the battle should go Clark's way. Accordingly, the OPFOR was reduced in strength by half, thus enabling Clark, despite deploying tactics of signal ineptitude, to triumph. His third star came down a few weeks later.

Battle exercises and war games are of course meant to test the fighting skills of commanders and troops. The army's most important venue for such training is the National Training Center at Fort Irwin, California, where Clark commanded from October 1989 to October 1991 and where his men derisively nicknamed him 'Section Leader Six' for his obsessive micro-management.

At the NTC, army units face a resident OPFOR that has, through constant battle practice coupled with innovative tactics and close knowledge of the terrain, become adept at routing the visiting 'Blue Force' opponents. For Clark, this naturally posed a problem. Not only were his men using unconventional tactics, they were also humiliating Blue Force generals who might nurture resentment against the NTC commander and thus discommode his career at some future date. To the disgust of the junior OPFOR officers Clark therefore frequently fought to lose, sending his men on suicidal attacks in order that the Blue Forces should go home happy and owing debts of gratitude to their obliging foe.

All observers agree that Clark has always displayed an obsessive concern with the perquisites and appurtenances of rank. Ever since he acceded to the NATO command post, the entourage with which he travels has accordingly grown to gargantuan proportions to the point where even civilians are beginning to comment. A Senate aide recalls his appearances to testify, prior to which aides scurry about the room adjusting lights, polishing his chair, testing the microphone etc prior to the precisely timed and choreographed moment when the Supreme Allied Commander Europe makes his entrance.

'We are state-of-the-art pomposity and arrogance up here,' remarks the aide. 'So when a witness displays those traits so egregiously that even the senators notice, you know we're in trouble.' His NATO subordinates call him, not with affection, 'the Supreme Being.' 'Clark is smart,' concludes one who has monitored his career. 'But his whole life has been spent manipulating appearances in the interests of his career. Now he is faced with a reality he can't control.'

May 19, 1999

THE WAR BEHIND THE BRIEFINGS
by Jeffrey St. Clair

Two months into the war, NATO's military high command is now settling into a routine for dealing with the collateral media damage caused by massacres of civilians by NATO bombs. The response to news that in one NATO raid on Korisa about 100 civilians had been blown apart and, in many cases, burned to a cinder as they slept provides an instructive guide to what is by now becoming a familiar routine.

First reports came complete with pictures so horrific that network news anchors in the US prefaced their coverage by warning that viewers might find the footage 'disturbing.' A Serb reporter for AFP, among the first to reach the scene, retrieved the fin of what was unquestionably an American bomb. NATO responsibility seemed clear and unquestionable. However, the Serb provenance of the reports allowed NATO authorities to swing effortlessly into a standard evasive maneuver by suggesting that the reporters were of course suspect as mere mouthpieces of Milosevic's propaganda machine. Addressing this point, John Simpson, chief foreign correspondent of the BBC, noted from Belgrade that, though tightly controlled by the Belgrade government, Serb reporters are:

> very much like Western journalists. Even under Tito, Yugoslav journalists were well-known for their relative objectivity. They will certainly report the official assessment of casualties in an attack, but, if their reporters on the scene give a different figure, they will broadcast that. And the reporters will use their own judgement. My experience

after fifty-four days of warfare here is that, when the first reports come
in that civilians have died in a NATO attack, they are almost always
correct.

Such informed caveats do not of course enter the briefings, formal
and background, of the Pentagon spinners and their counterpart in
Brussels, Jamie Shea. By the day after the Korisa killings, they had
moved to stage two of the damage control formula: the suggestion
that the true facts were unclear, along with hints that the Serbs did
it, or, as they informed the *Washington Post* for its May 16 edition,
'Serb artillery had been active in the area.'

At the NATO briefing on May 14, the day after the bombing,
spokesman Shea introduced his presentation with a large slide
projected on a screen bearing the words 'A Good Day.' Shea made
no mention of the Korisa attack in his presentation, though when
questioned, he promised 'a full investigation.' In fact, the high
command had already made its investigation. General Wesley Clark
had reportedly stayed up until 3 am on the night before Shea spoke
reviewing the pilot reports and video footage and had personally
edited the initial NATO statements.

Two days after the attack, in time for the Sunday papers, NATO
was ready to abandon the 'Serb artillery' defense and admit that they
had indeed killed the Kosovars. Now, however, the village of Korisa
had become a 'command center' and therefore a legitimate military
target. Background briefings suggested that the Serbs had hurriedly
removed signs of military activity, including an artillery bunker,
before allowing reporters on the scene.

By the beginning of the following week, NATO had settled into
the final phase of the operation: the massacres were wholly the
Serbs' fault, since the refugees had been 'herded' down from the
hills to act as 'human shields' against NATO bombs. (They would

hardly have been of much use as human shields unless, of course, NATO knew they were there and bombed anyway.)

The true facts of the matter appear to have been that the inhabitants of Korisa, some four thousand people, had fled their homes some two weeks before the bombing attack and taken to the hills. Just before the attack they returned, either at the behest of the Serb authorities, or, as one survivor told Paul Watson of the *Los Angeles Times*, because they were running out of food. The *Washington Post* did note on May 18 that 'A visit to the scene by a *Washington Post* reporter Saturday, and interviews with survivors conducted without the presence of Yugoslav authorities, provided no indication of a military presence near the field where the people were killed,' but that came in paragraph seven of a story that gave deferential weight to the bombers' view of events.

May 21, 1999

TOM FRIEDMAN: THE MADDEST DOG
by Alexander Cockburn

Liberals and social democrats who came of age politically amid protest against the war in Vietnam now talk in exactly the same phrases as did those Kennedy liberals back in the Sixties about the crusade that required planes, helicopters, Special Forces, troops, B-52 raids, the Phoenix program, My Lai and ultimately 2 million dead people.

Listen to the *New York Times*'s Thomas Friedman, the maddest dog in the war chorus:

> Only when [the Serbs] conclude that their nationalist fantasies have brought them to a very dark and lonely corner will they change. The

Balkans don't need a new Serbian leader, they need a new Serbian ethic that understands how to live in 21st-century Europe. NATO can't produce that transformation. But by intensifying the bombing and intensifying the diplomacy, it can create the conditions in which that transformation might begin. Stay the course.

And listen also to the Punch and Judy version of Friedman's ravings, coming out of the mouth of Bill Maher on *Politically Incorrect*, addressing the Serbs:

Let me be the first to say I am so sorry that supporting a genocidal regime has turned into such a hassle for you. I'm sorry if our bombing has delayed the delivery of your J. Crew catalog or screwed [laughter] screwed up your commute. And by the way, if I were you, I would write a strongly worded letter to the transit authority, because I've seen your bridges, and frankly, they're a mess. [laughter and applause] Believe me, we would never have started bombing them if we realized it was keeping you from getting to Tae-Bo class. So maybe what you yuppie fascists need to do is stop supporting an evil dictator who is hell-bent on eliminating an entire people just because their ancestors kicked your ancestors' asses 600 years ago. Let it go. You're yuppies, get some therapy. [laughter] Get your moral clock working. Let me give you a hint. If in your language you have ever used the phrase, 'Can I get to the mall if I make a left at the death camp?' [laughter] you might be a redneck.

(Maher learned later the consequences of swimming against the tide when he was swiftly fired for a minor infraction of the official propaganda line after 9/11.)

May 23, 1999

THE ANTIWAR LEFT
by Alexander Cockburn and Jeffrey St. Clair

At first the reaction of the antiwar left seemed very poor. Barely a twitch in the Bay Area in the first days of bombing, whereas at the start of the Iraq war demonstrators tied up the bridges almost at once.

But round the country there's been some spirited organizing and activity. In the Pacific Northwest, to take one region, one of our *CounterPunch* editors spoke to a lively audience at Humboldt State, all opposed to the war. *CounterPunch* readers David Messerve and Betsy Roberts contrasted the atmosphere handing out leaflets at the Arcata entry to route 101 in 1991, and today. Back then, they say, conservatives got back at the Arcata City Council (which had opposed the war) by putting up an enormous American flag next to the highway. This time Dave and Betsy saw the crusty old fellow – a local contractor – who had put up that flag and offered him a leaflet attacking the Serb bombing. He took it cordially, saying the US had no business in the Balkans. As a general rule the pacifist antiwar groups have been good and the human rights groups very bad. Amnesty International did issue a statement condemning the bombing of the TV station but conspicuously failed to denounce the bombing overall. Human Rights Watch has been bad.

May 27, 1999

EPIC POETRY
by Alexander Cockburn

In mid-May I traveled to Sacramento to give a talk at Time Tested Books, having been invited by Scott Soriano, who works at the store and who also publishes an excellent local newsletter, *Sacramento Comment*. My eye was caught by the cover of a slim volume on a high shelf behind the cash register, decorated with an engraving of a naked warrior with spear, and the title *Kossovo* (the older spelling), subtitled 'Heroic Songs of the Serbs,' translated by Helen Rootham.

The store's owner, Peter Keat, was generous enough to make a gift of the volume, published by Houghton Mifflin in 1920, with an intro by Maurice Baring and an informative historical preface by Janko Lavrin, citing both Jacob Grimm and Goethe on the genius of Serbian epic. Since there's plenty of patronizing comment in the press about Serbia's unwonted obsession with its past and with defeat (some of this comment written by British journalists brought up on obsessive school lessons about the Battle of Hastings and the retreat from Dunkirk), let us quote from Lavrin averring that 'the entire political mentality even of the modern Serbian peasant has been formed … chiefly by folk-poetry … That is the reason why his fervent patriotism has such a romantic, noble, and almost religious character.'

This enthusiasm for epic poetry could be studied with profit by our own legislators. Lavrin cites an historical memoir of Mrs. E. Lawton-Mijatovich:

> During the winter of 1873–74, happening to be in Kragrjevatz during the meeting of the National Assembly, I had the opportunity of hearing

a certain peasant, Anta Neshich, recite in blank verse to numerous audiences outside the Assembly Room the whole debate on the Bill for introducing the fresh monetary system into Serbia, concluding with the final acceptance of the Bill. The poet put the debate on the Budget in the same taking form, to the great delight of his many auditors.

War reporting in the fourteenth century could also be studied with profit by Wesley Clark, Jamie Shea and the others. Here's how the son of Sultan Murad recorded the death of his father, at Kosovo, writing to Suleiman-Bey, the Kadhia of Brussa:

When this my firman comes into your hands you should know that in accordance with Allah's will there was a battle on the field of Kossovo. My father, Sultan Murad, whose life had been happy and whose death was that of a martyr, prayed to Allah, after a vision whilst sleeping, to make him worthy of martyrdom. The battle being ended, he returned unhurt and in his full health, from the battlefield to his tent, which was elevated towards the heavens. And while we enjoyed the greatest pleasure in seeing how the cut heads of the Christian dukes rolled under the horses' hoofs, and how many of them with tied hands and others with broken legs stood, there suddenly appeared a fighter, by name Milosh Obilich. He came perfidiously, saying that he accepted Islam, and asking that he might so be ranked in the victorious army. When after his own wish he was allowed to kiss the feet of the illustrious Sultan, he drew a poisonous hanjar hidden in his sleeve, and boldly thrust it into the body of the Sultan, sorely wounding him. Thus he caused the illustrious Sultan to drink the sherbet of martyrdom. After this deed Milosh tried to escape through the soldiers who shone like stars in the sky, but was caught by them and cut in pieces.

Like almost all other chroniclers of battle, Murad II was being not entirely truthful. His father was stabbed and mortally wounded by Milosh before the battle began. As for Kosovo now, 'the plain of blackbirds,' the words of the epic poet need not be changed:

> Kad u jutru danak osvanuo, Ali lete dva vrana gavrana, Krvava im krila do ramena, Na kljunove b' jela pjena trgla ...
> On the morrow as the dawn is breaking, lo, there fly two ravens, two black ravens; Bloody are their wings up to the shoulders, From their beaks the blood-flecked foam is falling.

Peter Keat combines love of literature with activism as a member of the board of the Sacramento Municipal Utility District, a publicly owned utility that distributes electricity from hydro power generated off dams on the American River. As a publicly owned utility SMUD, a decade ago, gave Sacramento voters the chance to decommission the Rancho Seco nuclear power plant, which they duly did, simultaneously voting in a progressive SMUD board, of which Keat is a member.

SMUD is a model of its (sadly dwindling) kind. It has eliminated burdensome deposits, pushes energy conservation, cogeneration and solar programs. SMUD's rates are far lower than PG&E's; it has imposed no rate increase in eight years and has seen its bond rating go up steadily. Big companies have to pay their proper whack and are not, as is usually the case, subsidized by the ordinary consumers. All in all, SMUD is a fitting subject for Serbian epic poetry.

June 1, 1999

FIRST PICK YOUR WAR CRIMINAL
by Alexander Cockburn and Jeffrey St. Clair

Compared with Bill Clinton and his accomplices Milosevic is a piker when it comes to war crimes. Take Iraq. The sanctions imposed by the United States in 1991 have had a notoriously devastating effect on Iraq's civilian population, particularly the children. In May of 1996 the World Health Organization said that 'the vast majority of the country's population has been on a semi-starvation diet for years.' The hospitals have almost no medical supplies. The sewage treatment plants either barely function or don't work at all. Denis Halliday, who worked for the United Nations Development program in Iraq and who has issued many public denunciations of the sanctions, says that they are 'in contradiction of human rights provisions in the UN's own charter.'

In July 1991, Doug Broderick, a professional aid worker who was sent to Baghdad by the US charity Catholic Relief Services, predicted that as a consequence of sanctions 175,000 Iraqi children would certainly die because of the poor health conditions. He called it 'a disaster in slow motion.' It turned out that his prophecy was badly off. By the end of 1995 alone the United Nations Food and Agriculture Organization said that after careful investigation it had determined that as many as 576,000 Iraqi children have died as a result of sanctions. Using figures from Iraq's Ministry of Health the World Health Organization estimated that 90,000 Iraqis were dying every year in Iraq's hospitals, over and above those who would have expired at the normal rate.

In sum, it is beyond argument that the United States has engineered a program of enforced scarcity that has caused the deaths of hundreds of thousands of Iraqi civilians. In the final months of World War Two the Nazis tried to delay the advance of the Allies by opening the dikes in Holland. The man issuing this order was the German high commissioner in Holland, Seyss-Inquart. By the end of 1944 about 500,000 acres of land had been flooded, leading to what historian Gabriel Kolko called 'the most precipitous decline in food consumption any West European country suffered during the war.' Of the 195 Nazis indicted at Nuremberg, Seyss-Inquart was one of 24 sentenced to death.

Seyss-Inquart merely opened dikes in Holland. The historian Gabriel Kolko, who commented on that consequent fall in Dutch food consumption, was testifying about this German war criminal at the Vietnam tribunal, convened by Bertrand Russell in 1967 to hold hearings into US war crimes in Indochina. Kolko told the tribunal how the US Air Force had bombed the Toksan dam near Pyongyang. The plan was to destroy the irrigation system supplying 75 per cent of North Korea's rice farms. A subsequent USAF study of the bombing of the Toksan and Chasan dams noted: 'These strikes, largely passed over by the press, military observers and news commentators ... constituted one of the most significant air operations of the Korean war.' Of these deeds, the USAF historian remarked equably that the timing was aimed to be devastating in its psychological effect, when the exhausting labor of rice transplanting had been completed, but before the roots had become firmly embedded. There are probably Pentagon planners hard at work making similar calculations regarding the attrition of Serbian agriculture and commercial activity right now.

The bombing of the North Korean dams was a rousing success. Water bursting through the holes in the Toksan dam made by US bombs 'scooped clean' miles of valley below, with the added bonus of not only wiping out the rice paddies but also drowning Korean civilians in underground shelters. The USAF study exulted that '[t]o the Communists the smashing of the dams meant primarily the destruction of their chief sustenance – rice. The Westerner can little conceive the awesome meaning that the loss of this staple food commodity has for the Asian – starvation and slow death.' Another study detected 'Oriental fatalism' in the way the North Koreans carried on desperate repair efforts without regard for the delayed-action bombs also dropped around the target area.

Similar successful assaults were made on dams in Vietnam. In 1969 Henry Kamm, a *New York Times* reporter, recounted how a dam south of Hue had been 'blasted by American jets to deprive the North Vietnamese of a food supply.' Kamm returned later to find that the paddies had by then been destroyed by salt water encroaching from the South China Sea.

We don't have the trial transcript at hand, but no doubt Seyss-Inquart was asked why he had opened the dikes. Perhaps he answered in the same words as Secretary of State Madeleine Albright. In 1996 Albright was asked on CBS's *60 Minutes* by Lesley Stahl the following question: 'We have heard that half a million children have died [in Iraq]. I mean, that's more children than died in Hiroshima. And you know, is the price worth it?' The repulsive Albright famously replied: 'I think this is a very hard choice, but the price – we think the price is worth it.'

So, back in Nuremberg time, Albright would certainly have been hanged, if the standards applied to Seyss-Inquart had been leveled against her, and if she had been on the losing side. So would her commanding officer, Bill Clinton.

The protocols of the Geneva Convention of 1949 prohibit bombing not justified by clear military necessity. If there is any likelihood the target has a civilian function, then bombing is prohibited. In other words the vast majority of NATO targets have been criminally attacked. NATO's bombers have damaged and often destroyed hospitals and health care centers, public housing, infrastructure vital to the well-being of civilians, refineries, warehouses, agricultural facilities, schools, roads and railways. NATO spokesmen have directly stated their hope that the suffering of Serbs will prompt them to rise against Milosevic. (The same hope was publicly expressed by US officials amid the sanctions against Iraq, even though they knew well enough, after Bush had abandoned the Shia rebels in the late spring of 1991, that no matter how awful the effect of sanctions, Saddam and his regime would survive. NATO, in other words, is waging war on Serbian civilians – and Kosovar civilians for that matter.) If Milosevic goes on trial before the International Criminal Court, Clinton, Albright and Defense Secretary William Cohen should have their place on the court's calendar too.

Under the terms of the International Criminal Tribunal for the former Yugoslavia – a body set up by the UN Security Council in 1993 – anyone can file formal complaints for the Tribunal's prosecutor, Justice Louise Arbor, to consider within the terms of the Geneva Conventions. Thus far there have been three serious requests for investigation and indictment against the NATO leaders for their conduct against Serbia. Lawyers in Canada, Britain and France are now working together. Already the Canadian team has sent Arbor in The Hague requests for indictment against 67 persons for war crimes – said persons ranging from Bill Clinton to NATO spokesman Jamie Shea, whom Canadian lawyer Michael Mandel likened in role to William Joyce aka Lord Haw-Haw, a propagandist for the Nazis hanged by the Allies at the end of World War Two.

Prof. Mandel, who teaches law at Osgood Hall law school at York University in Toronto (of which, coincidentally, Louise Arbor is an alumna), says 'we have a great case. It will be a good test to see whether the law actually applies to powerful people.' Among the indictable war crimes in the complaint and request for indictment prepared by the Canadian lawyers are: the wanton destruction of cities, towns and villages, and kindred devastation, not caused by military necessity; the bombardment of undefended towns; the willful destruction of, or willful damage done to institutions dedicated to religion, charity or education (i.e., monasteries, hospitals and schools, all hit by NATO's bombs). 'They've admitted publicly the essentials of all these crimes,' Mandel says.

June 2, 1999

HUMANITARIAN ADOLF
by Alexander Cockburn

Jules Lobel and Michael Ratner, of the Center for Constitutional Rights, point out that on September 23, 1938 Hitler wrote to Prime Minister Chamberlain that ethnic Germans in Czechoslovakia had been 'tortured,' that 120,000 had been 'forced to flee the country,' that the 'security of more than 3,000,000 human beings was at stake,' and that they had been 'prevented from realizing also the right of nations to self-determination.' Hitler was also laying the basis for humanitarian intervention: a claim to intervene militarily in a sovereign state because of claimed human rights abuses. The Hitler precedent illustrates the mischief caused when countries assert humanitarian intervention as a pretext for acting in their own geopolitical interests, and it sets a dangerous precedent for other governments to take the same tack.

June 3, 1999

THE ANTIWAR RIGHT
by Alexander Cockburn

We'll say this for right-wing columnists like Novak or Feder: when they turn against a war, they do it right. In one column Robert Novak lashed out at NATO, excoriating liberal warmongers and reaching back in literary history to the social democrat H. G. Wells's *Shape of Things to Come*, where Britain is liberated from enemy occupation by an international armada. Novak also evoked Sumner Welles, FDR's Secretary of State, who thought bombers should be the weapon of an an international police force.

Try this from Feder:

It's argued that now that we're in the conflict, America must win it to remain credible. By 1973, we had lost 55,000 Americans in Vietnam, which gave us far more of a stake there than we have in Kosovo.

If we'd applied this do-or-die logic to the war in Southeast Asia, we would still be slugging it out in the rice paddies, and the Vietnam memorial would be a far more imposing structure.

I know, I know, if we don't take Belgrade and display Milosevic naked in a cage, malefactors and evildoers from Baghdad to Pyongyang will view us as a paper tiger.

But if I were Saddam Hussein, Kim Jong II or the Chinese politburo, I'd like nothing better than to see America wasting its limited military resources (very limited, thanks to our anti-defense commander in chief) in the Balkans.

Think of how thrilled Hitler would have been if, in the spring of 1939, England had decided to begin bombing Liechtenstein.

NATO cannot survive if it now abandons the campaign without achieving its objective, insists Henry Kissinger.

Who says NATO has to survive? Half of a century after NATO's birth, the Iron Curtain is a rust heap. Eastern Europe and the Baltic states are free. So, why NATO?

Presumably, if NATO loses credibility, it will limit the alliance's ability to pull us into future abysses. Wouldn't that be a pity?

The armed forces of the United States aren't the legions of the Roman Empire. The soldiers of a republic shouldn't be walking endless foreign battlements in a deranged and futile attempt to enforce a pax Americana.

It takes a robust Republican to throw NATO into the trashcan. Liberals never talk like that. For them, talking dirty about NATO is like attending a baptism and spitting in the font.

June 5, 1999

A FRAUD CALLED SANDERS

by Alexander Cockburn

The most useful parable about progressives is that offered by Bernard Sanders, self-styled 'socialist progressive independent' rep from Vermont. Sanders owes his political career to rage against the Vietnam War among radicals, many of whom moved into the state in the early 1970s. They forthwith planned a long-term, carefully organized, assault on Vermont's two-party structure. Sanders linked his political ambitions to this effort to organize a third force, the Progressive Alliance. He became mayor of Burlington and, later, congressman. At a rapid clip the emphasis moved from party-building to Sanders-building. At least five years ago it was apparent that the only movement B. Sanders was interested in was that of liberal money into his political campaign trough. One political piece of opportunism followed another, always forgiven by Vermont pwogwessives who are frightened of Sanders and fear to speak out against the loudmouth fraud, even though, last year, Sanders spoke vehemently in Congress in favor of sending his state's nuclear waste into a poor, largely hispanic, township in Texas called Sierra Blanca. He supported sanctions against Iraq. Then he voted in favor of this war. He did it once, he did it twice and on April 28, he did it again. This was the astounding 213–213 tie vote, which meant that the House of Representatives repudiated the war on Serbia launched by Clinton in violation of Article One of the US Constitution, which reserves warmaking powers to Congress. So if the 'socialist progressive' Sanders, who owes his entire career to antiwar sentiment, had not voted for the NATO bombers, the result would have been even more dramatic, a straight majority for the coalition of Republicans and radical Democrats such as Dennis Kucinich, Cynthia McKinney, Barbara Lee, Pete Stark and a handful of others.

On April 26, even before his most recent vote of shame, Sanders's office was occupied by fifteen radical Vermonters sickened by his stance. The last time any political rep from Vermont had an office occupied was when a group later known as the Winooski 44 sat in (Republican) Senator Robert Jefford's office in 1984, protesting Reagan's war in Central America. Jefford waited three days before asking the police to remove the protesters. Sanders waited six hours.

On Monday May 3, he held a town meeting in Montpelier attended by the fifteen protesters, wearing chains. The man in Sanders's Burlington office who told the protesters Sanders wouldn't speak to them was Philip Fiermonte, ironically one of the Winooski 44.

Readers of the *Washington Post* first edition can be forgiven if they missed the historic House vote refusing to approve the bombings. At first the *Post* reported the vote coyly on page A27. In the late edition the *Post* still played down the vote. The *New York Times* had a better sense of news and history and put the vote on its front page, above the fold: 'Deadlocked House Denies Support for Air Campaign.' The *Washington Times* did better too, with a front-page banner headline, 'House Refuses to Back Air War on Serbs: Separate Vote Denies Funds for Deploying Ground Forces.' In the Vietnam era it took years for resistance in the House even to approach that level.

June 7, 1999

THE COST
by Alexander Cockburn and Jeffrey St. Clair

The deal brokered by NATO's errand boy Chernomyrdin on June 2 was virtually identical to that offered by Milosevic to NATO – before the bombing started. The sole purpose of the bombing was to demonstrate to Serbia and to the world NATO's capacity to bomb, thus killing nearly 2,000 civilians, destroying much of Serbia's infrastructure, prompting the forced expulsion and flight of around a million Kosovars. Wars have been triggered by the frailest of excuses and prolonged on the slightest of rationales, but the

Cowards' War, as Nicholas von Hoffman aptly christened it, is hard
to beat for the effrontery of its supposed rationales.

The Rambouillet negotiations lasted from February 6 to February
23. The so-called 'contact group' of NATO powers – US, Germany,
France, Italy and UK – pushed for Kosovar autonomy, guaranteed by
the presence of NATO troops. Kept unrevealed at the time was a
secret Appendix B to the deal presented to NATO on the final day.
Not only were NATO troops to occupy Kosovo, but NATO troops
were to have the right to 'free and unrestricted passage and unimpeded
access throughout the FRY (Federal Republic of Yugoslavia) … This
shall include, but not be limited to, the right of bivouac, maneuver,
billet and utilization of any areas or facilities as required for support,
training, and operations.' This language comes in Article 8 of NATO's
secret demand in Appendix B. Article 10 allowed NATO cost-free
use of all Yugoslav streets, airports and ports. In other words NATO
was insisting that Yugoslavia – i.e. Serbia – surrender sovereignty.
NATO was setting impossible conditions, certain that Milosevic and
indeed every Serb would find them impossible to accept. It seems a
senior State Department official boasted of this at the time in deep
back briefings of US reporters, saying that the US 'had deliberately
set the bar higher than the Serbs could accept' and that 'they need
some bombing and that's what they're going to get.'

The final offer of the Serbs was for Kosovar autonomy, to be
guaranteed by a UN force with a Russian component. A NATO
presence in Serbia was unacceptable. The NATO powers rejected
this. Serbia refused to sign the Rambouillet agreement and so did
the Kosovars, until forced to by NATO powers on March 18. On
March 24 the bombing began.

On June 2 the deal agreed to by Milosevic and the Serb parliament
was for a UN force with a Russian component, plus a NATO force,
plus Kosovar autonomy within the Yugoslav federation. The unstated

agenda seems to be the partitioning of Kosovo. The KLA will be 'demilitarized' and Yugoslav troops allowed at some point to return in limited numbers to Kosovo. No international force either under UN or NATO auspices will enter Serbia. The Kosovar refugees will be able to return, but that was never a sticking point so far as Milosevic was concerned.

NATO forced a war and ended up with essentially the deal that could have been signed in late February. There will be some NATO helmets alongside the UN blue helmets in Kosovo, but only after a Cowards' War would this be called victory.

June 10, 1999

THE LIBERALS' WAR
by Alexander Cockburn and Jeffrey St. Clair

This was the Liberals' War, bombing a country for two and a half months from 30,000 feet. It was the Liberals' War waged by social democracy's best and brightest, intent on proving once again that wars can be fought with the best and most virtuous of intentions: the companion volume to Hillary Clinton's 'It Takes a Village' turns out to be 'It Takes An Air Force,' though Bill will no doubt claim one day it wasn't his idea and he only partly went along with Sandy Berger, Strobe Talbott and Madeleine Albright because he wanted to 'preserve my political viability,' the words he used in his famous draft-dodging shuffle in the Vietnam era. But war eroded his viability. Americans who had supported Bill's right to remain president even though he had kissed Monica Lewinsky began to turn sharply against him when he bombed Serbian schools.

Just as social democratic parties across Europe voted for war in 1914, so did they again in 1999. In Britain social democrats rallied to the pipsqueak bombardier, Tony Blair. There were honorable exceptions: Tony Benn and Yorkshire Labour Member of Parliament Alice Mahon who went to Belgrade and to Novi Sad and stood on the bridge with – as she later described – twelve nationalities including Albanians, defying NATO's bombers. Another fine Labour MP, Tam Dalyell, was a spirited opponent. So was Harold Pinter, whose fine denunciation we excerpted in a recent *CounterPunch*. So was our friend Tariq Ali, a veteran of the Sixties' anti-Vietnam War campaigns. The two leading liberal papers, the *Observer* and the *Guardian*, both favored the war.

In France most intellectuals fell into line behind NATO, though once again there were exceptions, notably Régis Debray, who went to Belgrade and Kosovo and wrote a fine denunciation which *Le Monde* put on its front page. Debray was then savaged by France's liberal intellectuals, including a vitriolic assault in *Libération*.

In Germany there was increasing division, even in the Social Democratic Party. After Economics Minister Oskar Lafontaine resigned rather than support the war, he also quit as leader of the party. Though Chancellor Schroeder ran for this position un-opposed, fully 30 per cent of the delegates at a special Social Democratic Party convention voted against him. There was also great dissension among the Greens against the conduct of Foreign Minister Joschka Fischer.

In Italy the resistance was strongest. There was a demonstration of 130,000 in Rome in late May, with the red banners of the Rifundazione Party of leftists paired bravely with the white banners of the Catholic Boy Scouts. The famous leftist Rosanna Rosanda appealed publicly in *Il Manifesto* for Italian soldiers to desert if required to fight in Yugoslavia. She received much public support.

The Pope flayed the war in his Easter Greeting, which was dropped from Britain's broadcasts. The Pope described NATO's bombing as an 'act of diabolical retribution.' From a man of God what stronger words could come?

Here in the US the war found almost all Democrats in Congress marshalled for war. The heroic exceptions were twenty-six Democrats in the House, led by Dennis Kucinich of Ohio – himself of Irish-Croat ancestry – who leagued with a majority of House Republicans twice to deny Clinton legitimation for his war. Most liberals favored the bombing. Susan Sontag termed it 'a just war.'

Among those opposing the war was a man who has written finely about this same *trahison*, Edward Said. Noam Chomsky, as always, set NATO's claims to humanitarian motive in clarifying context. Peace groups rallied and by late May there was evidence of intense organizing across the country. Here at *CounterPunch* we found, as we so often do, heartening evidence of interesting coalitions. Many people visiting our website and subsequently calling us up are not from traditional left constituencies, but were delighted by our commentaries and have declared their admiration and pleasure at our stance. Wars are never beaten nor even greatly inconvenienced in the law courts, but we should note that Clinton has had to face the suit brought by Tom Campbell, Republic rep from San Jose, charging Clinton with unconstitutional warmaking, with the suit being lodged for him, twenty-three other Republicans and two Democrats – Kucinich and Marcy Kaptur, also of Ohio – by the Center for Constitutional Rights. We should also note the complaints to the International Tribunal on War Crimes about war crimes by NATO leaders. We don't care for the tribunal, which we see merely as a judicial errand boy for the NATO powers, but here we see a win–win. Either it will discredit itself by indicting only Milosevic or it will give us the enormous pleasure of seeing Clinton,

Blair and the others accused of war crimes. Either way, it spells death to the public viability of the tribunal.

June 13, 1999

THE McCAIN STORY
by Jeffrey St. Clair

The top warmonger in Congress has been Senator John McCain, Republican from Arizona, seeker of the Republican presidential nomination. In one rhetorical bombing run after another, McCain has bellowed for 'lights out in Belgrade' and for NATO to 'cream' the Serbs. At the start of May he began declaiming in the US Senate for the NATO forces to use 'any means necessary' to destroy Serbia.

McCain is often called a 'war hero,' a title adorning an unlovely résumé starting with a father who was an admiral and graduated fifth from the bottom at the US Naval Academy, where he earned the nickname 'McNasty.' McCain flew twenty-three bombing missions over North Vietnam, each averaging about half an hour, total time ten hours and thirty minutes. For these brief excursions the admiral's son was awarded two Silver Stars, two Legions of Merit, two Distinguished Flying Crosses, three Bronze Stars, the Vietnamese Legion of Honor and three Purple Hearts. *US Veteran Dispatch* calculates our hero earned a medal an hour, which is pretty good going. McCain was shot down over Hanoi on October 26, 1967 and parachuted into Truc Boch Lake, whence he was hauled by Vietnamese, and put in prison.

A couple of years later he was interviewed in prison camp by Fernando Barral, a Spanish psychiatrist living in Cuba. The interview appeared in *Granma* on January 24, 1970. Barral's evaluation of McCain is quoted by Amy Silverman, author of many excellent pieces on McCain in the Phoenix-based *New Times* weekly. Here's how Barral described 'the personality of the prisoner who is responsible for many criminal bombings of the people.' Barral goes on:

> He (McCain) showed himself to be intellectually alert during the interview. From a morale point of view he is not in traumatic shock. He was able to be sarcastic, and even humorous, indicative of psychic equilibrium. From the moral and ideological point of view he showed us he is an insensitive individual without human depth, who does not show the slightest concern, who does not appear to have thought about the criminal acts he committed against a population from the absolute impunity of his airplane, and that nevertheless those people saved his life, fed him, and looked after his health and he is now healthy and strong. I believe that he has bombed densely populated places for sport. I noted that he was hardened, that he spoke of banal things as if he were at a cocktail party.

McCain is deeply loved by the press. As Silverman puts it, 'as long as he's the noble outsider, McCain can get away with anything it seems – the Keating Five, a drug-stealing wife, nasty jokes about Chelsea Clinton – and the pundits will gurgle and coo.'

William Safire, Maureen Dowd, Russell Baker, the *New Yorker*, the *New York Times Magazine*, *Vanity Fair*, have all slobbered over McCain in empurpled prose. The culmination was a love poem in *60 Minutes* from Mike Wallace, who managed to avoid any inconvenient mention of McCain's close relationship with Savings & Loan fraudster Charles Keating, with whom the senator and his kids romped on Bahamian beaches. McCain was similarly spared scrutiny for his astonishing claim that he knew nothing of his wife's scandalous dealings. His vicious temper has escaped rebuke.

McCain's escape from the Keating debacle was nothing short of miraculous, probably the activity for which he most deserves a medal. After all, he took more than $100,000 in campaign contributions from the swindler Keating between 1982 and 1988, while simultaneously log-rolling for Keating on Capitol Hill. In the same period McCain took nine trips to Keating's place in the Bahamas. When the muck began to rise, McCain threw Keating over the side, hastily reimbursed him for the trips and suddenly developed a profound interest in campaign finance reform.

The pundits love McCain because of his grandstanding on soft money's baneful role in politics, thus garnering for himself a reputation for willingness to court the enmity of his colleagues. In fact colleagues in the Senate regard McCain as a mere grandstander. They know that he already has a big war chest left over from his last senatorial campaign, plus torrents of pac money from the corporations that crave his indulgence as chairman of the Senate Commerce Committee. Communications companies (US West, Bell South, ATT, Bell Atlantic) have been particularly effusive in McCain's treasury, as have banks, military contractors and UPS. They also know he has a rich wife.

McCain is the kind of Republican that liberals love: solid military credentials as a former POW, ever ready with acceptable sound-bites on campaign finance reform and other cherished issues. Thus it was that McCain drew enthusiastic plaudits last year when he rose in the Senate chamber to denounce the insertion of $200 million worth of pork in the military construction portion of the defense authorisation bill. Eloquently, he spoke of the 11,200 service families on food stamps, the lack of modern weapons supplied to the military, the declining levels of readiness in the armed forces. Bravely, he laid the blame at the doors of his colleagues: 'I could find only one commonality to these projects, and that is that 90 per cent of them happened to be in the state or districts of members of the Appropriations Committees.'

Sternly, in tones befitting a Cato or a Cicero, he urged his colleagues to ponder their sacred duty to uphold the defense of the Republic rather than frittering away the public purse on such frivolous expenditure: 'We live in a very dangerous world. We will have some serious foreign policy crises. I am not sure we have the military that is capable of meeting some of these foreseeable threats, but I know that what we are doing with this $200 million will not do a single thing to improve our ability to meet that threat.'

In the gallery, partisans of pork-free spending silently cheered while those who hoped to profit from portions of the $200 million gnashed their teeth in chagrin. Yet such emotions were misplaced on either side. This was vintage McCain. Had he wished to follow words with deeds, he could have called for a roll-call on the items he had just denounced so fervently. That way the looters and gougers would have had to place their infamy on the record. But no, McCain simply sat down and allowed the offending expenditure to be authorized in the anonymous babble of a voice vote ('All those in favor say Aye'). Had McCain really had the courage of his alleged convictions he could have filibustered the entire $250 billion authorisation bill, but, inevitably, no such bravery was in evidence. Instead, when the $250 billion finally came to a vote, he voted for it.

This miserable display provides useful insights into the reasons for McCain's ineffectiveness on issues such as campaign finance that have garnered him so much favorable publicity. A conservative Senate staffer offers these observations on McCain's fundamental weakness of character:

… the real question is why this senator did not use the strong leverage he has to insist that his 'ethical' position be incorporated into a major bill. After all, Senator McCain couched his concerns in issues of the highest national importance: readiness, modernization, and the military's ability to defeat the threats we face (whatever they are). Pragmatism is the most commonly heard excuse. If McCain had made a pain out of himself in insisting on keeping the unneeded and wasteful pork out of the milcon authorization bill, some people would argue he would have lost comity with his Senate colleagues. They wouldn't respect him anymore. They would have been angry with him, because he kept them up late (it was about 10.30 pm), and they would have been embarrassed by his showing them up as pork-meisters. This would weaken his ability to get things done.

'This argument assumes politics in the US Senate is a popularity contest: if you want to get anything done around here, you have to go along and get along. Well, this place is a popularity contest, but it is supposed to be one with the voters, not one's colleagues. Besides, this place doesn't really operate that way. Here, they have contempt for fluffy show pieces. Show them you mean business, and you're someone who has to be dealt with (rather than a talk-only type), and you'll begin to get some results. Get ready for a fight, though, because there are some on the other side who are no push-overs. Obviously, Mr McCain was not prepared to make that investment.

June 20, 1999

HERE COMES ELIE WIESEL
by Alexander Cockburn

Usually, when Elie Wiesel is trundled before the cameras, it's a signal that some spectacular piece of moral fraudulence is about to be foisted onto the American people and the powers-that-be reckon that Wiesel's unctuous kiss of approval is required.

Last week this ardent supporter of the war on Serbia appeared on *Larry King Live*, with Wolf Blitzer standing in for King. 'I think it [the bombing] had to be done,' Wiesel said piously, 'because all the other options had been explored. I do not believe that we have the right to send troops or even airplanes to bomb unless we have exhausted all the other possibilities, and we did try. Milosevic, apparently, disappointed everybody.' This balderdash puts Wiesel, morally speaking, on a par with Cardinal Spellman, blessing the B-52s as they set off to drop napalm on little children in the Vietnam era. 'All the other possibilities' were never explored, because NATO wanted to bomb Serbia. It didn't matter what Milosevic agreed to.

On the same show Wiesel appeared on, no less a person than Brent Scowcroft told Blitzer bluntly that what he had called 'the Rambouillet diktat' had been changed in the final agreement. Blitzer then asked whether by the phrase 'Rambouillet diktat' Scowcroft was referring to 'the peace agreement that the Serbs rejected in February.'

'That's right,' Scowcroft answered. 'Because that, to Milosevic, meant that he would never see Kosovo again – absolutely unacceptable to him personally. It also gave the right for NATO troops to roam around inside Serbia – another no-no. That was changed [in the final agreement].'

Scowcroft clearly thought the whole attack on Serbia pretty unpalatable, though he didn't say so directly, merely insisting that possibly the 'war' wasn't a perfect recipe for the future.

July 10, 1999

A DIME'S WORTH OF DIFFERENCE?
by Alexander Cockburn

Not long after the official end of the war on Serbia I crossed the Bay Bridge to honor a commitment to debate Michael Lerner on the immorality and lawlessness of this same war. Arriving at James Lick High School in Noe Valley I found that Lerner – who once ravished Hillary Rodham Clinton with his sermons on the politics of meaning – had felt no such obligation, baling by fax the previous day. Lerner, an ardent armchair bombardier, told the organizers he had no desire to have the delicately nuanced nature of his support for the war distorted by that odious perverter of truth, Cockburn.

So the meeting, organized by a left group called Socialist Action, proceeded without him, most of the panel's speaking time being consumed by a woman giving a detailed history of the Balkans across the last generation. In my own brief remarks I urged the crowd to look on the bright side. At least we had learned in the war that all the awful things we'd ever felt about liberals were true. And we'd also learned that as leftists we have many friends on the right. The backbone of opposition to the war had, after all, been conservative. It was Jack Kemp who had written in the *Washington Times* that the war on Serbia had been 'an international Waco.'

In the question period I listened gloomily as at least three members of the audience, plus both my fellow panelists, criticized the hope I'd expressed at the end of my chat that there could be a coalition of left and right against business as usual. It reminded me of the invective rained on my head by a self-proclaimed anarchist talk radio host in Detroit a few years ago when I told him that I'd found exciting political energy and gut hatred of corporate power at a local 'Gunstock,' a rally of supposed right-wingers that had been the target of this same anarchist's ripest venom. The saddest but most enduring truth in political life is that most people cling with desperate strength to the prejudices that they are pleased to call 'informed opinions.'

In August 1996 Norman Mailer published in *Esquire* his interview with Pat Buchanan, a brave effort to explore what common terrain can be shared by left and right in America, against the center. The article ended with Buchanan's remark to Mailer that 'left and right come together basically in opposition to big business, government, big corporations – against the oppressive weight of gigantic institutions upon the individual. You get a broad coalition of Left and Right. They feel they are going to lose the country they grew up in. That is the underlying focus.' Mailer ran Buchanan's quote, then closed with the line: 'Four years to the millennium!'

Buchanan went nowhere in 1996 and the left's anti-corporate crusader, Ralph Nader, ran a pro-forma listless campaign. Now we're six months from the millennium and things are, at least on the surface, even worse. Politics always draw their vitality from the extremes. George Wallace and Malcolm X, even though he was killed three years earlier, set the political thermostats in 1968, and with the addition of the Weather Underground, did the same in 1972.

In every spavined sentence in the numbing argot of the Democratic and Republican party platforms there lurks, albeit often in barely detectable volume, the DNA of what was once a robust, even 'extreme' political idea. But today the trace elements of such DNA have become so infinitesimally small that even the most powerful microscopes scarcely register a presence. Take Al Gore and George W. Bush, currently favored as the presidential contenders in 2000. The only real difference between them is the fact that at this point in the political season George W. has raised twice as much money as Al, who himself has hauled in record-breaking truckloads of cash. Oh, at the level of rhetoric there are minute deviations. George W. just took a swing through the Pacific Northwest and declared himself a friend of the chainsaw and the logging deck, thus sending a message to big timber money that George W. is a better investment than Gore, the Tree-Hugger. And the timber men will no doubt pony up for George W., happily aware that for them there's no downside, since the ancient forests of the Pacific Northwest have been cut down at a bracing rate all through the Clinton–Gore years.

Gore and George W. are alike as two peas, right down to the same slightly dazed look that comes of having big-time politicians as fathers and interesting encounters with powerful drugs in their formative years. I don't know anything about Gore's mother, but Barbara Bush was one of the nastier women I've ever interviewed (a half-hour session in 1979, when George Sr was fighting Ronald Reagan for the nomination). Maybe there's a difference here.

In fact a debate between Al and George W. on the subjects of parents – their parents – might be the sole means of putting together an exciting debate in 2000. Imaginatively staged, with both men injected with sodium pentothal, and moderated by Geraldo Rivera and Gail Sheehy, such an encounter might scrape off the dreadful rime of banality that cakes their public personae and reveal the wounded egos beneath.

At the level of political performance in the White House, 2001–2004, we can say with some certainty that it would make not an iota of difference whether Gore or Bush is the leaseholder. Corporations will plunder the Earth at the same rate, embryos be dislodged from their mothers' wombs at the same pace, constitutional rights and freedom be abused with the same frequency, drug wars fought with the same intensity or growing disillusion. The same small countries will be bombed, the same infants die, the same thirteen-year-old girls glue Nike shoes together. The same men and women will pass from Death Row to their graves, regardless of whether Al trounces George W. or George W. trounces Al, or whether Bill Bradley surges past Al, or whether Steve Forbes or Lamar Alexander turn George W. into the Ed Muskie of the millennium. (Since it's a quarter of a century ago I'd better remind the younger crowd that Muskie was the front-runner for the Democratic nomination in 1972, proceeding with majestic solemnity towards certain triumph, until he tumbled in a less-than-expected showing in New Hampshire.) Within the conventional political arena we have come to a dead end. As Bill Clinton remarked to the *Los Angeles Times*, George W. is merely pulling the same political scam in 1999 with his 'compassionate conservatism' as did Bill himself with DLC 'New Democrats' in 1992.

As a force capable of reinvigorating our political DNA the left is in terrible shape. Its national champions – Bernard Sanders, Jesse Jackson, Michael Moore, Jim Hightower – are all phonies. The radical right – which has contributed 80 per cent of the political energy in the country for the past twenty years – is almost as impotent, although more healthily endowed with a hostility to state power. The left will never break away from the Democratic Party to any important degree, since the institutional ties between labor and the Democrats will never allow it. The right might well tear itself loose from the Republicans. Bob Smith of New Hampshire seems keen on leading such a breakaway. I certainly hope he does so. Who else might precipitate a reinvigoration of the system? Now, Jesse Ventura is a demagogue, a quality highly esteemed by the ancient Greeks, for whom the word contained the simple sum of its two parts, *demos* meaning the people, the populace, the commons, and *agogos*, meaning leader, or leading. As the Oxford English Dictionary puts it, a demagogue in its initial meaning is defined as 'a popular leader or orator who espoused the cause of the people against any other party in the state.' To Hobbes and Dryden, half-way through the seventeenth century, the word still carried this sense. At the same time, amid the storms of the English civil war, royalists gave demagogue its current sense of someone wantonly and cynically inflaming base political passions for selfish ends. The word fell victim to a class mugging.

Yet in the first sense, we need demagogues desperately. Part of our present problem is that there are no leaders with the demagogic virtue to rally and arouse the people. Ventura fulfills at least one initial part of the demagogic requirement, by his evident capacity to speak directly in a way that people can understand and believe. Here's how he dealt with the death penalty issue, on Geraldo Rivera's show on MSNBC on July 6. RIVERA: Well, what about the death penalty, then? Gov. VENTURA: I don't support the … RIVERA: Because they've moved now to make it fifteen, fourteen, thirteen, twelve, infancy. Gov. VENTURA: I disa – disagree with the death penalty altogether now, and – I've t – I've taken … RIVERA: Really? Gov. VENTURA: Yeah. I've taken that position, because u – upon becoming governor, Geraldo, I wouldn't want that weight on my shoulder, especially in the light of DNA evidence that they have today. I mean, if you sentence someone to die, and five years later it's proven that they didn't do the crime, I would have a hard time living with that. But what I say is let's make life, life. Life is not life imprisonment. That's phony. They sentence someone to life and they let them out in ten years. If you're going to make it life, let's make it life, but I do not agree with the death penalty.

And this came directly after Ventura affirmed his belief in the Second Amendment while making the entirely accurate observation that at the precise moment the gun control crowd screams for guns to be taken out of the hands of children, the army is drafting teenagers and shoving automatic weapons in their hands and training them to kill. In the same conversation he came out, in coherent terms, against the drug war and in favor of medicinal use of marijuana, plus agro-industrial cultivation of hemp.

So here we have Al Gore, who campaigned in New York in 1988 by pasting Mike Dukakis as the man who paroled Willie Horton. And we have George W. who's never met a death warrant in Texas he didn't like. And we have Ventura who admits he doesn't want to be the man who puts to death innocent people, a man who admits, unlike George W., that this would cause him to lose sleep. My friends, at this desperate hour we have at least the makings of a decent demagogue. Six months to the millennium, and right now the prospect of ultimate political Y2K, plunging us into mental darkness: Al versus George W.

July 27, 1999

WHERE TOMORROW'S BOMBS WILL FALL
by Jeffrey St. Clair

No more Mr Nice Guy, says NATO. Next time we bomb someone, we're going to do it right. No shilly-shallying. Power stations and water-treatment plants will be blown up on the first night. This end to any pretense that bombs are aimed at military targets is disclosed in what is described by Tim Butcher and Patrick Bishop of the London *Daily Telegraph* as a private preliminary review by NATO experts of the seventy-eight-day Allied Force bombing campaign against Serbia. The report apparently concludes that the bombing campaign had almost no military effect, that despite thousands of bombing sorties they failed to damage the Yugoslav army tactically in Kosovo. NATO's current assessment is that only a handful of tanks, guns and armored personnel carriers were damaged. You may recall that at one point in the bombing NATO cried exultantly that thousands of Serb soldiers had been killed and that Serb forces were therefore on the verge of losing all operational viability.

The NATO report also concludes that it was a big mistake to have opened the campaign with bombs that wreaked little havoc but firmed up civilian morale. In the chilling words of the *Telegraph*, the NATO report intimates that 'Any future operation by NATO is likely to involve heavier, more ruthless attacks on civilian targets such as power stations and water-treatment plants earlier in the campaign.' Recall that the Geneva Convention of 1949 prohibits bombing of any target that has a civilian function. NATO's strategists are now concluding that the only point of bombing is to destroy civilian-related infrastructure. So, the Clinton–Albright war prompted at its onset the slaughter of thousands of Kosovars by the

Serbs, the flight or expulsion of hundreds of thousands more, the killing via bomb and missile of around 1,600 Yugoslav civilians, the destruction of Serbia's economy, the ruin of the Danube river trade and environmental catastrophe. And NATO says that next time it will try to make it all a lot worse.

July 29, 2002

INSIDE PAKISTAN AND AFGHANISTAN WITH RAWA

by Anne Brodsky

I just returned from another six weeks with RAWA (Radical Afghan Women's Association), five weeks in Pakistan and one amazing week in Afghanistan. RAWA's work is very busy and the need is still enormous – this includes some cities in Pakistan where refugees are actually flowing in, not out. They are doing creative things such as working to help other established schools rather than taking the time to start their own. In one example an eight-year-old Afghan high school in Peshawar thought it would have to close for lack of funds and losing students. RAWA started funding them and even made tuition free for the first time in the history of this school, and now not only can they pay their teachers, but they have more students than they did before and the demand is growing because students who could never afford to attend now can.

RAWA's work in Afghanistan is keeping everyone quite busy as the need and possibility to help is actually expanding. Many, many women and girls are in their literacy and sewing classes, many who are either too old to attend the newly reopened schools for girls (there is an age limit for entering the lower grades, which many need to attend after five years without any education) or whose families still will not let them attend schools for safety reasons. The women and girls say that five years of Taliban rule only strengthened their resolve and commitment to education and made their families realize its importance. Most of these women have never been in school before, but still are interested in joining and learning. Most classes have more demand than RAWA has teachers and funds.

About 80–90 per cent of the women we saw in Kabul were in burqa still. In Jalalabad we saw no women without burqa. The interim government is starting to require 'permission' for everything, as a veiled attempt to keep many things under control. Even visiting a public high school required special permission. As this trend increases it will make things very dangerous for RAWA. They have many enemies in the government with so many Northern Alliance (NA) and warlords in positions of control, so continue to operate quite underground. There is no doubt that the need is great and their particular message of humanitarian as well as political change is a necessity, especially for the women.

Because we drove to Kabul from Pakistan, I was able to see a remarkable slice of the landscape and life. It is true that Afghanistan is an amazingly beautiful country. Even that small stretch, which took ten hours across destroyed roads, was incredibly diverse with blue-green rivers, undulating valleys with fields of rounded stones, flat mesa plateaus, sandstone hills with natural caves, steep shale peaks turned sideways, jagged mountains and roads that zigzag through mountain switchbacks. We drove through small villages where the influence of the Taliban was still very evident, and the men treated me and the RAWA member who accompanied me as if we had no right to be in public except for their curiosity. In the US the response to them would be a sarcastic 'Haven't you ever seen a woman before?' or 'You really should get out more". Here both of the statements, which played in my head, were fact, not sarcasm. To change the men in this town would be a revolution. In many other places Abdul Haq, Massood and Rabbani's pictures were everywhere but Karzai's was not.

Just for some perspective on life, our taxi-drivers from Pakistan to Afghanistan were both former Taliban and former mujahideen. They talked quite openly to the male supporter who was with us about their time with both groups and were probably Taliban for money and to further their private gains, but nonetheless it points out that former Taliban, both foot soldiers, middle managers, like these drivers, and the leadership, are still everywhere. Many people said that the only ones who couldn't identify the former Taliban in their midst were the foreigners who were employing them and giving them government positions. Everyone else knows but is too scared to say.

The reconstruction in Kabul is evident in some places, but it is like time stood still in others, where the ten-year-old destruction is evident as if it happened yesterday. People live and run shops side by side with buildings riddled with bullet holes and shells of buildings destroyed by rocket attacks. I also saw the result of US bombings. The refugees are returning to difficult lives and many cannot find jobs and are living in tents and unprotected commercial buildings without windows or doors. They say that jobs are hard to come by, for those willing to do hard manual labor as well as for those with higher education. Many jobs are reportedly going to Panjshiris only and others are available only with bribes. Some from refugee camps in Pakistan say they had more help there and are starving here without any assistance. I talked to a number of refugees who had only returned because harassment from the Pakistani police in Islamabad in particular made them feel too unsafe in Pakistan.

They are actually doing worse now in Kabul. Many think that there will be a wave of refugees back to Pakistan come winter, when it is too cold to live in Kabul without shelter and jobs.

I was afforded a really unique view of life in Kabul because all of my meetings and interviews and the humanitarian projects I saw were in private homes in Kabul and surrounding villages/suburbs. Many of these were the equivalent of middle-class homes, but in none did I see running water or indoor toilets. Even in the capital city people rely on wells and public pumps. Electricity in most parts of the city is available only every other night. In the outer villages, the electric lines were stolen ten years ago and still these homes have no electricity, even as wall lamps and chandeliers remain in their homes. The library at the University of Kabul has virtually no electricity because all of the wiring was stolen by the various factions and Taliban. As in the older refugee camps, most people live in high-walled enclosures with gardens and small farmyard animals, even in the city. Construction however is sturdier than in the older camps and here glass windows and screens gave a more permanent and comfortable environment. The one TV news broadcast I saw did have a woman broadcaster, but she never looked up from the page she was reading and the whole broadcast had a very amateur feel to it. There is so much to be reconstructed here.

The people are cautiously optimistic, but this seems only because of the presence of the peacekeepers and the continued hope that the international community will follow through on its promises of aid and that someone will actually stop the warlords. The presence of NA soldiers in dark unmarked cars is ominous. There are other types of soldiers and police in various uniforms, many ill-fitting. It is hard to judge who will have a weapon and who not. Often young boys with the NA had weapons and older more mature and responsible-looking men in Afghan army uniforms were unarmed. I saw taped interviews of Loya Jirga attendees in which they too were expressing their concern about the needs for peace and security and controls on the warlords, who were too evident in the Loya Jirga process.

For more information on RAWA go to: http://www.RAWA.org
Anne Brodsky is an Assistant Professor of Psychology at the University of Maryland, Baltimore County.

August 10, 1999

THE FIRST LADY AS THERAPEUTIC COP
by Alexander Cockburn

Hillary Rodham Clinton was an enthusiastic advocate for the cluster bombs that now litter the Serbian and Kosovan landscapes, set to kill or cripple for the next half-century. But memories are short. Perhaps we will soon see HRC clutching some Balkan infant, bent over the maimed tyke, and who will then recall that she bears some responsibility for that lost limb? 'I urged him to bomb,' she confided to Lucinda Franks in *Talk*. 'You cannot let this go on at the end of a century that has seen the major holocaust of our time. What do we have NATO for if not to defend our way of life?'

In fact it's scarcely surprising that Hillary should have urged the First Man to drop cluster bombs on the Serbs to defend 'our way of life.' The First Lady is a social engineer. She believes in therapeutic policing, and the duty of the state to impose such policing. War is more social engineering, fixitry via high explosive, social therapy via the nose-cone of a cruise missile.

There's not much of a left any more. But there are plenty of therapeutic cops around, and Hillary is their leader, the very quintessence of social worker liberalism. All it takes to usher in the New Jerusalem are counselors, community action programs and tougher gun laws, which is what Hillary called for after Columbine, not long after she gave the First Man that bit of advice about bombing the Serbs.

As a tough therapeutic cop, Hillary does not shy away from the most abrupt expression of the therapy, the death penalty. In this perspective perhaps we ought to look at her commitment to Choice as at least in part another piece of therapeutic policing. Steve Levitt, an economist at the University of Chicago, and John Donohue III, a law prof at Stanford, have been circulating a paper – reported in the *Chicago Tribune* on August 8 – arguing that the legalizing of abortion in the early 1970s has contributed to the falling crime rate in the 1990s. Indeed they claim that legalized abortion may account for as much as half the overall crime drop between 1991 and 1997. Levitt says abortion 'provides a way for the would-be mothers of those kids who are going to lead really tough lives to avoid bringing them into the world.' The authors cite statistics from five states that legalized abortion before the *Roe v. Wade* decision of 1973. These five states with high abortion rates in the early 1970s had greater crime drops in the 1990s. The *Trib*'s story quotes Cory Richards, a policy wonk at the Guttmacher Institute, as saying: 'This is an argument for women not being forced to have children they don't want to have. This is making the point that it's not only bad for the women, but for children and society.'

So, from the social engineering, crime fighting point of view the reintroduction of the death penalty in 1977 had the legalization of abortion in 1973 – the *Roe v. Wade* decision – as its logical precursor and concomitant. And the death penalty for undesired embryos has had the advantage of being a lot more certain, and cheaper to administer, than the death penalty for undesired adults. I don't think it's the way the women's movement saw the Choice issue back in the early 1970s, but I can certainly imagine Hillary arguing for abortion as socially therapeutic.

She comes from the liberal social engineering tradition that sponsored the great sterilizing boom earlier in the century, whose rampages in Vermont are only now coming to light. As in many other states, progressives with a devout belief in the ability of science to improve Vermont's gene pool lobbied successfully for passage of a sterilization law in 1931. The law targeted poor rural Vermonters, Abenaki Indians and others deemed 'unfit' to procreate.

Hillary, never forget, is a Methodist, and that bleak creed of improvement is bedrock for her. She's a social cleanser. This is the cold steel that stiffens her spine and carries her forward, self-righteous amid the untidy mess of all her contradictions.

August 30, 2000

THE PENTAGON'S PRESIDENTIAL AUCTION
by Andrew Cockburn

Gore's famous embrace of Tipper before his speech at the Democratic convention may pale beside his prospective ecstasies with the Joint Chiefs of Staff. In AD 193 the Roman Praetorian Guard murdered the Emperor Pertinax and proceeded to auction off the imperial throne to the highest bidder. Until this year the most strenuous emulation of this feat by the US military came in 1980, when the Joint Chiefs of Staff took bids on the White House from the ramparts of the Pentagon. Despite fierce bidding by Jimmy Carter, the Chiefs had no hesitation in accepting Republican pledges and in proclaiming that only Ronald Reagan would keep the Empire strong.

We are in the climactic moments of the 2000 auction. By now the ritual is well established. Stage One: senior Praetorians and associated intellectual prostitutes repine the pitiful condition of America's fighting folk and the decrepitude of the US military arsenal. Frank Gaffney Jr, a Defense Department official in the Reagan years, set the tone in an article in the *Washington Times* in early August: 'Future defense capabilities may be seriously inadequate. History suggests that the consequence of such a practice is a vacuum of power that hostile nations often feel invited to fill.' Then Gaffney relayed the Praetorians' reserve price on the imperial throne: 'A nation with a projected $1.9 trillion budget surplus can afford consistently to allocate a minimum of 4 per cent of its gross domestic product to ensure its security.'

Already on July 21, Adm. Jay Johnson had said, as he stepped down from his post as the Navy's top officer, that national security requires a defense expenditure of 4 per cent of GDP. On August 16, Gen. James Jones, Commandant of the Marine Corps, used the occasion of an interview with *Defense Daily* to call for a 'gradual ramp up' in defense spending 'to about 4 to 4.5 per cent of the US gross domestic product.' Two days after Jones's comments, Gen. Gordon Sullivan, formerly Army Chief of Staff and now president of the 100,000-strong Association of the US Army, confirmed the Praetorians' floor demand: 'We must prepare for the future of the security of our nation. We should set the marker at 4 per cent.'

The Praetorians have avoided spelling out what 4 per cent actually means in dollar terms. The latest figures from the Office of Management and Budget project GDP at $10.9 trillion in 2002, rising to $13.9 trillion in 2007. So a military budget set at 4 per cent of GDP in 2002 would amount to $438 billion, and in 2007 to $558 billion. This year's budgetary tribute to the Praetorians is just on $300 billion. The combined spending of all putative foes of the United States – Russia, China and our old friends the rogue states, including Iran, Syria, Iraq, Libya, North Korea, Serbia, Cuba and Sudan – amounts to a little over $100 billion.

It is not well understood that though the number of ships, planes and troops available to guard the nation has declined sharply, the actual flow of dollars into the pockets of the Praetorians and their commercial partners has remained at cold war levels. It is true that in the immediate aftermath of the cold war, US military spending under George Bush I diminished slightly. Clinton reversed this trend with enough brio to allow Gore, speaking to the Veterans of Foreign Wars in the 1996 campaign, to declare that the Democratic bid to the Praetorians that year was far superior to that of the Republicans.

In his offer to the Praetorians this year, George W. Bush has offered Star Wars plus a pay raise for the armed forces. This is scarcely enough. An August 23 *Washington Post* editorial relayed the Praetorians' contempt: 'It is Mr. Bush who, despite some muscular rhetoric, is sounding weak on defense.' In other words, 'George, it's your bid.' The Praetorians know well that the missile defense scheme endorsed by Bush is a fantasy and that missile defense spending has been more or less constant since the early Sixties.

The appeal of a pay raise from a Republican emperor is undercut by lavish disbursements such as the recent 10 per cent raise enacted by Emperor Clinton, who further solidified the loyalty of the senior officer class by smoothing out wrinkles in the practice of double- dipping. These days, an officer can retire on full pension and then return to work at the Pentagon in civilian capacity at a hefty salary, with pension unimpaired. 'There are retired colonels in this building,' a Pentagon number cruncher remarked recently, 'who are taking home $200,000 a year.' 'I'm proud,' Gore told the VFW five days after he kissed Tipper, 'that we won the largest military pay increase in twenty years.'

Gore's commitment to the Praetorians was well advertised by his choice of running mate. Senator Joe Lieberman has been the faithful errand boy of Connecticut's arms firms. The Praetorians are licking their lips at the prospect of a delightful bidding war stretching over the presidential debates. We can look forward to Lieberman chastising Dick Cheney for his temerity, as President Bush's Defense Secretary, in cutting the military budget and even canceling such egregious boondoggles as the A-12 Stealth fighter.

There may be a deeper reason for the 4 per cent solution. The military share of the economy has been going down. There are no convincing external enemies, and it's been getting harder to claim a prime role for military R&D in setting the agenda for technological innovation. Thanks to Hollywood and our militarist heritage, the Pentagon still has a powerful cultural hold. The Democrats had Tom Hanks, the rescuer of Private Ryan, in camera view in the Staples Center, when Lieberman extolled the most powerful military force on Earth. But as the Pentagon's weight in the overall economy diminishes, so too does the clout of the Praetorians, and there may come a day when their bluff is called.

For now, let us await the next bid. Oh, and by the way, if the Praetorians get their 4 per cent out of a bidding war between Gore and Bush, Pentagon analyst Franklin Spinney accurately remarks: 'The 4 per cent defense solution would be tantamount to a declaration of total war on Social Security and Medicare in the following decade. Such a war could be justified only if our nation's survival were at stake.'

Andrew Cockburn is the co-author of Saddam Hussein: An American Obsession.

October 26, 1999

GENOCIDE IN KOSOVO?

by Alexander Cockburn and Jeffrey St. Clair

It's an important issue, since the NATO powers, fortified by a chorus from the liberal intelligentsia, flourished the charge of genocide as justification for bombing that destroyed much of Serbia's economy and killed around 2,000 civilians, with elevated death levels predicted for years to come. Whatever horrors they may have been planning, the Serbs were not engaged in genocidal activities in Kosovo before the bombing began. They were fighting a separatist movement, led by the KLA and behaving with the brutality typical of security forces, though to a degree more restrained than those backed by the United States in Central America. One common estimate of the number of Kosovar Albanians killed in the year before the bombing is 2,500. With NATO's bombing came the flights and expulsions and charges that the Serbs were accelerating a genocidal plan; on some accounts, as many as 100,000 were already dead. An alternative assessment was that NATO's bombing was largely to blame for the expulsions and killings.

After the war was over, on June 25, Bill Clinton told a White House press conference that on Slobodan Milosevic's orders tens of thousands of people had been killed in Kosovo. A week before, from the British Foreign Office, came the statement from Geoff Hoon that 'according to the reports we had gathered, mostly from the refugees, it appeared that around 10,000 people [that is, Kosovar Albanians] had been killed in more than 100 massacres.' Of course, the US and British governments had an obvious motive in painting as horrifying a picture as possible of what the Serbs had been up to, since the bombing had come under increasingly fierce attack, with rifts in the NATO alliance. The NATO powers had plenty of reasons to rush charges of genocide into the headlines. For one thing, it was becoming embarrassingly clear that the bombing had inflicted no significant damage on the Serbian army. All the more reason, therefore, to propose that the Serbs, civilians as well as soldiers, were collectively guilty of genocide and thus deserved everything they got.

Throughout the end of June and July there were plenty of press accounts running along lines similar to a July 4 dispatch in the *New York Times* from John Kifner with this sentence in its lead paragraph: 'The bodies keep turning up, day after day, and are expected now to number 10,000 or more. On August 2 Bernard Kouchner, the UN's chief administrator in Kosovo, said that 11,000 bodies had already been discovered in mass graves in the province.'

According to a useful and interesting analysis put out on October 17 by Stratfor.com (an independent operation based in Austin, Texas, that offers intelligence briefings on the Internet), Kouchner cited the International Criminal Tribunal for the former Republic of Yugoslavia as his authority, but the tribunal has said it hadn't provided any such information.

Nonetheless, the 10,000 figure became the baseline, with some estimates soaring far higher. Teams of forensic investigators from fifteen nations, including a detachment from the FBI, have been at work since June. To date they've examined about 150 of 400 sites of alleged mass murder.

There's still immense uncertainty, but at this point it's plain there are not enough bodies to warrant the claim that the Serbs had a program of extermination. The FBI team has made two trips to Kosovo and investigated thirty sites, containing nearly 200 bodies. In early October, the Spanish newspaper *El Pais* reported what the Spanish forensic team had found in its appointed zone in northern

Kosovo. The UN figures, said Perez Pujol, director of the Instituto Anatomico Forense de Cartagena, began with 44,000 dead, dropped to 22,000 and now stand at 11,000. He and his fellows were prepared to perform at least 2,000 autopsies in their zone. To date they've found 187 corpses. Pujol said he had the impression that the Serbs had given families the option of leaving. If they refused, or came back, they were killed. Like any murder of civilians, these were war crimes, just as any mass grave, whatever the number of bodies, indicates a massacre. But genocide?

One persistent story held that 700 Kosovars had been dumped in the Trepca lead and zinc mines. On October 12 Kelly Moore, a spokeswoman for the international tribunal, announced that the investigators had found absolutely nothing. There was an alleged mass grave containing 350 bodies in Ljubenic that turned out to hold seven. In Pusto Selo, villagers said 106 had been killed by the Serbs, and NATO rushed out satellite photos of mass graves. Nothing to buttress that charge has yet been found. Another eighty-two were allegedly killed in Kraljan. No bodies have as yet been turned up.

Although surely by now investigators would have been pointed to all probable sites, it's conceivable that thousands of Kosovar corpses await discovery. But as matters stand, the number of bodies turned up by the tribunal's teams is in the hundreds, not thousands, which tends to confirm the view of those who hold that NATO bombing provoked a wave of Serbian killings and expulsions, but that there was and is no hard evidence of a genocidal program.

Count another victory for the Big Lie.

October 29, 1999

BILL'S GOOD SIDE
by Alexander Cockburn

Our itinerant president seems to be wearying of the formalized mendacity that forms a substantial portion of his daily round. In a recent meeting with the two most prominent Kosovar Albanians, Clinton fidgeted irritably as Hacim, a man who clambered to his present eminent position over the bodies of many serious rivals, discoursed on the 'reconciliation' now under way in Kosovo. Finally Clinton could stand it no longer. 'That's nonsense,' he cried, 'and you know it.' Then he rounded on Rugova, who was chanting an interminable ode of gratitude, and curtly bid him be silent.

The president is most certainly right. Amid growing embarrassment among the war crime investigators at the scanty evidence of 'genocide' as supposedly perpetrated by the Serbs, the Kosovar Albanians are methodically driving out or slaughtering Serbs, as well as other minorities such as Gypsies, 90,000 of whom have now been expelled according to the Society of Endangered Peoples in Göttingen, Germany. The Society's president, Tilman Zuelch, said in early September that 'dark-skinned people can no longer walk the streets of most towns in Kosovo without risking injury to their very lives.'

June 20, 2002

SERBIAN RESERVATIONS
by James T. Phillips

'Did you come to see the zoo?'

A teenage girl wearing a colorful headband and dangling earrings stared at me as she asked about my intentions. The look on her face was a mixture of defiance and bemusement. Journalists prowling around her turf were once a common sight and, since the neighborhood is a small Serb enclave in the center of Pristina, noticing a man with a camera wasn't very difficult.

The teenager's home is located in a six-story block of apartments. One hundred and seventy-four Serbs live in the apartments, and other buildings housing thousands of Albanians surround the enclave. The Serbs have access to one small store, a fitness center, and, when I asked where do the children play, the teenage girl pointed to a dusty courtyard that functions as a football pitch. Twenty British KFOR soldiers live in one of the apartments, and they guard the Serbs day and night. The soldiers are alert, well armed and, like the Serbs in the courtyard, easy targets for those staring in through invisible bars that encircle the enclave.

'We are like prisoners here,' said the girl. 'We live like animals in a zoo.'

Yugoslavia was once multi-ethnic and modern, a member of the United Nations and, until 1991, ruled by communists. Eleven years after the beginning of the endless warfare in the Balkans, the nation of Yugoslavia has been cleaved into pieces by various nationalist leaders identified in the international press as freedom fighters (Croats), democrats (Bosnian Muslims), rebels (Albanians) and

butchers (Serbs). With the assistance of politicians, diplomats and
bomber pilots from the US – and compliant members of NATO
and the UN – the leaders of these various entities have succeeded
in creating ethnically pure regions carved out of the carnage of
war.

Capitalism has replaced communism in these new nations and,
although many of the same leaders continue to rule, the cleansing
operations during the past decade have assured the people of the
former Yugoslavia a future free from oppression, fear and ethnically
incompatible neighbors.

Except, of course, in Kosovo.

During the Balkans wars (1991–2002), Slovenes, Croats, Bosnians
(Croat, Serb and Muslim), Macedonians and Albanians fought and
died for the right to be independent and free. The Serbs living in
Kosovo also fought and died, yet three years after the end of NATO's
brutal war against Yugoslavia they are still not free.

Statistics about the success or failure of the mission in Kosovo,
gathered and published by KFOR, UNMIK and humanitarian aid
groups – and reported by journalists and writers looking to confirm
their own biases and agendas – are available in many busy offices
located in the bustling city of Pristina. The dissemination of this
information and propaganda sometimes seems to take priority over
the delivery of food and supplies to the people concentrated in a
few ethnically pure enclaves scattered throughout Kosovo. The
simple stories about the lives of Serbs, Roma and other minorities
living in these enclaves have gone missing, and the less-than-equal
undesirables of Kosovo continue to live in fear, loathing the rise of
a government dominated by Albanians and the fall of their own
precarious living standards.

★

'I'm sorry,' said the man sitting next to me. 'My son, he is full of energy.'

I met Jovica Rajkovic and his seven-year-old son Milan on the train that runs from Zvecan to G. Jankovic. Milan was sitting in the seat across from me, and he was kicking the edge of my seat. His father gently admonished the boy. Milan stopped kicking and tried to stand up on his seat and look out the dirt-encrusted window. Jovica reached over and took hold of his son's arm. Milan sat down. He remained still for less than five seconds.

Zvecan is a small town located north of Mitrovica, the 'flashpoint' city where Serbs and Albanians live, separated by the polluted Ibar river. Serbs live north of the river and Albanians live in the southern areas of the segregated city. The railroad station in Zvecan sits in a cleft between crumbling hills and shares a small valley with the rusting remains of the Trepca mining complex, the source of the pollution that flows in the Ibar river. G. Jankovic is a large town located near the border crossing between southern Kosovo and northern Macedonia, and it is the end of the line.

Three years ago, in the spring of 1999, the same train and the same tracks were used to transport thousands of Albanians to the Blace refugee camp in Macedonia. On a hot and humid day in June of 2002, a Serb father and son boarded the ancient train and traveled the short distance to their home in Kosovo Polje. Armed KFOR soldiers from Greece provided protection for the passengers as the train chugged slowly through areas populated by Albanians. The damage done to the Albanian towns and villages during the war has been repaired, and the new houses dotting the landscape would be considered small mansions in North America.

Jovica peered through the window. He pointed towards blackened shells of burned-out houses in abandoned Serb villages.

'Look there,' said Jovica. 'The Albanians have destroyed our homes.'

There was very little rebuilding or remodeling occurring in the Serb villages, and there were no large homes being financed and constructed for Serbs, as was being done for the free and independent Albanians of Kosovo. Since the end of the war between NATO and Yugoslavia, thousands of new structures have been built by Albanians and paid for by the international community. However, three years after the war ended, many Serbs continue to live in tents and small prefabricated shelters, surviving on what little aid and assistance is trickling down to them after the Albanians have siphoned off most of the money, goods and services being provided by the international community.

'It is a catastrophe for my people,' said Jovica.

When we arrived at the station in Kosovo Polje, Jovica and Milan said goodbye and stepped down onto a platform crowded with passengers waiting to board the southbound train. Gripping his son's hand tightly in his own huge fist, Jovica quickly threaded his way through groups of Albanians standing in and around the railway platform. The atmosphere was tense. Hostile stares and smirking laughter by the Albanians quickened the pace of the Serb father and son, and they were out of my sight within seconds.

UNMIK is the acronym for the United Nations Mission in Kosovo, the international organization responsible for reorganizing a shattered land and people. Although the landscape of Kosovo has seen some definite improvements, many of the people still live broken lives. And, fittingly for this surreal province of Serbia, UNMIK has not even been able to provide a secure environment for its own Serb civilian employees.

'This is terribly humiliating,' said Marija, a young Serb woman who works for UNMIK.

I was escorting Marija to her job in Pristina. She lives only three blocks from her office, but is afraid to walk through the streets alone. Although she speaks excellent English and passes herself off as an American, the young woman, a hard-edged and proud Serb, is scared to acknowledge her ethnicity.

Marija is not her real name. A Serb working in Albanian areas of Kosovo can easily become a target of Albanians who want to continue the cleansing of the ethnic minorities that began immediately after the end of the war in June of 1999. UNMIK also disapproves of any disparaging comments from the local staff. Marija could lose her life or her job if her real name was published. Like other Serbs, Marija has lost her identity as well as her freedom.

'The internationals want to get rid of us,' said Marija, referring to the enclaves populated by minorities and protected by UNMIK and KFOR. 'They want to get rid of a problem, and the problem is the Serbs.'

'The Serbs are not free.'

David Pierson is a 48-year-old American from Colorado working as an UNMIK policeman in the city of Pristina; he agrees with Marija.

'They are always under escort,' said Pierson. 'I don't call that free. The Serbs have to come and go in groups.'

Officer Pierson was sitting at a table outside a small kiosk, drinking coffee and watching the people pass by, when I stopped and said hello. His perch was only a few blocks from Marija's office. There are more than 500 American policemen currently working in Kosovo. They try to offer protection to the minority communities, but walking a beat in Pristina usually means driving around in a brand-new Sports Utility Vehicle painted to resemble a Coca-Cola can with wheels. Their contact with the people is limited to responding to calls for assistance from Serbs, and ordering coffee at Albanian cafés.

'Crime is down, murders are down,' said Barry Fletcher, a press spokesman for UNMIK. Fletcher is also an American policeman. 'Now, it's just street crime, car thefts and sexual assaults. But if we pull out of here in the next few years, the situation will return to what it was in 1999.

'Both sides view themselves as victims,' said Fletcher. 'They do not accept that they are also the perpetrators. Only time will heal the hate.'

The Albanians once lived under Serbian rule, and they rebelled against their alleged oppressors. With the assistance of other Americans – politicians and diplomats, aid workers and soldiers – the Albanians won their war of liberation and have created a society that is discriminating against the Serbs, Roma and other minorities. The policemen now stationed throughout Kosovo have to deal with the problems.

'It's apartheid,' said Fletcher, the UNMIK spokesman, acknowledging the fact that good cops cannot change bad behavior, and giving credence to the Serb complaints about whether the international community really cares about protecting innocent lives. 'If you give us information about a crime, and give us a name, we'll book them. We'd love to.'

Marija thinks it is a crime when her right to walk to work is denied, and does not believe that freedom for the ethnic minorities of Kosovo is very high on the agendas of the Albanians or the Americans.

'The internationals want to get rid of the Serbs,' she said as I escorted her to her job at UNMIK headquarters. 'The Serbs are going to remain in a cage.'

James T. Phillips is a freelance reporter. He has covered wars in Iraq, Croatia, Bosnia, Kosovo and Macedonia.

March 6, 2003

'LIBERATION' FOUR YEARS AFTER
by Chad Nagle

'That is Kosovo,' says my Macedonian driver, pointing out the window at a ravine by the roadside, piled high with garbage. Four years later, 'liberation' in this forlorn patch of the former Yugoslavia looks like a destitute landscape of scrubby fields and abandoned industrial enterprises, ransacked or destroyed buildings, and social breakdown in town after lifeless town. It is a desolate reminder to the world that wars seldom if ever bring the sort of rosy results pledged by those who wage them, and that Iraqis – as they watch their homeland destroyed by American bombs and missiles – have much to beware of when the US promises to bring them freedom and democracy by force of arms.

Kosovo is an economic wasteland, a new welfare state adopted by the West in an ex-Yugoslav district that once numbered perhaps 2 million, but which has been 'ethnically cleansed' of most of the non-Albanians who lived there. Kosovar Albanians once enjoyed a life free of taxes or even – for the most part – bills within the Federal Republic of Yugoslavia. Now they are the West's dependants. Except for a weird construction boom that has produced mile upon mile of ugly three- and four-story, unoccupied red-brick houses, nothing of any substance is produced in Kosovo today. Aid from the 'international community' has endowed the inhabitants with copious quantities of construction materials to build new residential monstrosities, but these structures now stand empty and windowless, as if in preparation for a mass population drive.

'They've tricked the West into giving them money and materials to rebuild damaged homes,' says my driver. 'But these damaged homes don't exist, and they just use the resources to put up these houses. They're speculating in real estate by taking over church land, moving in and announcing the ground is their property. They all do exactly the same thing, like a tribe planning its future.'

The heavily guarded and conspicuously gigantic US military base, Camp Bondsteel, sprawls as far as the eye can see a short distance south of Kosovo's main city, Pristina, and serves as the center of economic activity in the province. The locals highly prize the prospect of a job in Bondsteel – in one of the bowling alleys or fast-food outlets on the base – since employment opportunities in Kosovo as a whole are so scarce. Despite the paucity of regular jobs for ordinary folk, enough Kosovar Albanians manage to travel to the West to justify regular available flights to destinations like Zurich and Frankfurt from Pristina airport (regular flights to the Serbian capital, Belgrade, have not been restored since the 1999 war). Smuggling and prostitution are rampant, and people in Serbia and Macedonia seem unable to talk about Kosovo without mentioning illegal trade in narcotics, cigarettes, guns and alcohol.

In Pristina, which numbers anywhere between a quarter of a million and 400,000 inhabitants depending on who you ask, electricity is available a mere four hours a day. Only buildings like the Hotel Grand – once buzzing with people from the press or international organizations – can count on electrical power around the clock. But even this is thanks to private generators, and guests of the Grand still have to do without running water after midnight.

The social and economic disaster in Kosovo can be forgiven, many say, because NATO halted 'genocide' by the Yugoslav armed forces. Yet the figures of 500,000 Albanians killed were debunked even before the bombing stopped, and only a few hundred bodies were eventually found, many Serbs or Albanians killed by NATO itself. The Kosovar Albanian guerrilla war for 'national liberation' had nothing to do with a drive to avert mass murder, but even after the propaganda-driven war was over the West had to bolster the lie as truth. Those watching the Iraq war on TV in the West should therefore be prepared to recognize similar myth-making by Western governments about crimes, atrocities and 'weapons of mass destruction' in Iraq before and after hostilities end.

Today, Kosovo is covered with signs of such 'myth maintenance,' mostly in the form of gaudy memorials to legendary fallen heroes of the Kosovo Liberation Army (KLA). Giant cornucopias of plastic flowers and hideous roadside cemeteries lie scattered all over the province, testaments to the gratitude with which ordinary Albanians supposedly view the sacrifices of their paramilitary brethren. In fact, the state of many of these ugly monuments is evidence of a less than sincere reverence on the part of Kosovo's current inhabitants for the agents of their freedom struggle.

According to the official history, the US-led assault on Yugoslavia was largely prompted by a massacre of Albanians on January 15, 1999, at the Kosovar village of Racak, where the American envoy of the Organization for Security and Co-operation in Europe (OSCE), William Walker, alleged Serbs had gunned down forty Albanian peasants on a hillside in a crime 'the like of which has not been seen before.' Many have disputed Walker's account, raising questions as to whether the US diplomat may have fabricated the incident or been involved in an even more sinister way, like a model of the 'Quiet American' from the recent film of Graham Greene's novel. Walker's credibility in the Racak affair was shaky to begin with, since he had served as US ambassador to El Salvador when death-squad activity there was at its zenith (1988–92). Even if the episode did in fact occur as told by Walker, Racak should surely have become 'sacred ground' to any Kosovar Albanians retaining memories of victimization by the Serbs. So what does Racak look like today?

The site of the slaughter is a patch of hillside covered with the usual unsightly plastic flower display and fascistic KLA hagiography, while entrance to the makeshift cemetery is through a dark metal archway with Albanian wording above it. The path up to the Racak massacre site winds past heaps of garbage on either side, and at the base of the hillside down which the murderous Serbs were alleged to have approached the Albanians on that fateful day, junked cars, refrigerators and other large and rusting kitchen appliances contribute to the scenery of this Kosovar Albanian version of Arlington Cemetery. 'Immediately after the NATO war, the Albanians took international aid and bought new cars and kitchen appliances,' says my driver. 'They just threw their old stuff out into the streets and fields, even if it worked perfectly. They wanted new things, like children, and they got them.'

But is Kosovo safe and peaceful now? 'Security decreases every day,' says a Serb shop owner in Gracanica, site of a fourteenth-century Serbian Orthodox monastery. 'Before, the bus to Belgrade used to have a Swedish escort, but not any more. Maybe they think it's safer now but I don't think it's so rosy. I can't even go to Pristina.' What about the free market economy? 'Investment here is all mafia,' he says. 'None of it is the product of an honest day's sweat.'

Then there is the 'tyrant' Milosevic, and the democratization of Yugoslavia, another purported result of the West's war. Even if the people of the former Yugoslavia have a few problems, at least they have democracy instead of a vicious dictatorship – so the official line goes. But after Serbian Prime Minister Zoran Djindjic was killed by a single sniper's bullet as he was getting into his Mercedes limousine on March 12, the climate of fear that gripped Belgrade was palpable even to an outsider. The government of Djindjic's Democratic Party (DS) decreed a 'state of emergency' and started arrests, which reached 1,000 a little over a week later, according to official reports. As if rubbing home a point, televised news endlessly replayed video camera footage of the moment of Djindjic's death, showing the fifty-year-old's tall frame shudder for an instant as a bullet entered his shoulder, pierced his heart, and exited his stomach before he was pushed into the back of the waiting vehicle. One of his bodyguards also took a hit with the same kind of ammunition banned by the Geneva Conventions – an expand-on-impact dumdum bullet. While the temptation to blame Milosevic for the killing was obvious, no one could seriously believe the ex-president of Yugoslavia was behind it.

'I believe the state of emergency is being used to create a one-party state,' says Zoran Belinovac, legal affairs adviser to the Democratic Party of Serbia (DSS), once a partner with the DS in government but now powerless, without a single minister in the cabinet. 'Not even in wartime can you arrest someone and detain them for thirty days without right to a lawyer.' The media in Serbia, says Belinovac, already resembles a one-party state's, because a government organ called the Media Bureau controls all media access and content and is completely controlled by the DS. 'The situation was barely better before the state of emergency,' claims Belinovac. 'Under Tito, media always talked about the "rule of the workers". Under Milosevic, state media talked about the "national interest". But the DS's media game is smarter and more complex. Now it's all about "reform". It's enough to say you are a "democrat" and "reformer" without having to prove anything.' Ironically, in the aftermath of the Djindjic murder the DS removed two judges who had been appointed under Milosevic's presidency.

Most leading representatives of Serbia's main political parties apparently accept the government's official line: Djindjic started cracking down on organized crime and was rubbed out. But most also accept that the pro-Western Djindjic had long made deals and compromises with mobs like Zemun and Surcin in an effort to consolidate the power of his government and the DS. In fact, Serbian Minister of Internal Affairs Dusan Mihaijlovic – the man directing the state of emergency – even described one rascal as a 'respected citizen' in a public statement last year.

'Right now state institutions in Serbia are very weak,' says Nenad Stefanovic, a correspondent for the news magazine *Vreme*. 'The mafias are stronger and better organized than the state.'

'I have twenty-four years of service to the state and speak four languages,' says a career Yugoslav civil servant who asks not to be named. 'Yet they put me out on the street for no reason. I was a state representative, and they have destroyed the state. The economy doesn't work, there are no more professionals in the civil service, and you are obliged to pay taxes on income you earned ten years ago. I have no pension and unemployment benefits are practically nil. Health services are completely destroyed, and now everything is 'private' because of the DS government.'

'The current state structures obviously have no authority or influence now,' says Dusan Jelicic of the Socialist Party of Serbia (SPS), still formally chaired by Slobodan Milosevic, now on trial for war crimes in The Hague. 'Djindjic was doing a balancing act with the mafia and switched sides from Zemun to the Surcin clan,' he claims. 'A Croat businessman named Stanko Subotic had even provided Djindjic with a private plane for his official trips. None of this inspired much confidence in the public that the government was acting in the best interests of the people.' Now, Jelicic says, no one can criticize the DS or the government. 'We can all be arrested.'

Even assuming Djindjic was actually trying to clamp down on Serbian organized crime, the West probably cared little about any problems he was having. Former Swiss magistrate Carla Del Ponte, now chief prosecutor at the War Crimes Tribunal at The Hague, had been handing Djindjic longer and longer lists of people to be extradited, until finally Djindjic – himself the key figure responsible for the extradition of Milosevic – had to put up his hand.

'Djindjic told Del Ponte it was ridiculous to indict every single Serb who had been in Kosovo during the war in 1999, but she just kept coming with the lists,' says *Vreme*'s Nenad Stefanovic, a frequent reporter on developments at The Hague. 'Del Ponte has often said she didn't care about the political circumstances inside individual countries, only the trial of war criminals,' says Stefanovic. 'Yet the international community and the Hague Tribunal paid a lot of attention to the domestic problems of Croatia, and [UN high representative in Kosovo] Michael Steiner also used to say at diplomatic meetings that although there were clearly a lot of war criminals in Kosovo, if we sent them to The Hague the KLA could retaliate. Nobody paid any attention to Serbia.' After the Serbian premier's murder, Del Ponte stated publicly that she had met with Djindjic weeks before his death, and said he had told her in a one-on-one meeting: 'They will kill me.'

The 'international community' has generally treated Carla Del Ponte as above moral reproach, but back in 1999 before her appointment at The Hague, articles from the Swiss and Italian press suggested that Del Ponte tipped off banks in Lugano, Switzerland, that they would be investigated for laundering money from cigarette smuggling. At the height of the Kosovo war, when Del Ponte was prosecuting the Mabetex scandal (in which construction tenders were awarded by the Kremlin to a KLA-tied Albanian named Beghijet Pacolli), Moscow's opposition to NATO's war suddenly evaporated just as Russian President Boris Yeltsin and his family were being implicated. Shortly after that, Del Ponte won the Hague job. However effective her actions in the service of NATO's war aims, Del Ponte probably did little to fortify the rule of law in the Balkans or elsewhere.

Although Zoran Djindjic likely played a destructive role in strengthening Serbian political institutions, his violent removal looks set to plunge the country into further chaos.

So dire has the political, social and economic situation in Serbia become that many people have evidently placed hopes in the ruling government's 'state of emergency.' A recent poll showed 86 per cent of respondents support the policy as a way of restoring the authority of state institutions in Serbia, and it is no exaggeration to say that memories of the Communist period are overwhelmingly positive among large swathes of the citizenry. Many in Belgrade now pine for the Tito days, just as in neighboring Bulgaria pensioners remember Communist leader Todor Zhivkov's era as a time when the police did their jobs, pensions were paid, and schoolchildren didn't abuse drugs and carry handguns to school.

The assassinations and mafia rule in Serbia and Kosovo are a sad testament to the merit of 'democratization' and 'reform' that has come to the region as a legacy of the country's 'liberation' by the West, much in the way that Afghanistan under Western puppet Hamid Karzai – featuring regular assassination attempts and bloody warlords ruling the countryside – offers another example of the hollowness of Western trumpeting of democracy and freedom.

Chad Nagle is a lawyer and freelance writer who traveled to Serbia and Kosovo in March on behalf of the British Helsinki Human Rights Group.

PART TWO

OVERVIEW

March 6, 2002

FORMER SENIOR CIA OFFICER: WHY THE 'WAR ON TERROR' WON'T WORK
by Bill Christison

On January 15 the Attorney General of the United States, John Ashcroft, held a press conference in order to describe the initial criminal charges that the government would make against John Walker, the twenty-year-old American citizen who had joined the Taliban military forces. In his talk, Ashcroft said this: 'The United States does not casually or capriciously charge one of its own citizens with providing support to terrorists. We are impelled to do so today by the inescapable fact of September 11, a day that reminded us in no uncertain terms that we have enemies in the world and that these enemies seek to destroy us. We learned on September 11 that our way of life is not immune from attack, and even from destruction.'

The guts of what Ashcroft said is: 'We have enemies in the world and these enemies seek to destroy us.'

I submit to you that this is simply not a true statement. The evidence I've seen shows that the real objective of the Muslim extremists led by Osama bin Laden was to rid the Muslim world itself of American domination and influence. They wanted NOT to destroy the United States; rather they wanted the US out of their own land. Bin Laden and his supporters also wanted, and those yet alive still want, to unite Muslim nations behind an extreme version of Islam, believing that the Islamic world can thereby better control its own future. I think they realize full well there is no possibility they can 'destroy' the United States, and their objective, while still pretty grandiose, is considerably more limited. Their aim, according to one recent analysis that appeared in the *New York Review of Books*, 'is to create one Islamic world. This is a call to purify the Islamic world of the idolatrous West, exemplified by America. The aim is to strike at American heathen shrines, and show, in the most spectacular fashion, that the US is vulnerable, a paper tiger.'

These Islamic extremists are not nice people. Those still alive, and other future adherents to their cause, will continue to try to kill innocent people in the US and elsewhere. But what the extremists see themselves as trying to do is to stop the United States from continuing its drive for global hegemony, including hegemony over the Islamic world. I think it's important to understand this, because if people in the United States believe that some enemy is trying to 'destroy' the US – and actually has some possibility of doing so – then waging an all-out war against that enemy can be more easily justified.

But what if the US is not trying to prevent its own destruction, but instead is trying to preserve and extend its global hegemony? In that case, I think we should all step back and start demanding of our government a serious public debate over future US foreign policies. We should be strenuously debating the degree to which the people in this country, given all of our own domestic problems, want the US government to continue foreign policies intended to strengthen US hegemony over and domination of the rest of the world in the political, economic and military arenas.

In short, Ashcroft's claim that enemies are seeking to destroy the United States makes it easier for the US government to avoid any limits that might otherwise be imposed on its 'war against terrorism' by an informed public opinion. President George W. Bush's references in his own speeches to America's enemies as 'the evil ones' tend in the same direction. Although acts of terrorism – which I'm defining here as killings of, or other violence against, innocent noncombatants – are always inexcusable, simply labeling perpetrators as 'the evil ones' makes it easier for the US government to avoid any inconvenient discussion of ways in which the US might modify its foreign policies to reduce the likelihood of future terrorist acts. But are all Afghans 'evil ones'? Or all members of the Taliban? Or did only a few Taliban leaders know about the planned terrorist attacks before September 11? In any case, is it clear that all Taliban members were accomplices of Al Qaeda and Osama bin Laden? And if they were accomplices, is it not true that the better legal systems of the world do not punish accomplices to a crime as severely as the criminals themselves? Is it right that in this war the US is punishing the accomplices just as much as the criminals themselves? It seems to me that the use of the term 'evil ones' is intended to avoid discussion of a lot of nuances.

My own view is that the United States is now, almost five months after September 11, heading into an extraordinarily difficult time, when substantial changes in our foreign policies will be required. Yet all the polls seem to show that up to 90 per cent of the people in this country still don't even want to listen to anyone who proposes alternatives to our present foreign policies. So I guess that shows that only 10 per cent of Americans care much about our policies toward the rest of the world.

The first and most basic belief I have about the current situation is that military action will never be effective in solving the problem of terrorism against the United States. At best it will only prevent terrorism temporarily. As I've already mentioned, there's little doubt that the US will somehow kill or capture or otherwise neutralize Osama bin Laden and most of his lieutenants. The US has already pretty much pulverized Afghanistan by bombing, and has incidentally killed an unknown number of innocent noncombatants in the process. The US government, by the way, seems uninterested in even estimating how many innocent noncombatants have in fact been killed, but it is possible that the number is as large as or larger than the 3,000 killed in the US on September 11. Whatever the military success of the US, however, a couple of years hence new extremists just as clever as bin Laden, and hating the US even more, will almost certainly arise somewhere else in the world. That's why we need to understand the root causes behind the terrorism.

If I am right that military action will not prevent future terrorism, but only delay it, we should start working on these root causes right away. We should not wait until the military actions are finished before looking at root causes, as some people would urge us to do.

So let's go. I'm going to list six major root causes of the terrorism that I think are important. The critical thing you should keep in mind on all of these six issues is that there is a great deal of disagreement in Washington and elsewhere over the relative importance of one compared to another. With that caveat, here are the six root causes of terrorism against the US. I've arranged them in a rough order that starts with those I think are most difficult to deal with, but the order does not necessarily reflect their relative importance. My personal feeling is that all six are of equal importance.

★

ONE My number one root cause is the support by the US over recent years for the policies of Israel with respect to the Palestinians, and the belief among Arabs and Muslims that the United States is as much to blame as Israel itself for the continuing, almost thirty-five-year-long Israeli occupation of the West Bank and the Gaza Strip.

My first comment on this issue is that it is a more controversial root cause than any of the others on our list. The government of Israel, and many supporters of Israel in the United States, really did not want to talk about any root causes immediately after September 11. Top leaders in the United States, most of whom strongly support Israel, preferred to talk only in general terms – about how the terrorists were mad and irrational, and how they had attacked 'freedom itself,' out of mindless hatred. More recently, when pressured to talk about root causes at all, the Israelis and their supporters have gone to great lengths to reject arguments that Israel's behavior toward the Palestinians, or US support for Israel, are in any way even a partial cause of the terrorism. When forced to say something positive about root causes, they tend to allege a broader Islamic religious hatred of the West and its modern technology than I think exists. They also emphasize the internal tensions within the Arab world, the lack of democracy and the dictatorial rulers of Arab nations, who are depicted as trying to distract their people from their own internal grievances by whipping up hatred of Israel.

I need to digress for a moment. In a situation where there are clearly multiple root causes of terrorism, it's in the interest of any person or nation that might be blamed for one of the root causes to emphasize instead the other root causes. In the last couple of months, a sizable propaganda campaign has been launched suggesting that Saudi Arabia is the most important root cause of the

September 11 terrorism. I certainly agree that the dictatorial and decrepit Saudi government and its support throughout the Muslim world for a harsh and immoderate version of Islam can be seen as one – but only one – of the root causes behind the recent terrorism. I'll have more to say about this later. What I want to point out here is that I suspect supporters of Israel are aggressively pressing this campaign against Saudi Arabia, in the hope of persuading other world leaders that the issue of Palestine is NOT a significant root cause. *The New York Times* columnist Thomas Friedman is a leading practitioner of this pro-Israel campaign. The United States' strong support for Israel and for its occupation and colonization of the West Bank and the Gaza Strip is indeed a major root cause of the terrorism against the US.

Two My number two root cause is the present drive of the United States to spread its hegemony and its version of big-corporation, free-enterprise globalization around the world. At the same time, the massive poverty of average people, not only in Arab and Muslim nations but also in the whole Third World, has become more important as a global political issue. The gap between rich and poor nations, and rich and poor people within most of the nations, has grown wider during the last twenty years of globalization or, more precisely, the US version of globalization. Animosities against the United States have grown among the poor of the world, who have watched as the US has expanded both its hegemony and a type of globalization based on its own economic system, while they themselves have seen no or very little benefit from these changes.

This problem of poverty around the world is so immense that it's almost impossible to grasp. Global statistics are far from perfect, but they show that the world's population hit 6 billion last year. 2.8 billion people, almost half of the world's total, have incomes of less than two dollars a day. Here's another statistic: the richest 1 per cent of the world's people receive as much income as the poorest 57 per cent. And here's a final statistic: the richest 25 million people in the United States receive more income than the 2 billion poorest people of the world – one third of the world's total population. Can we even comprehend the magnitude of the injustice that these figures represent? And have no doubt – we in the United States are, rightly or wrongly, blamed for these figures.

The catalog of reasons for animosity toward the US throughout the world includes a number of things in addition to our overbearing assertion of both economic and political hegemony: our arrogance in insisting that whatever we say goes, our penchant for abrogating or ignoring international treaties that we don't happen to like, as well as the influence of US corporations that exploit cheap labor in Third World countries to make consumer goods for Americans. Take all these things together and you have a wide sense among the poor people of the world of being oppressed by the United States. This in turn made it possible for Osama bin Laden and the fundamentalists around him to instill and spread intense hatred of us, just as a sense of being oppressed by the Allies after World War One made it possible for Hitler to arouse the kind of fear and hatred among Germans that led both to the slaughter of Jews and to World War Two.

The pressures arising from the complex and related problems of US hegemony, globalization and the immense gap in wealth will grow steadily more explosive. My proposal is that the US should immediately develop and implement, with active participation of the UN and the European Union, a new, very large, and long-term 'Marshall Plan' type of aid program for all of the poor nations of the world. This plan should specifically be aimed at reducing the size of the income gap between the poorest and richest nations, and at reducing the income gap between the rich and poor within nations. This type of plan could contribute significantly to reducing the likelihood of future terrorism against the United States. It would also show a far more generous side of the United States to people who at present see only a US version of globalization that seems to them highly selfish and beneficial largely to big corporations and the rich of the world.

I've been talking about a massive aid program for the world's poor since last October, when I spoke to a number of peace groups in Santa Fe. More recently, the British Chancellor of the Exchequer, Gordon Brown, has proposed a similar plan, in the amount of $100 billion for each of the next four years. My own suggestion as to the amount is $350 billion spread over three years. $350 billion is, after all, just about what the US military budget will probably amount to in the next ONE fiscal year. One would think that we could find an equal amount to spend over a three-year period for what I would regard as a better purpose.

About now some of you are probably thinking, how unrealistic can this guy get! He of all people – meaning me – should be aware of how corrupt the governments of most Third World nations are, and you can just see all this money simply going down the drain. My answer is that solving the problem of massive income inequalities around the world is absolutely critical to the future stability of the world, and so far the US version of globalization has not improved the situation at all. I think there are enough intelligent people in the UN, US, Europe and the underdeveloped countries themselves that we could set up a planning and monitoring group to oversee the wise use of such large funds and to hold the level of corruption to a minimum. The United States should not run such a program unilaterally, and the institutions set up to manage it should not be used to perpetuate and strengthen US global hegemony, as is the case now with the International Monetary Fund and the World Bank. When you hear charges of unrealism before some new program is even in the detailed planning stages, I think you're entitled to ask if those making the charges aren't really opposing the new program for some other reason. My own feeling is that the world is in such a mess, and the inequality problem is so severe, that maybe we should worry less about alleged 'unrealism' and more about getting on with the business of planning, followed by real action, to do something about the problem.

THREE The number three root cause I want to discuss is the continuing sanctions and lack of food and medicines for the people of Iraq, deaths of Iraqi children, and the almost daily bombing of Iraq by the US and Great Britain. Right or wrong, the Arab and Muslim 'street' blames this on the US, not on Saddam Hussein.

I don't have much to comment about on this one. The sanctions and the bombings have been in effect for ten years, and have neither brought about the ouster of Saddam Hussein nor significantly weakened him. And they have caused the deaths of children variously estimated at up to or over a million. The US government's position is that Saddam himself is to blame for the troubles of the Iraqi people, but the fact remains that after all these years, the Iraqi people are the ones hurt by US actions, not Saddam.

My view is that simple justice argues for an end to both the sanctions and the bombings. My proposal is that we do precisely that.

FOUR My number four root cause is the continued presence of US troops in Saudi Arabia.

Ten years ago this was the principal cause of Osama bin Laden's hostility toward the United States. (His hostility on account of US actions against Iraq and then the massive US support for Israel came later and in both cases may be tactical – an effort to broaden his own popularity in the Arab world.) Today the thousands of US military personnel in Saudi Arabia are a constant irritant in Saudi–US relations. The Saudi people clearly do not want them there. Unless we plan to invade Iraq again, I doubt there is any longer a vital reason to keep men and US ground-based military facilities there.

My proposal? The obvious one – that we remove the troops. I understand, of course – you'd have to be blind and deaf not to know this – that some people at high levels in the US government do want to invade Iraq again. All I can say is, I hope such people do not carry the day. I can't think of a thing that would do more to broaden this 'war on terrorism' into a Judeo-Christian war against Islam – despite any US governmental protestations to the contrary.

FIVE The fifth root cause on my list is the dissatisfaction and anger of many average and even elite Arabs and Muslims over their own authoritarian, undemocratic, and often corrupt governments, which are supported by the United States.

My first comment here is that Osama bin Laden is a good example of this particular root cause. His extremist wrath was directed as much against the Saudi government, for example, as it was against the United States. His opposition to what used to be his own government was probably the main reason why he had the support of a majority of the young men under twenty-five in Saudi Arabia. He received similar support from many young men in other Arab and Muslim states as well. Right now these groups of angry young men obviously no longer have a viable leader in Osama bin Laden, but other extremist leaders are almost sure to arise. In addition, the next generation of leaders in at least some of these states may well emerge from among these young men. If any of them do come into power, their future governments will likely be more anti-American than the present governments, which Washington likes to call 'moderate,' but which are really nothing of the sort. If we have not reduced our energy dependence on oil in the meantime, we may face serious trouble.

In my view, this is a truly difficult problem. My proposal is that we should adopt draconian measures immediately to reduce our overall energy usage, including but not limited to cutting our dependence on Mideast oil. We should, for example, change our tax structure to make energy as expensive to consumers in the United States as it is in Europe and Japan. This will require significant life-style changes in the US. I think we kid ourselves if we believe that we can solve any coming energy crunch by expanding alternative power sources or by increasing 'clean coal' usage, nuclear power usage, and Alaskan oil usage. The shortages will be too great; so will the long-term environmental costs; and so will the political costs in our relationships with other nations that have already accepted higher energy prices for consumers as a necessary burden of twenty-first-century life.

We also should not count on new oil supplies from Central Asia allowing us to forget about the need for conservation and to stop being concerned about the stability of Saudi Arabia or other areas of the Middle East. Even assuming that massive supplies of oil from Central Asia become available quickly, all we'll be doing is transferring our support from the dictatorships of Saudi Arabia and the Gulf States to the dictatorships of Central Asia. That is not a prospect that we should blithely accept. In my view, conservation is the route we must follow.

I think we should, at the same time, gradually reduce the closeness of our ties with the present authoritarian governments in Arab and Muslim states, and try to develop a better understanding of and improved relations with groups in these states that oppose their own present governments. We should seek out groups that appear to be democratically inclined and 'moderate' in the true meaning of the word. Difficult? Of course it will be. But it is the best shot we've got, in my opinion, to have a decent relationship with many Muslim states in the future. It's also the best shot we've got if we wish to diminish, over time, the support for future Osama bin Ladens that arises from the anger of Arabs and Muslims with their own governments.

SIX The sixth and last root cause on my list arises directly from the US 'war on terrorism.' It has to do with the kind of war the US is now able to fight. On three recent occasions – the Gulf War of 1990–1991, the Kosovo War of 1999 against Yugoslavia, and the current war against Afghanistan – the United States has easily achieved victories by relying almost exclusively on air power, on missiles launched from a great distance, and now even on drone aircraft with no humans on board. The US has won these wars with practically no casualties among its own forces. But while few Americans get killed, sizable numbers of other nationalities do.

Most people in the United States are proud both of these victories and of the low US casualties in these three wars. From the viewpoint of anyone who supports the wars, this prowess of US armed forces deserves to be honored. But elsewhere in much of the world, especially the underdeveloped world, this overwhelming invincibility of the US military intensifies the frustrations about and hatred of the United States. This in turn makes future terrorist acts against the US – or what is now called by US strategic thinkers asymmetrical warfare – even more likely. Those in underdeveloped lands who oppose the US drive for worldwide hegemony are increasingly coming to see no means other than terrorism as an effective method of opposing the United States.

This is an issue that demands a lot more discussion than it's been getting, and it goes to the heart of our future foreign policies. For the immediate future, perhaps the next five or ten years, it's going to be tempting for any government of the United States to implement and enforce whatever foreign policies it chooses by going to war, because it will be confident – even overconfident – that it won't lose a military confrontation and won't suffer many casualties. The US government in fact has already started moving in this direction, by threatening to launch preemptive wars against nations that are trying to develop nuclear weapons or other weapons of mass destruction. Another thing the US is already doing is to militarize the United States to an unprecedented, and wholly unnecessary, degree in comparison with other nations. An editorial in the March 3 *New York Times* puts it bluntly. 'If Congress cranks up the Pentagon's budget as much as President Bush would like, the United States will soon be spending more on defense than all the other countries of the world combined.' To me, this is absurd – but there you are. These military expenditures will clearly lead to cuts in spending on domestic US problems such as poverty and healthcare, and make it harder to do anything about solving the problems of global poverty and income inequality that I've already discussed. In this same five- to ten-year period, the readily available military option will also encourage the US to avoid facing up to the hard decisions necessary for a peaceful resolution of our more intractable foreign policy problems.

This leads me to a very important conclusion. Since the greater willingness to initiate and fight wars intensifies hatred of the US, it is in the US interest to show restraint and voluntarily stop employing warfare based on bombing in order to combat future acts of terrorism. The fact that US bombs and missiles have already killed innocent civilians is tragic and puts us on a par with the extremists who committed the September 11 acts. The US should stop, right now, all further military action that risks killing more civilians. At the same time, I want to emphasize that I am quite sure there is enough evidence of Osama bin Laden's complicity in the September 11 terrorist actions to arrest and indict him. Assuming he is still alive, I would therefore support covert or Green-Beret-type operations to capture, but not assassinate, him. Maximum precautions should be taken, however, to prevent such operations from killing or injuring any more innocent civilians. Once captured, bin Laden should be prosecuted and tried in an international court.

I fully understand that compared to most views you hear concerning the US 'war on terrorism,' my views are RADICAL. But I believe that unless the US moves in the directions I've been suggesting, in five or ten years the terrorism against the United States will become so intense that our global relationships with other nations will be in a shambles. On the other hand, if the US government voluntarily moves toward the kind of foreign policy changes I've been talking about, I think that its actions might start a trend toward a considerably more peaceful, and stable, twenty-first century than now seems likely.

Bill Christison was an analyst for the CIA from 1950 to 1979. At various times, he worked on Soviet and European affairs, on global nuclear proliferation, and later, on Asian and African affairs. In the 1970s, he served as a National Intelligence Officer and as the Director of the CIA's Office of Regional and Political Analysis. He now lives in Santa Fe, NM.

February 26, 2001

W: FIRST BLOOD
by Alexander Cockburn and Jeffrey St. Clair

Bombing the Iraqis should properly be listed as part of the Inaugural ceremonies, a man not being truly President of the United States till he drops high explosive on Baghdad or environs. The new team evidently felt that the Commander-in-Chief could not be allowed to leave the jurisdiction, even to Mexico, without unleashing planes and bombs against Saddam, for whom the bombardment produced the effect of widespread sympathy across the world for Iraq.

Bill Clinton delayed this portion of his inaugural ceremonies to June 27, 1993, when he was urged by Vice-President Al Gore to order a salvo of cruise missiles supposedly in retaliation for an alleged Iraqi plot to kill George Bush Sr when he visited Kuwait in April of 1993. Both Clinton and Bush were somewhat reluctant about the sortie. 'Do we have to take this action?' Clinton muttered to his national security team, as the cruise missiles on two carriers in the Persian Gulf were being programmed. Gore advised that a demonstration of national resolve was of paramount importance. Clinton's reservations were amply justified. Eight of the twenty-three missiles homed in with deadly imprecision on a residential suburb in Baghdad, one of them killing Iraq's leading artist, Leila al-Attar.

Feasting on shrimp, cocktail canapés and Diet Coke, the White House group watched CNN's Wolf Blitzer announce the strike; the misfortune of the errant missiles and al-Attar's death were never mentioned. Clinton's pollster Stan Greenberg, who did daily surveys on the popular sentiment, reported to the gratified Commander-in-Chief that bombardment of Iraq caused an uptick of eleven points.

Since the Clinton administration was at that time in the process of its first meltdown, this was a welcome ray, and one no doubt remembered by the new Bush team, possibly eager to shift the focus from the headline-hogging former president. Bomb your way into favorable headlines has been the policy of every president since World War Two.

Of course, these bombardments all violate international law. There is no UN provision for such assaults. UN Resolution 688, sometimes referred to as a document legitimizing the no-fly-zone bombardment, makes no reference to a right to take over Iraqi airspace. There was nothing new about the declared motive for last week's bombing raids, described as 'protective retaliation.' Just over a year ago, after similar raids, the British Defence Secretary, Geoff Hoon, invoked the sorties as being 'in pursuit of legitimate self-defence,' a phrase hard to read without laughing out loud.

There's nothing new about this particular bombing, which the Iraqis say killed some civilians. The US and Britain have been routinely bombing Iraq for much of the past decade, with no discernible effect beyond the slaughter of about 500 Iraqis overall, a death count which only looks scrawny in comparison to the million or so, mostly children, who have died as a consequence of sanctions since they were imposed a decade ago.

Secretary of State Colin Powell had barely settled into his new office before he was affirming this murderous sanctions policy, whereby a US-dominated UN committee in New York routinely plays God in decreeing what can and cannot be shipped to Iraq. UN officials working in Baghdad have long agreed that the root cause of child mortality and other health problems is not simply lack of food and medicine but the lack of clean water (freely available in all parts of the country prior to the Gulf War) and of electrical power, now running at 30 per cent of its pre-bombing level, with consequences for hospitals and water-pumping systems that can be all too readily imagined.

Of the 21.9 per cent of contracts vetoed as of mid-1999 by the UN's sanctions committee, a high proportion were integral to the efforts to repair the water and sewage systems. The Iraqis submitted contracts worth $236 million in this area, of which $54 million worth – roughly one-quarter of the total value – have been disapproved. 'Basically, anything with chemicals or even pumps is liable to get thrown out,' one UN official revealed. The same trend has been apparent in the power supply sector.

The proportion of approved/disapproved contracts does not tell the full story. UN officials refer to the 'complementarity issue,' meaning that items approved for purchase may be useless without other items that have been disapproved. For example, the Iraqi Ministry of Health once ordered $25 million worth of dentist chairs, said order being approved by the sanctions committee – except for the compressors without which the chairs are useless and consequently gathering dust in a Baghdad warehouse. In February of 2000 the US moved to prevent Iraq from importing fifteen bulls from France. The excuse was that the animals, ordered with the blessing of the UN's humanitarian office in Baghdad to try to restock the Iraqi beef industry, would require certain vaccines which, who knows, might be diverted into a program to make biological weapons of mass destruction. For sheer bloody-mindedness, however, the interdiction of the bulls pales beside an initiative of the British government, which banned the export of vaccines for tetanus, diphtheria and yellow fever on the grounds that they too might find their way into the hands of Saddam's biological weaponeers.

It has been the self-exculpatory mantra of US and British officials that 'food and medicine are exempt from sanctions.' This, like so many other Western policy pronouncements on Iraq, has turned out to be a lie.

So now the wheel turns full circle. Back in 1991 Defense Secretary Dick Cheney and top uniformed Pentagon man Colin Powell urged bombardment and President Bush I approved. In 2001 Powell and Cheney are at Bush II's elbow as he approves his administration's first military adventure. Is there a strategy, beyond Inaugural chest-thumping? Well, it changes the subject from what the Bush administration proposes to do about a man who would probably fare as ill in a UN Tribunal on War Crimes as Saddam, viz., Ariel Sharon, Israel's new prime minister.

Beyond this 'signal' to the world about priorities in Bush time, there could be the outlines of a new Iraq policy, whereby the new government is signaling its readiness to embark on a far tougher stance towards Iraq, beefing up aid to the main opposition group in exile, the Iraqi National Congress (INC), led by Ahmad Chalabi. In the late 1990s Chalabi's cause was pressed by Republicans in Congress, most notably Jesse Helms and Trent Lott. A bizarre alliance, stretching from Helms to *The New Republic* to *Vanity Fair*'s Christopher Hitchens, pressed Chalabi's call for the US to guarantee 'military exclusion zones' in northern Iraq and in the south near Basra and the oil fields, to be administered by the INC. Such guarantees could set the stage for a new military assault on Saddam.

Against the continuation of sanctions and bombing sorties this is an unlikely prospect, but George W. Bush could at least be toying with the thought that at last the Clinton–Gore campaign's slurs against his father for not finishing off Saddam will be avenged.

September 12, 2001

WHO SAW IT COMING?
by Alexander Cockburn and Jeffrey St. Clair

Tuesday's onslaughts on the World Trade Center and the Pentagon are being likened to Pearl Harbor, and the comparison is just.

Not in terms of destructive extent, but in terms of symbolic obliteration the attack is virtually without historic parallel, a trauma at least as great as the San Francisco earthquake or the Chicago fire.

There may be another similarity to Pearl Harbor. The possibility of a Japanese attack in early December of 1941 was known to US Naval Intelligence and to President Roosevelt. Last Tuesday, derision at the failure of US intelligence was widespread. The *Washington Post* quoted an unnamed top official at the National Security Council as saying: 'We don't know anything here. We're watching CNN too.' Are we to believe that the $30 billion annual intelligence budget, immense electronic eavesdropping capacity, thousands of agents around the world, produced nothing in the way of a warning? In fact Osama bin Laden, now prime suspect, said in an interview three weeks ago with Abdel-Bari Atwan, the editor of the London-based *al-Quds al-Araby* newspaper, that he planned 'very, very big attacks against American interests.'

Here is bin Laden, probably the most notorious Islamic foe of America on the planet, originally trained by the CIA, planner of other successful attacks on US installations such as the embassies in East Africa, carrying a $5 million FBI bounty on his head proclaiming the imminence of another assault, and US intelligence was impotent, even though the attacks must have taken months, if not years to plan. Back in the 1960s and 1970s, when hijacking was a preoccupation, the possibility of air assaults on buildings such as the Trade Center were a major concern of US security and intelligence agencies. But since the 1980s and particularly during the Clinton–Gore years the focus shifted to more modish fears, such as biochemical assault and nuclear weapons launched by so-called rogue states.

This latter threat had the allure of justifying the $60 billion investment in Missile Defense, aka Star Wars. One of the biggest proponents of that approach was Al Gore's security advisor Leon Fuerth, who wailed plaintively amid Tuesday's rubble that 'In effect the country's at war but we don't have the coordinates of the enemy.'

But the lust for retaliation traditionally outstrips precision in identifying the actual assailant. By early evening on Tuesday America's national security establishment were calling for a removal of all impediments on the assassination of foreign leaders. Led by President Bush, they were endorsing the prospect of attacks not just on the perpetrators but on those who might have harbored them. From the nuclear priesthood is coming the demand that mini-nukes be deployed on a preemptive basis against the enemies of America.

The targets abroad will be all the usual suspects: rogue states (most of which, like the Taliban or Saddam Hussein, started off as creatures of US intelligence). The target at home will of course be the Bill of Rights. The explosions of Tuesday were not an hour old before terror pundits like Anthony Cordesman, Wesley Clark, Robert Gates and Lawrence Eagleburger were saying that these attacks had been possible 'because America is a democracy,' adding that now some democratic perquisites might have to be abandoned. What might this mean? Increased domestic snooping by US law enforcement and intelligence agencies; ethnic profiling; another drive for a national ID card system. Tuesday did not offer a flattering exhibition of America's leaders. For most of the day the only Bush who looked composed and in control in Washington was Laura, who happened to be waiting to testify on Capitol Hill. Her husband gave a timid and stilted initial reaction in Sarasota, Florida, then disappeared for an hour before resurfacing at a base in Barksdale, Louisiana, where he gave another flaccid address with every appearance of being on tranquilizers. He was then flown to a bunker in Nebraska, before someone finally had the wit to suggest that the best place for an American president at time of national emergency is the Oval Office.

The commentators were similarly incapable of explaining with any depth the likely context of the attacks. By contrast, the commentary on economic consequences was informative and sophisticated. Worst hit: the insurance industry. Likely outfall in the short-term: hiked energy prices, a further drop in global stock markets. George Bush will have no trouble in raiding the famous lock-box, using Social Security Trust Funds to give more money to the Defense Department. That about sums it up. Three planes are successfully steered into three of America's most conspicuous buildings and America's response will be to put more money in missile defense as a way of bolstering the economy.

September 20, 2001

THE PRICE, MRS ALBRIGHT?
by Alexander Cockburn and Jeffrey St. Clair

What moved those kamikaze Muslims to embark, so many months ago, on the training that they knew would culminate in their deaths as well of those (they must have hoped) of thousands upon thousands of innocent people? America has led a charmed life amid its wars on people. The wars mostly didn't come home and the press made as sure as it could that folks including the ordinary workers in the Trade Towers weren't really up to speed on what has been wrought in Freedom's name. In Freedom's name America made sure that any possibility of secular democratic reform in the Middle East was shut off. Mount a coup against Mossadegh in the mid-1950s, as the CIA did, and you end up with the Ayatollah Khomeini twenty-five years later. Mount a coup against Kassim in Iraq, as the CIA did, and you get the Agency's man, Saddam Hussein.

What about Afghanistan? In April of 1978 an indigenous populist coup overthrew the government of Mohammed Daoud, who had formed an alliance with the man the US had installed in Iran, Reza Pahlevi, aka the Shah. The new Afghan government was led by Noor Mohammed Taraki, and the Taraki administration embarked, albeit with a good deal of urban intellectual arrogance, on land reform, hence an attack on the opium-growing feudal estates. Taraki went to the UN, where he managed to raise loans for crop substitution for the poppy fields.

Taraki also tried to bear down on opium production in the border areas held by fundamentalists, since the latter were using opium revenues to finance attacks on Afghanistan's central government, which they regarded as an unwholesome incarnation of modernity that allowed women to go to school and outlawed arranged marriages and the bride price.

At that time the mujahideen were getting money not only from the CIA but from Libya's Muammar Qaddafi, who sent them $250,000. In the summer of 1979 the US State Department produced a memo making it clear how the US government saw the stakes, no matter how modern-minded Taraki might be or how feudal the mujahideen. The memo was dispatched to US embassies around the world, including the one in Tehran. A few months later the embassy was occupied by Iranian students and the occupants taken hostage. The diplomats and CIA residents shredded their secret files but the students laboriously reassembled them, and ultimately they were published in sixty-eight paperback volumes. Among the documents was the following memo, written shortly after the Taraki coup:

> The United States' larger interest ... would be served by the demise of the Taraki–Amin regime, despite whatever setbacks this might mean for future social and economic reforms in Afghanistan. The overthrow of the DRA [Democratic Republic of Afghanistan] would show the rest of the world, particularly the Third World, that the Soviets' view of the socialist course of history being inevitable is not accurate.

Taraki was killed by Afghan army officers in September 1979. Hafizullah Amin, educated in the US, took over and began meeting regularly with US embassy officials at a time when the US was arming Islamic rebels in Pakistan. Fearing a fundamentalist, US-backed regime in Afghanistan, the Soviets invaded in force in December 1979.

The back-office staffs, messenger boys, cleaners, and other workers throughout the Trade Center didn't know that history. There's a lot of other relevant history they probably didn't know but which those men on the attack planes did. How could those people in the Towers have known, when US political and journalistic culture is a conspiracy to perpetuate their ignorance? Those people on the Towers were innocent portions of the price that Albright insisted, in just one of its applications, was worth it. It would honor their memory to insist that in future our press offers a better accounting of how America's wars for Freedom are fought and what the actual price might include.

September 25, 2001

RETRIBUTION
by Alexander Cockburn and Jeffrey St. Clair

We're passing from appalling human loss and suffering, live in the front yard of the media capital of the world, to the traditional parameters of imperial retribution. It won't be bombs that settle the issue, and the Pentagon has small appetite for any substantial foray into Afghanistan on the ground. Cash will be the lubricant of victory, and since unlimited supplies of cash are available to buy support for the US among the Afghan factions, it may not be long before the Taliban are chased out. The only inauspicious factors from Bush's point of view are that the bribing will be the province of the CIA, whose record for screw-ups is ample, and the inter-mediary is to be Pakistani military intelligence, which sponsored the Taliban's triumph and which has its own agenda, not one dedicated to peace and reconstruction for Afghanistan.

Much has been been made of the doom awaiting martial forays into Afghanistan, the British debacles of the nineteenth century and the Soviets' in the 1980s. But the British were exceptionally stupid and the Russians didn't suffer unduly. Across ten years they lost some 13,000 in Afghanistan. A Russian colonel, veteran of the campaign, recently disclosed to Patrick Cockburn that about 33 per cent of these mortalities were due to accidents (tanks falling off roads and so forth), which brings down the number of Russians actually killed by the muj to under a thousand a year. The muj, including bin Laden, held out against the Russians and in the end forced their withdrawal because they enjoyed the limitless support of the Pakistani military and of the US, in the form of the CIA running the largest covert op in its history at a cost of $3.5 billion.

Who have the Taliban got? A starving, discontented domestic population and external enemies on all sides, wallowing in promises of huge American dispensations. Their original sponsors in the Pakistani military have far larger satisfactions than temporary loss of a client regime in Kabul before a new one can be cobbled together. Pakistan is now certified as OK to be a member of the nuclear club, with its debts rescheduled.

The globe-spinners talk about bin Laden's dangerous appeal to Muslims around the world chafing at the despotism and corruption of their leaders, the occupation of Jerusalem by the Jews and their US protector, the starving of Iraqi children, but if the Arab world is so much of a tinder box, why didn't bin Laden try to apply the match there? All talk of fragile Araby notwithstanding, the regimes there have been astoundingly stable across years of political turmoil.

October 5, 2001

'SMALL IS BEAUTIFUL'
by Jeffrey St. Clair

'At a bare minimum, tactical nuclear capabilities should be used against the bin Laden camps in the desert of Afghanistan. To do less would be rightly seen by the poisoned minds that orchestrated these attacks as cowardice on the part of the United States and the current administration.' These are not the words of a columnist for the rabidly pro-war *New York Post*. No. These are the considered sentiments of Thomas Woodrow, a former officer at the Defense Intelligence Agency.

The Pentagon has come to a remarkable conclusion with regard to nuclear weapons: smaller is better. These days the Wizards of

Armageddon are palpably anxious to develop a new class of nuclear weapons, the so-called 'deep penetrator' warheads. Over the past decade the Pentagon and its weapons designers have been quietly busy crafting a variety of new weapons. Indeed, although the Clinton administration generated a lot of hoopla by supporting the comprehensive test ban treaty (which it promptly violated with a string of subcritical tests), the Department of Energy and the Pentagon were busy developing new breeds of weapons. In 1997, they unveiled and deployed the B61-11, described as a mere modification of the old B61-7 gravity bomb. In reality it was largely a new 'package,' the prototype for the 'low-yield' bunker-blasting nuke that the weaponeers see as the future of the US arsenal.

The nuclear priesthood is salivating at the prospect of a new generation of nukes and new infusions of cash under the Bush regime, which has been stockpiled with nuclear hawks, ranging from Richard Armitage and Paul Wolfowitz to Assistant Secretary of Defense Jack Couch, who a couple of years ago wrote that the US should consider dropping a small nuke on North Korea to teach them a lesson.

The Pentagon, of course, isn't the only one pushing new bombs. So are the nuclear labs and their legions of contractors.

October 20, 2001

THE LEFT AND THE 'JUST WAR'
by Alexander Cockburn

The left is getting itself tied up in knots about the Just War and the propriety of bombing Afghanistan. I suspect some are intimidated by laptop bombardiers and kindred bullyboys handing out white

feathers and snarling about 'collaborators' and being 'soft on fascism.'
A recent issue of *The Nation* carried earnest efforts by Richard Falk
and an editorial writer to mark out 'the relevant frameworks of
moral, legal and religious restraint' to be applied to the lethal
business of attacking Afghans. I felt sorry for Falk as he clambered
through his moral obstacle course. This business of trying to define
a just war against Afghanistan is what C. Wright Mills used to call
crackpot realism.

War, as the United States has been fighting it in Iraq and
Yugoslavia, consists mostly of bombing, intended to terrify the
population and destroy the fabric of tolerable social existence.
Here's how a couple of Pentagon briefers described the infliction
of terror, as reported by Jonathan Landay of the *San Jose Mercury
News* on October 17: "'If you're on the ground and get hit with a
bomb from a B-52 it's over," the officer said. "But if you're there
and you hear an AC-130 coming, with its Gatling gun going, the
experience can be even more frightening.'" Marine Corps Lieut.
Gen. Gregory Newbold provided further context: 'The psychological effect was intended to convince the Taliban leadership that
they have made an error and their calculus some day will be in their
interests to see that.'

Those AC-130s were over Kabul. What else can the consequence be but to terrify and kill civilians, whose anguish may or
may not impinge upon the 'calculus' of the Taliban leaders?
Remember, too, that bombs mostly miss their targets. Colonel John
Warden, who planned the air campaign in Iraq, said afterwards that
dropping dumb bombs 'is like shooting skeet. 499 out of 500 pellets
may miss the target, but that's irrelevant.' There will always be
shattered hospitals and wrecked old folks' homes, just as there will
always be Defense Department flacks saying that the destruction
'cannot be independently verified' or that the hospitals or old folks'

homes were actually sanctuaries for enemy forces, for 'command and control.'

How many bombing campaigns do we have to go through in a decade to recognize all the usual landmarks?

There can be no 'limited war with limited objectives' when the bombing sets matches to tinder from Pakistan and Kashmir to Ramallah, Bethlehem, Jerusalem. 'Limited war' is a far less realistic prospect than to regard September 11 as a crime, to pursue its perpetrators to justice in an international court, using all relevant police and intelligence agencies here and abroad.

The left should be for peace, which in no way means ignoring the demands of either side. Bin Laden calls for an end to sanctions on Iraq, US troops out of Saudi Arabia, justice for Palestinians. The left says Aye to those, though we want a two-state solution, whereas bin Laden wants to drive Jews along with secular and Christian Palestinians into the sea. The US government calls for a dismantling of the Terror Network, and the left says Aye to that too. Of course we oppose networks of people who wage war on civilians.

So we're pretty close to supporting demands on both sides, but we know these demands are not going to be achieved by war. What is this war about? On Bush's side it's about the defense of the American Empire; on the other, an attempt to challenge that Empire in the name of theocratic fundamentalist Islam. On that issue the left is against both sides. We don't want anyone to kill or die in the name of the American Empire, for the 'war on terror' to be cashed in blood in Colombia or anywhere else, or for anyone to kill or die in the name of Islamic fundamentalism. Go to the UN, proceed on the basis that September 11 was a crime. Bring the perpetrators to justice by legal means.

A final word about 'rationalizing.' After the Columbine school killings, people called for more security in schools. They also asked big questions: How could we have raised such children? Was it distance parenting, violence in culture, bullying? If you asked such questions, no one confused explanation with justification. No one charged you with being soft on teen killers.

Leave the final word to Seth Bardacke, who remarked to his father Frank, the afternoon of September 11: 'I guess now we know that bombing civilians is wrong.'

November 10, 2001

FBI EYES TORTURE
by Alexander Cockburn and Jeffrey St. Clair

'FBI and Justice Department investigators are increasingly frustrated by the silence of jailed suspected associates of Osama bin Laden's al Qaeda network, and some are beginning to say that traditional civil liberties may have to be cast aside if they are to extract information about the Sept. 11 attacks and terrorist plans.'

Thus began a piece by Walter Pincus on page 6 of the *Washington Post* on Sunday, and if you suspect that this is the overture to an argument for torture, you are right. The FBI interrogators have been getting nowhere with the four key suspects, held in New York's Metropolitan Correctional Center. None of these men have talked, and Pincus quotes an FBI man involved in the interrogation as saying that 'it could get to that spot where we could go to pressure … where we won't have a choice, and we are probably getting there.' Pincus reports that 'among the alternative strategies under discussion are using drugs or pressure tactics, such as those employed occasionally by Israeli interrogators, to extract information. Another idea is extraditing the suspects to allied countries where security services sometimes employ threats to family members or resort to torture.'

Some FBI interrogators are thinking longingly of drugs like the so-called 'truth serum,' sodium pentothal; others of the 'pressure tactics,' i.e., straightforward tortures, used by Shin Bet in Israel, banned after savage public debate a few years ago, which included sensory deprivation (an old favorite of British interrogators in Northern Ireland), plus many agonizing physical torments. Another idea is to send the suspects to other countries for torture by seasoned experts.

The FBI claims it is hampered by its present codes of gentility. If so, there's no need to eye Morocco or France as subcontracting torturers. As a practical matter torture is far from unknown in the interrogation rooms of US law enforcement, with Abner Louima, the Haitian immigrant brutalized by New York police, the best-known recent example.

The most infamous disclosure of consistent torture by a police department in recent years concerned cops in Chicago in the mid-Seventies through early Eighties who used electroshock, oxygen deprivation, hanging on hooks, the bastinado and beatings of the testicles. The torturers were white and their victims black or brown. A prisoner in California's Pelican Bay State Prison was thrown into boiling water. Others get 50,000-volt shocks from stun guns. Many states have so-called 'secure housing units' where prisoners are kept in solitary in tiny concrete cells for years on end, many of them going mad in the process. Amnesty International has denounced US police forces for 'a pattern of unchecked excessive force amounting to torture.'

Last year the UN delivered a severe public rebuke to the United States for its record on preventing torture and degrading punishment. A ten-strong panel of experts highlighted what it said were Washington's breaches of the agreement ratified by the United

States in 1994. The UN Committee Against Torture, which monitors international compliance with the UN Convention Against Torture, has called for the abolition of electric-shock stun belts (1,000 in use in the US) and restraint chairs on prisoners, as well as an end to holding children in adult jails. It also said female detainees are 'very often held in humiliating and degrading circumstances' and expressed concern over alleged cases of sexual assault by police and prison officers. The panel criticized the excessively harsh regime in maximum security prisons, the use of chain gangs in which prisoners perform manual labor while shackled together, and the number of cases of police brutality against racial minorities.

So far as rape is concerned, because of the rape factories more conventionally known as the US prison system there are estimates that twice as many men as women are raped in the US each year. A Human Rights Watch report in April of this year cited a December 2000 *Prison Journal* study based on a survey of inmates in seven men's prison facilities in four states. The results showed that 21 per cent of the inmates had experienced at least one episode of pressured or forced sexual contact since being incarcerated, and at least 7 per cent had been raped in their facilities. A 1996 study of the Nebraska prison system produced similar findings, with 22 per cent of male inmates reporting that they had been pressured or forced to have sexual contact against their will while incarcerated. Of these, more than 50 per cent had submitted to forced anal sex at least once. Extrapolating these findings to the national level gives a total of at least 140,000 inmates who have been raped.

Since its inception the CIA has taken a keen interest in torture, avidly studying Nazi techniques and protecting their exponents such as Klaus Barbie. The FBI could ship the four key suspects to plenty of countries taught torture by CIA technicians, including El

Salvador. Robert Fisk reported in the London *Independent* in 1998 that after the 1979 revolution Iranians found a CIA film made for SAVAK, the Shah's political police, on how to torture women. William Blum, whose *Rogue State* (Common Courage, 2000) gives a useful overview of the United States' relationship to torture, cites a 1970 story in Brazil's extremely respectable *Jornal do Brasil*, quoting the former Uruguayan chief of police intelligence, Alejandro Otero, as saying that US advisers, particularly Dan Mitrione, had instituted torture in Uruguay on a routine basis, with scientific refinement in technique (such as the precise upper limits of electric voltage before death intervened) and psychological pressure, such as a tape in the next room of women and children screaming, telling the prisoner that his family was being tortured.

The CIA's official line is that torture is wrong and is ineffective. It is indeed wrong. On countless occasions it has been appallingly effective.

November 15, 2001

ALTER ASKS: 'CAN WE TORTURE JUST A TEENSY BIT?'
by Alexander Cockburn

Open the November 5 edition of *Newsweek* and here's Jonathan Alter, munching on the week's hot topic, namely the propriety of the FBI torturing obdurate September 11 suspects in the bureau's custody here in the United States. Alter says no to cattle prods, but continues the sentence with the observation that something is needed to 'jump-start the stalled investigation.' The tone is lightly facetious: 'Couldn't we at least subject them to psychological torture, like tapes of dying rabbits or high-decibel rap?' There are respectful references to Alan Dershowitz (who's running around the country promoting the idea of 'torture warrants' issued by judges) and to Israel, where 'until 1999 an interrogation technique called "shaking" was legal. It entailed holding a smelly bag over a suspect's head in a dark room, then applying scary psychological torment … Even now, Israeli law leaves a little room for "moderate physical pressure" in what are called "ticking time bomb" cases.'

As so often with unappealing labor, Alter arrives at the usual American solution: outsource the job. 'We'll have to think about transferring some suspects to our less squeamish allies,' he says. What's striking about Alter's commentary and others in the same idiom is the abstraction from reality, as if torture is so indisputably a dirty business that all painful data had best be avoided. One would have thought it hard to be frivolous about the subject of torture, but Alter managed it.

Would one know from his commentary that under international covenants – signed and ratified by the United States – torture is illegal? One would not, and one assumes that as with the war against the Taliban's Afghanistan, Alter regards issues of legality as entirely immaterial. Would one know that in recent years the United States has been charged by the UN and also by human rights organizations such as Human Rights Watch and Amnesty International with tolerating torture in prisons, by methods ranging from solitary, twenty-three-hour-a-day confinement in concrete boxes for years on end, to activating 50,000-volt shocks through a mandatory belt worn by prisoners? Would one know that one of the darkest threads in postwar US imperial history has been the CIA's involvement with torture, as instructor, practitioner or contractor?

Remember Dan Mitrione, kidnapped and killed by Uruguay's Tupamaros and portrayed by Yves Montand in Costa-Gavras's film

State of Siege? In the late 1960s Mitrione worked for the US Office of Public Safety, part of the Agency for International Development. In Brazil, so A. J. Langguth (a former *New York Times* bureau chief in Saigon) related in his book *Hidden Terrors*, Mitrione was among the US advisors teaching Brazilian police how much electric shock to apply to prisoners without killing them. In Uruguay, according to the former chief of police intelligence, Mitrione helped 'professionalize' torture as a routine measure and advised on psychological techniques such as playing tapes of women and children screaming that the prisoner's family was being tortured.

Alter expresses a partiality for 'truth drugs,' an enthusiasm shared by the US Navy after the war against Hitler, when its intelligence officers got on the trail of Dr Kurt Plotner's research into 'truth serums' at Dachau. Plotner gave Jewish and Russian prisoners high doses of mescaline and then observed their behavior, in which they expressed hatred for their guards and made confessional statements about their own psychological makeup.

As part of its larger MK-ULTRA project the CIA gave money to Dr Ewen Cameron at McGill University. Cameron was a pioneer in the sensory-deprivation techniques for which Jonathan Alter has issued his approval. Cameron once locked up a woman in a small white box for thirty-five days, deprived of light, smell and sound. The CIA doctors were amazed at this dose, knowing that their own experiments with a sensory-deprivation tank in 1955 had induced severe psychological reactions in less than forty hours.

Start torturing, and it's easy to get carried away. Torture destroys the tortured and corrupts the society that sanctions it. Just like the FBI today, the CIA in 1968 got frustrated by its inability to break suspected leaders of Vietnam's National Liberation Front by its usual methods of interrogation and torture. So the agency began more advanced experiments, in one of which it anesthetized three prisoners, opened their skulls and planted electrodes in their brains. They were revived, put in a room and given knives. The CIA psychologists then activated the electrodes, hoping the prisoners would attack one another. They didn't. The electrodes were removed, the prisoners were shot and their bodies burned. Alter can read about it in Gordon Thomas's book *Journey into Madness*.

The Israelis? They're still torturing. In July, AP and the *Baltimore Sun* relayed charges from the Israeli human rights group B'tselem of 'severe torture' by police: Palestinian youths as young as fourteen being badly beaten, their heads shoved into toilet bowls and so forth. But Israel outsourced too. After Israel finally retreated from its 'security strip' in southern Lebanon, run by its puppet South Lebanese Army, the journalist Robert Fisk visited Khiam prison. His report for the *Independent*, May 25, 2000, began thus:

> The torturers had just left but the horror remained. There was the whipping pole and the window grilles where prisoners were tied naked for days, freezing water thrown over them at night. Then there were the electric leads for the little dynamo – the machine mercifully taken off to Israel by the interrogators – which had the inmates shrieking with pain when the electrodes touched their fingers or penises. And there were the handcuffs which an ex-prisoner handed to me yesterday afternoon. Engraved into the steel were the words: 'The Peerless Handcuff Co. Springfield, Mass. Made in USA.' And I wondered, in Israel's most shameful prison, if the executives over in Springfield knew what they were doing when they sold these manacles.

If handcuffs are sold these days to the FBI's subcontractor of choice, at least the executives will know they have Jonathan Alter to explain the patriotic morality of their bottom line.

November 28, 2001

WHERE WERE THEY WHEN IT COUNTED?
by Alexander Cockburn

The weekend before Thanksgiving, as the Taliban fled into the Hindu Kush and America's children flocked to Harry Potter, the nation's opinion formers discovered that the Bush administration had hijacked the Constitution with the Patriot Act and the military tribunals. *Time* magazine burst out that 'war is hell on your civil liberties.' The *New York Times* suddenly began to run big news stories about John Ashcroft. But well before the end of September Ashcroft's proposals to trash the Bill of Rights were available for inspection and debate.

At the time when it counted, when a volley of barks from the watchdogs might have provoked resistance in Congress to the Patriot Bill and warned Bush not to try his luck with military tribunals, there was mostly decorum from the opinion-makers, aside from amiable discussions of the propriety of torture. Taken as a whole, the US press did not raise adequate alarums about legislation that was going to give the FBI full snoop powers on the Internet, deny habeas corpus to non-citizens, expand even further warrantless searches unleashed in the Clinton era with new powers given in 1995 to secret courts operating under the terms of the Foreign Intelligence Surveillance Act passed in the Carter years, in 1978.

In the run-up to Bush's signing of the USA Patriot Act on October 25, the major papers were spiritless about the provisions in the bill that were horrifying to civil libertarians. It would have only have taken a few fierce columns or editorials, such as were profuse after November 15, to have given frightened politicians cover to join the only bold soul in the US Senate, Russell Feingold of Wisconsin. Now it was Feingold, remember, whose vote back in the spring let Ashcroft's nomination out of the Judiciary Committee, at a time when most of his Democratic colleagues were roaring to the news cameras about Ashcroft's racism and contempt for due process. The *Times* and the *Post* both editorialized against Ashcroft's nomination.

But then, when the rubber met the road, and Ashcroft sent up the Patriot Bill, which vindicated every dire prediction of the spring, all fell silent except for Feingold, who made a magnificent speech in the US Senate on October 25 citing assaults on liberty going back to the Alien and Sedition Acts of John Adams, the suspension of habeas corpus sanctioned by the US Supreme Court in World War One, the internments of World War Two (along with 110,00 Japanese Americans there were 11,000 German Americans and 3,000 Italian Americans put behind barbed wire), the McCarthyite blacklists of the 1950s and the spying on antiwar protesters in the 1960s. Under the terms of the bill, Feingold warned, the Fourth Amendment as it applies to electronic communications would be effectively eliminated. He flayed the Patriot Bill as an assault on 'the basic rights that make us who we are.' It represented, he warned, 'a truly breath-taking expansion of police power.'

Feingold was trying to win time for challenges in Congress to specific provisions in Ashcroft's bill. In vain. The USA Patriot Act passed into law and Feingold's was the sole vote against it in the Senate. There weren't even articles about his reasons for being the sole hold-out.

Though Rep. Dennis Kucinich voted for war-making, he has since tried to get the 'left' in Congress to pull the plug on Bush's military tribunals, but as of November 28 could only find thirty-seven colleagues to agree with him, one of whom is Bob Barr, the conservative former prosecutor who also was among those attacking from the earliest days the provisions of the USA Patriot Act. And guess who wrote this: 'Today, America is being stampeded into a new undeclared war, against Iraq. This is a time for truth, a time for Congress to do its duty, and debate and decide on war or peace. We do not need to have our politics poisoned for yet another generation by the mutual recriminations of a War Party and a Peace Party in the aftermath of yet another undeclared war. No more undeclared wars. No more presidential wars.' It was Patrick Buchanan who, like Safire, wrote speeches for Richard Nixon.

We've always said that the true contours of American politics are in no way reflected by the conventional political maps.

December 7, 2001

FATHERS AND SONS: THE BUSHES AND BIN LADENS GO WAY BACK

by Jeffrey St. Clair

Chances are that George W. Bush didn't need to be tutored on how to pronounce Osama bin Laden's name, after the President was informed about the events of 9/11 while reading that story about the goat to grade-schoolers in Sarasota, Florida. The bin Ladens and the Bushes go way back.

Exactly how far back remains a matter of conjecture. But, like many ultra-rich Saudis, the bin Laden brood has always had a thing for Texas. The patriarch of the bin Laden clan, Mohammed bin Laden, the son of a Yemeni bricklayer who moved to Saudi Arabia and struck it rich in the construction business, flew frequently to

Dallas to seal deals with his associates in the oil industry, often in his private jet. There's much speculation, though no hard proof, that Mohammed knew George Bush the First and his cohort of oil, banking and political cronies in the Lone Star state.

Mohammed died in a plane crash in Saudi Arabia. One of his elder sons, Salem, died near Houston when his ultra-light airplane hit power lines. Of all the bin Ladens, it was Saleem who had the close relationship to the Bushes. The connection was a Houston wheeler-dealer named James Bath, who haunted the darker back corridors of the Bush–Reagan years, amid the fragrance of scandals ranging from Iran/contra to BCCI to the Silverado Savings and Loan debacle to Iranian weapons mogul Adnan Khashoggi.

Bath was an Air Force fighter pilot in Vietnam who ended up in the National Guard in Houston, where he first met George W. Bush, who had fled to the Guard in order to avoid combat. Bath and Bush became fast friends, with Bush later recalling that 'Bath is a lot of fun.'

In the mid-1970s, Bath became vice-president of Atlantic Aviation, one of the world's top business-aircraft sales companies. At the time, Atlantic was owned by Edward DuPont, of the DuPont chemical empire. DuPont's brother, Richard, served on the board of Atlantic. According to Gerard Colby's excellent book, *DuPont Dynasty*, Richard's own company, Summit Aviation, was a longtime CIA contractor.

In 1976, Bath met Osama bin Laden's brother Salem. Salem was entranced by planes and he and Bath hit it off almost immediately. Soon Salem had Bath named as trustee for the bin Laden family operations and considerable investments in the United States. It was through the bin Ladens that Bath was introduced to one of their old family friends, Adnan Khashoggi. According to Robert Lacey's book, *The Kingdom: Arabia and the House of Saud*, Mohammed bin

Laden was a patient of Khashoggi's father, a prominent Iranian physician. The young Khashoggi became a middleman for the bin Laden conglomerate in the late 1950s, getting his start by negotiating a big truck sale that earned the Iranian $25,000.

It wasn't too long after Bath met bin Laden that he made a $50,000 investment in Arbusto Energy, a small oil company that was George W. Bush's first business venture. Arbusto means Bush in Spanish. Bath later claimed in court records that the $50,000 came from the bin Laden family.

Investigative journalist Peter Brewton asserts in his book on the Bush clan that one of Bath's former business partners, Charles White, claims that it was in this very same year of 1976 that George W. Bush, then director of Central Intelligence for the Ford administration, recruited Bath to work for the CIA. Brewton cites White as saying one of Bath's jobs was to report on the investments of Saudi millionaires. White, by the way, was another fighter pilot and went to Annapolis with Oliver North.

Through the bin Ladens, Bath was also introduced to Sheik Khalid bin Mahfouz, the CEO of the National Commercial Bank, Saudi Arabia's biggest bank. The NCB was a prime lender for Khashoggi. In 1985, at a time when the arms dealer was moving weapons to Afghanistan, Iran and the contras, NCB loaned Khashoggi $35 million. Bath would team with Khalid, and former Texas governor John Connally, in buying the Main Bank in Houston, an institution that helped finance the campaigns of many Texas politicians through the late 1970s and 1980s.

Khalid's banking empire would eventually extend to a stake in the Bank of Credit and Commerce International, the institution that catered to crooks and spooks. Among other nefarious enterprises, BCCI served as Khashoggi's chief bank for his arms deals with Iran, a depository for Oliver North's covert action funds, and the conduit for CIA money bound for the mujahideen in Afghanistan. In 1992, Khalid was indicted on fraud charges stemming from his involvement with BCCI. The Federal Reserve Board found that Khalid and his NCB had violated US banking laws when he teamed with BCCI to try to take over the Washington-based First Bancshares. His assets in the US were frozen and his Fifth Avenue New York penthouse was seized.

Bath was also an investor in Skyways Leasing, a Grand Cayman-based firm, controlled by Khalid and, according to White, the CIA. Skyways was also part of North's contra supply network. Two of Skyways' original owners, David Byrd and William Walker, were also officers in IC, Inc., which channeled some $3.6 million in funds for North's enterprise.

But the bin Laden group's ties to the Bushes and the elite of the US military and intelligence establishment extend far beyond the curious career of James Bath. The bin Laden construction empire has enjoyed the benefits of numerous contracts with the Pentagon, perhaps none so lucrative as those for the construction of the new airstrips and barracks following the 1996 truck bombing of the US army base in Dhahran, which killed eighteen people – a bombing that many have blamed on Osama bin Laden. The bin Laden family has also invested at least $2 million in the Carlyle Group's Partner's II Fund, which specializes in the acquisition of aerospace companies. The Carlyle Group is the DC investment house, run by former Pentagon staffers, which specializes in the financing of weapons companies and security firms. The chairman of the Carlyle Group is Frank Carlucci, secretary of defense during the second Reagan administration. Its counselor is James Baker. And, despite his pledge not to trade in his presidency for a spot on corporate boards, it also employs George H. W. Bush as a senior adviser for the group's Asian Fund.

The bin Ladens' money has been zealously courted by the Carlyle Group. Baker, Bush and Carlucci have all made pilgrimages to Jeddah, Saudi Arabia, headquarters of bin Ladin [sic] Enterprises. Bush Sr has met with the bin Ladens at least twice at the behest of the Carlyle Group – once in November 1998 and again in January of 2000. Baker has also courted the bin Ladens. He even flew from Washington to Saudi Arabia on the bin Laden family jet.

Carlucci's ties are even more involved, dating at least as far back to his days as chairman of Nortel Networks, the telecommunications giant, which engaged in several joint ventures with the bin Laden group.

The attention appears to have more than paid off. The *Wall Street Journal*, in a September 27 story, quoted an international financier with ties to bin Ladin Enterprises as saying that the family's investments in the Carlyle Group are substantially larger than $2 million, saying that the holdings in the aerospace fund were 'just an initial deposit.'

Until 1997, the Carlyle Group used to own a security outfit called Vinnell, which, as Ken Silverstein details in his book *Private Warriors*, holds a contract to train the Saudi Arabian National Guard. The National Guard's primary duty is to protect Saudi military bases and the nation's oil infrastructure. According to Silverstein, many of Vinnell's operatives are veterans of the CIA and the US Army's Special Forces. Vinnell's roots can be traced to Vietnam, where it did some of the nastier work for the Pentagon and earned the nickname 'our little mercenary force.' During the Gulf War, Vinnell operatives basically led Saudi units. Today Saudi Arabia remains one of Vinnell's top clients. The company maintains more than 1,000 employees in the country, many of them working full-time to protect Saudi assets against attacks from homegrown militants, such as Osama bin Laden and his followers.

December 15, 2001

PEBBLES AND POPPIES
by Alexander Cockburn

First the tumult of war, now the fruits of peace. From Afghanistan come tidings of the new era of tolerance, now that the Taliban have, at least for the time being, slunk off the stage of history. Shortly before the turn of the year Justice Minister Karimi declared that Afghanistan's new government will still impose sharia Islamic law on its people but with less harshness.

The details were fleshed out by Judge Ahamat Ullha Zarif, who has told the French news agency Agence France Presse that public executions and amputations will continue, but there will be changes: 'For example, the Taliban used to hang the victim's body in public for four days. We will only hang the body for a short time, say 15 minutes.' Very Warholian.

Kabul's sports stadium, financed by the International Monetary Fund, was where the Taliban used to carry out public executions and amputations every Friday. No longer. 'The stadium is for sports. We will find a new place for public executions,' says Judge Zarif.

Judge Zarif makes it clear that the ultimate penalty will remain in force for adulterers, both male and female. They would still be stoned to death, Zarif told the French news agency, 'but we will use only small stones.' Now there's progress!

This adjustment in the size of the executive munitions will, the judge explains, allow the condemned person a chance to escape. 'If they are able to run away, they are free.' It turns out that this avenue of escape is only available to those adulterers who admit their sexual misdeeds. 'Those who refuse to confess their wrongdoing and are condemned by a judge will have their hands and feet bound so that they cannot run away. They will certainly be stoned to death,' Zarif said.

The winds of change can be felt on another front. Afghanistan's farmers faced bankruptcy after Mullah Omar ordered a halt to the planting of opium poppies last year. In the years that the CIA was rallying Afghanistan's landlords and mullahs against the Soviets, Afghanistan became the West's prime supplier of heroin and morphine. Mullah Omar's ban has been variously explained as an effort to ingratiate the Taliban regime with the US in hopes of getting aid, or as an effort to restrict supply and thus hike prices. Whatever the motive, the prohibition led to a 96 per cent fall in Afghanistan's production of raw opium – from more than 453,500 kilograms in 1999 to 18,500 kilograms in 2001, according to the United Nations Drug Control Program.

Now news reports, such as this from Craig Nelson, describe renewed poppy cultivation in lyrical terms: 'Everyone is planting,' says Ashoqullah, a twenty-five-year-old landowner. 'In a few months, these fields will be covered in a blanket of spectacular red and white flowers. We'll draw the ooze from the flower bulbs, pack it in plastic bags or small soap cartons and sell it at the bazaar.' From the bazaars the raw opium will make its way north or south to processing labs in Pakistan or Tadzikistan, two members of the great anti-terror coalition, and then westward to the veins of addicts in Europe and the United States. But Afghanistan's swift return to preeminent status as the USA's number one heroin supplier is surely a small price to pay for the extinction of the Taliban and routing of Al Qaeda.

Alas, this raises the question of just how extinct the Taliban is. Fudge the numbers as you may, not too many of them ended up dead, aside from those prisoners killed at Mazar al Sharif or suffocated on their way to other prisons. Presumably the rest dispersed to their homes, awaiting further instructions from their Pakistani supervisors.

Osama bin Laden? Suppose he pops up in Kashmir, calling for renewed jihad against the Indian occupiers. Now that would set the cat among the pigeons!

So perhaps it's not quite so clear how much has really been achieved in the great crusade, but for sure, it is a famous victory!

December 20, 2001

ANTHRAX AS NORMALCY: 500 CASES A YEAR
by Jeffrey St. Clair

Imagine if the anthrax attacks had killed nearly 500 people, instead of the four in the US who have died from the bacteria so far. Consider further the outrage that would most certainly erupt had it come out that the US government knew about the anthrax outbreak in advance, but failed to take any action to protect people from the disease. Then factor in the big drug companies, which have refused to administer out life-saving vaccines because to do so might undermine their lucrative patents.

Sound far-fetched? Hardly. This is a rough description of what has been going on in Haiti since the mid-1970s, where nearly 500 people contract anthrax every year. You can search the major media and the US government in vain for coverage of what can only be called an ongoing crisis. At most, *CounterPunch* has been able to locate a few press releases from the State Department warning US tourists about this danger and a move by the Commerce Department to restrict the import of certain goods made from animal hides, though not major league baseballs, which are manufactured in Haiti by workers making about twenty cents an hour.

Here is the text of an advisory from the Commerce Department:

Consumers who may have goatskin items such as bongo drums, wineskins, hassocks, small rugs, decorative wall coverings (mosaics), 'balancers,' ladies' purses or unfinished goatskin hides known to have been imported from Haiti should place the products in a sealed plastic bag and call a local or State health department for disposal instructions. Consumers should not attempt to sterilize the product, incinerate it, or throw it away because of the risk of additional contamination.

The fact that so many American textile corporations have moved their sweatshop operations to Haiti to exploit pathetically low wages doesn't seem to have prompted much concern for the health of their workers. Indeed, the only detailed analysis of the situation that we can find comes from the college of veterinary medicine at Louisiana State University. According, to the LSU study, '27% to 50% of goatskin products are contaminated. During 1973–77 there were 1,587 human anthrax cases reported in the southern peninsula or 317 per year; 85 cases in 1983; and 1,396 cases during 1985 to 1988, or 349 per year.' Then, amazingly, between 1989 and 1993, no one even surveyed human anthrax cases. When the surveys resumed again in 1993, it turned out that in that year more than 100 people contracted the disease. In 1995, 449 people contracted anthrax. During these years, more than 700,000 cows and goats were vaccinated against the disease. No humans were given vaccinations.

'We have an emergency medical clinic in Cap Haitien, dealing mostly with burns, but have been working in the north of Haiti for over 30 years,' Eva DeHart, of For Haiti With Love, tells *CounterPunch*. 'Anthrax is normally ingested in Haiti. The animal gets sick, they slaughter it in the market quickly and unsuspecting victims take it home, cook it, eat it, and because of their already malnourished condition and lack of available medical care they die. They also contract the disease from the factories. An entire family on our support program died of pulmonary anthrax. They lived downwind from a tannery when they were tanning infected hides. I can't remember a time where you were not advised to avoid skins and hides with hair for items being bought to bring home, and we have been working down there for 30 years. It is a poor country, you just accept certain restrictions for your own safety.'

February 27, 2002

DANIEL PEARL: SHOULD HIS EDITORS HAVE SENT HIM THERE?
by Alexander Cockburn

Daniel Pearl's dispatches reminded me somewhat of Peter Kann's in the days when he was the *Wall Street Journal*'s most light-heartedly stylish reporter, before assuming the imperial purple and becoming the company's CEO. It was Kann, back in the late 1970s, who traveled to Afghanistan and reported that the place was a dump covered with flies and that it was hard to understand why any Great Power would want any truck with the place.

Ironically, since his captors charged him with being an agent of the American Empire and of Zionism, Pearl was not afraid to file reports contradicting the claims of the State Department or the Pentagon or even of the mad dogs on the *Journal*'s editorial pages whose ravings fulfill on a weekly basis the most paranoid expectations of a Muslim fanatic. Just about the time they were killing

Pearl, had they paused to buy a copy of the *Wall Street Journal* his killers would have found a reprint on the editorial pages of a particularly feverish article from *Commentary*, in-house periodical of the American Jewish Committee, stating flatly that to be opposed to Israel was to be anti-Zionist, and to be anti-Zionist was to be anti-Semitic. It's the familiar two-step logic of the Israeli lobby: oppose the sale of Apache helicopters to Sharon or the bulldozing of Palestinian homes and you become a co-conspirator in the Holocaust.

The *Wall Street Journal* editorial page wrote, the day after news of Pearl's death was confirmed, that it showed 'evil' was still stalking the world, 'evil' being the current term of art for 'awfulness beyond our comprehension.' Now, these editorial writers have spent years writing urgent advisories to whatever US president happens to be in power that the most extreme reactionary forces in Israel must be given unconditional backing. It would take any Islamic fanatic about fifteen minutes in a clips library to demonstrate that if bombs are to be dropped on Palestinians, peace overtures shunned, just settlements rejected, then the *Wall Street Journal*'s editorial page is on board, full-throat.

Why was it left to Pearl's wife to offer herself to the kidnappers in lieu of her husband? Why did not the *WSJ*'s editorial page editor, Paul Gigot, proffer himself, or if he had protested that his credentials were not yet sufficiently seasoned since he has only recently plumped his behind into the editorial chair, why not bring Robert Bartley out of retirement and send him to Karachi for discussion of the relationship of editorial writing in the *Wall Street Journal* to overall moral responsibility for US policies in the Middle East and South Asia?

So if that *WSJ* editorial writer who invoked 'evil' had been honest, he might have written: 'It may well be that Danny Pearl was killed because his murderers held him responsible for positions on the Middle East conflict and on Islam oft expressed in these editorial pages. If so, then he died for principles that we honor and will always uphold,' or something of that sort, while simultaneously emphasizing that reporters are not editorial writers and that Pearl bore no responsibility for the editorials.

Might it not have occurred to Pearl's editors, those who assigned him to South Asia, that the fact that he was an Israeli citizen might put him in extra peril, given the fact that he was seeking to contact an extremely dangerous crowd of Muslim terrorists in Karachi? The fact of his citizenship only emerged after his death, in a report, February 24, in the Israeli newspaper *Ha'aretz*, by Yossi Melman:

> Professor Yehuda Pearl, father of murdered Wall Street Journal reporter Daniel Pearl, has told *Ha'aretz* that he fears that making public his son's Israeli citizenship could adversely affect investigative efforts by Pakistani police to apprehend the killers and track down the murdered reporter's body. In a telephone conversation from his Los Angeles residence, Professor Pearl expressed regret and anger over the revelation by the Israeli media of his family's 'Israeli connection.' The US media, which was aware of the information, complied with the family's request not to make it public.

Then Melman concluded with this minor bombshell:

> The American media was asked to comply with this request after information was obtained that confirmed reports that the 38-year-old reporter was dead.

It seems to me almost certain that those Pakistani terrorists would have killed any reporter for a US news organization who had the ill-fortune to come seeking an interview at that particular time. Robert Fisk, of the London *Independent*, has probably written more pieces sympathetic to the Palestinian cause than almost any other mainstream reporter, yet that didn't prevent him from nearly being beaten to death by Afghans in a frontier town a few weeks ago. On February 23, Fisk wrote:

> In Pakistan and Afghanistan, we can be seen as Kaffirs, as unbelievers. Our faces, our hair, even our spectacles, mark us out as Westerners. The Muslim cleric who wished to talk to me in an Afghan refugee village outside Peshawar last October was stopped by a man who pointed at me and asked: 'Why are you taking this Kaffir into our mosque?' Weeks later, a crowd of Afghan refugees, grief-stricken at the slaughter of their relatives in a US B-52 bomber air raid, tried to kill me because they thought I was an American ... Over the past quarter century I have witnessed the slow, painful, dangerous erosion of respect for our work. We used to risk our lives in wars – we still do – but journalists were rarely deliberate targets. We were impartial witnesses to conflict, often the only witnesses, the first writers of history. Even the nastiest militias understood this. 'Protect him, look after him, he is a journalist,' I recall a Palestinian guerrilla ordering his men when I entered the burning Lebanese town of Bhamdoun in 1983.

After discussing the trend whereby journalists clamber into uniforms (as US correspondents did in Vietnam) Fisk continues:

> When the Palestinians evacuated Beirut in 1982, I noticed that several French reporters were wearing Palestinian kuffiah scarves. Israeli reporters turned up in occupied southern Lebanon with pistols. Then in the 1991 Gulf war, American and British television reporters started dressing up in military costumes, appearing on screen – complete with

helmets and military camouflage fatigues – as if they were members of the 82nd Airborne or the Hussars. One American journalist even arrived in boots camouflaged with painted leaves, although a glance at any desert suggests that this would not have served much purpose. In the Kurdish flight into the mountains of northern Iraq more reporters could be found wearing Kurdish clothes. In Pakistan and Afghanistan last year, the same phenomenon occurred. Reporters in Peshawar could be seen wearing Pushtun hats. Why? No one could ever supply me with an explanation. What on earth was CNN's Walter Rodgers doing in US Marine costume at the American camp outside Kandahar? Mercifully, someone told him to take it off after his first broadcast. Then Geraldo Rivera of Fox News arrived in Jalalabad with a gun. He fully intended, he said, to kill Osama bin Laden. It was the last straw. The reporter had now become combatant.

Perhaps we no longer care about our profession. Maybe we're all to quick to demean our own jobs, to sneer at each other, to adopt the ridiculous title of 'hacks' when we should regard the job of foreign correspondent as a decent, honourable profession … Can we do better? I think so. It's not that reporters in military costume – Rodgers in his silly Marine helmet, Rivera clowning around with a gun, or even me in my gas cape a decade ago – helped to kill Daniel Pearl. He was murdered by vicious men. But we are all of us – dressing up in combatant's clothes or adopting the national dress of people – helping to erode the shield of neutrality and decency which saved our lives in the past. If we don't stop now, how can we protest when next our colleagues are seized by ruthless men who claim we are spies?

Pearl's style was totally alien to the bloodthirsty rantings of his editorial colleagues. He sent excellent dispatches questioning the claims of the Clinton administration that it had been justified in the 1998 destruction via cruise missile of the El Shifa Pharmaceutical

Industries plant in the Sudan. Again, he and fellow *WSJ* reporter
Robert Block entered some effective reservations about allegations
of Serbian genocide in Kosovo. In fact Slobodan Milosevic might
make use of them in mounting his vigorous defense in the US-
sponsored kangaroo court in The Hague against charges of
genocide. Pearl and Block stigmatized the Serb armed forces as
having done 'heinous things,' while also writing that 'other
allegations – indiscriminate mass murder, rape camps, cremato-
riums, mutilation of the dead – haven't been borne out in the six
months since NATO troops entered Kosovo. Ethnic-Albanian
militants, humanitarian organizations, NATO and the news media
fed off each other to give genocide rumors credibility. Now, a
different picture is emerging.' David North, of the Trotskyist Fourth
International, wrote on the World Socialist website on February
23: 'On the very day that Pearl's murder was confirmed, US
Secretary of Defense Donald Rumsfeld admitted that US troops
had mistakenly killed 16 anti-Taliban Afghan fighters, but refused
to apologize. It does not require exceptional political insight to
realize that in the decision to murder Pearl, the desire for revenge
was a major subjective factor.'

North then remarked that the outlook of the Pakistani terrorists
is not so different from that of Thomas Friedman, the repellent
columnist of the *New York Times*, also recently recruited as a kind
of Charles Kuralt of globalization by PBS's *Lehrer News Hour*. North
cited a recent Friedman column which praised Bush's Axis of Evil
speech in these terms:

Sept. 11 happened because America lost its deterrent capability. We
lost it because for 20 years we never retaliated against, or brought to
justice, those who murdered Americans ... innocent Americans were
killed and we did nothing. So our enemies took us less and less seriously

and became more and more emboldened ... America's enemies smelled weakness all over us, and we paid a huge price for that.

North very properly comments:

By changing only a few words, the Pakistani terrorists could use Friedman's argument to justify their murder of Pearl: 'We have failed to retaliate against America ... innocent Arabs, Afghans and Moslems were killed and we did nothing ... America took us less and less seriously and became more and more emboldened.' The thought patterns of the pompous and belligerent American columnist and the Islamic terrorist have far more in common than either imagine. Both think in terms of ethnic, religious and national stereotypes. Both believe in and are mesmerized by violence.

Leave the last beautiful, true words to Daniel Pearl's widow:

Revenge would be easy, but it is far more valuable in my opinion to address this problem of terrorism with enough honesty to question our own responsibility as nations and as individuals for the rise of terrorism. My own courage arises from two facts. One is that throughout this ordeal I have been surrounded by people of amazing value. This helps me trust that humanism ultimately will prevail.

My other hope now – in my seventh month of pregnancy – is that I will be able to tell our son that his father carried the flag to end terrorism, raising an unprecedented demand among people from all countries not for revenge but for the values we all share: love, compassion, friendship and citizenship far transcending the so-called clash of civilizations.

March 6, 2002

POLITICS OF A BUMPER CROP: OPIUM AND AFGHANISTAN
by Alexander Cockburn and Jeffrey St. Clair

Though Britain has been blaring its support for America's 'War on Terror,' there is public disquiet in the UK at one aspect of the new era of freedom now prevailing in Afghanistan: the renewal of opium cultivation, banned with unprecedented and near total success by Mullah Omar in July of 2000. In order to receive US aid, Hamid Karzai's coalition had to make a pro forma announcement in January that opium cultivation is still forbidden, but the extent of this renewed commitment to abstention from Afghanistan's prime cash crop was almost simultaneously displayed in the unceremonious ejection of Afghanistan's drug control agency from its offices in Kabul, with the drug tsar's desk being kicked physically into the street.

A couple of weeks ago the London *Guardian* reported in a headline that 'MI5 fears flood of Afghan heroin.' The ensuing story by Nick Hopkins and Richard Norton-Taylor led with the news that 'Police and intelligence agencies have been warned that Britain is facing a potentially huge increase in heroin trafficking because of massive and unchecked replanting of the opium crop in Afghanistan. The expectation is that the 2002 crop will be equivalent to the bumper one of three years ago, which yielded 4,600 tonnes of raw opium.'

The *Guardian* went on to report a new assessment by the UN office for drug control and crime prevention, based in Vienna, that after the war the West stands to lose the 'best-ever opportunity' to suffocate the illegal trade. Afghanistan is the source of 75 per cent of the world's heroin and 90 per cent of Britain's supply.

Opium poppies are primarily grown in the south and east of

Afghanistan, the regions dominated by the Pashtuns, the ethnic fraction that sustained the Taliban until such support became an obvious poor bet. In political terms, it's a safe forecast to say that no serious effort will be made to interfere with the opium crop. To do so would be to deal the Karzai regime as serious a blow as did Mullah Omar to loyalty to the Taliban when he banned opium cultivation (an act variously explained as a last-ditch attempt to get recognition from the West, or as a price-support tactic, restricting supply).

These developments lend a certain irony to the enormously costly ads bought by the US government on Superbowl Sunday to inform America's consumers of illegal drugs that to buy cocaine or heroin is to help terrorism. To the contrary, at least so far as Afghanistan is concerned, to buy heroin and morphine is to provide a sure market for Afghanistan's farm sector, which employs as many as 200,000 in the fields harvesting the opium from the poppy heads. A sure income to the opium farmers means a cut for the rural barons whose support in essential for the future well-being of America's selected government, headed by Karzai.

Meanwhile, readers here in the US of the magazine *Vanity Fair* can marvel at the tact displayed by Maureen Orth in her article in the March issue on 'Afghanistan's Deadly Habit,' about 'the symbiotic connection between drugs and terrorism.' The impression given by Orth is that only with the coming to power of the Taliban in 1996 did the opium industry 'grow so quickly that in 1999 Afghanistan produced 5,000 tons of opium, more than 70 per cent of the world's supply.'

It is true that deep into the article Orth makes very fleeting reference to the CIA's possible role in the late 1970s and 1980s in the expansion of opium cultivation in Afghanistan. The facts are easily available (and cited at some length in that very fine book *Whiteout, The CIA, Drugs and the Press*, coauthored by Jeffrey St. Clair and Alexander Cockburn). One of President Jimmy Carter's White House advisors on the drug trade said later that 'We were going into Afghanistan to support the opium growers in their rebellion against the Soviets. Shouldn't we try to pay the growers if they will eradicate their production?' David Musto, one of President Carter's drug policy advisers, went public with his concerns in an op-ed in the *New York Times* in 1980.

Reports issued by the UN and Drug Enforcement Administration in the early 1980s stated that by 1981 Afghan heroin producers may have captured 60 per cent of the heroin market in Western Europe and the United States. In New York City in 1979 alone, the year the CIA-organized flow of arms to the mujahideen began, heroin-related deaths increased by 77 per cent. There were no Superbowl ads that year about doing drugs and aiding terror. You could say that those dead addicts had given their lives in the fight to drive back Communism.

The only possible way to curb the trade is to offer farmers enough income to grow something else, at a reasonable level of profit. Decade after decade there have been efforts. Mohammed Mossadegh tried crop substitution in Iran in the early 1950s and was soon toppled with the help of the CIA, which found some of its allies among the big land barons running the opium trade. In Afghanistan, Noor Taraki's short-lived new Afghan government attacked the opium-growing feudal estates and got loans for crop substitution. Orth does say frankly that 'the Taliban ban on poppy growing was the largest, most successful interdiction of drugs in history.' And in history's dustbin is where that interdiction speedily ended up. Will the US press for crop substitution? Probably not, always for the same reason: to suppress drug cultivation requires putting money in the pockets of peasants and that means expensive aid programs and also enormous political risks of offending important, if unpalatable, allies.

August 7, 2002

KARZAI'S BODYGUARD
by Gary Leupp

One often hears that Afghanistan is the most ferociously independent of countries, the graveyard of invaders. So the news that Hamid Karzai has been fitted with a battery of American bodyguards must give us pause. Why, one might ask, in this battle-hardened country brimming with warriors, in which Kalashnikovs outnumber men, should its head of state require this foreign guardianship?

The Pope in the Vatican has his Swiss Guards; but the mini-state has no competent armed population to draw on, and there's a long history behind that quaint convention. Why should Karzai, or his American handlers, opt to surround him with gun-toting aliens, when there ought to be so many local, loyal troops?

We have been told that Karzai received overwhelming support at the Loya Jirga in June. If that were the case, why can't he muster a trustworthy Afghan entourage? (First of all, it isn't the case, actually; former king Zahir Shah enjoyed wide support but was forced to withdraw his bid to become head of state by Defense Minister and warlord Mohammed Fahim, whom a Western official quoted by the *Washington Post* has likened to a 'street thug,' and US special envoy and kingmaker Zalmay Khalilzad.) The fact is that Karzai, having been placed in power by the US as next-best thing to the late CIA operative Abdul Haq, has reason to fear his own people. His 'political base remains weak,' notes the *Washington Post* (August 5), and his 'authority barely extends beyond Kabul.'

Two members of Karzai's administration have been assassinated, cases still unresolved. On February 14, Transport and Tourism Minister Abdul Rahman was assassinated at Kabul Airport. Karzai and Foreign Minister Abdullah gave entirely different accounts of the incident. On July 6, Abdul Qadir, one of the vice-presidents, was also assassinated for reasons that remain unclear. (Karzai blamed 'terrorists,' George Bush suggested that opium interests might have been involved, and others blamed Northern Alliance forces for slaying a rising Pashtun leader.)

More significant than these acts of political violence is the emergence of a political opposition movement rooted among the common people. There have been ongoing protests in Kabul about that July 1 wedding party raid, in which according to the official Afghan government report, forty-eight civilians were killed by US bombs; and demonstrators have targeted both the US military and the president so intimately associated with it. Anti-government demonstrations have occurred in Gardez and Khost as well.

Fahim, sometimes at loggerheads with Karzai (and should the two part ways, he will command far greater native military support), has long expressed the view that there should be minimal foreign military presence in the country. (His line since December has been: 'Thanks for the bombs that broke the Taliban, but we Northern Alliance forces can handle things from here.') He is furious about Karzai's Yankee bodyguard. Those defenders are an admission of Karzai's vulnerable position in the lawless environment the bombing has produced, and of the well-founded fear that tends to encompass puppets making Faustian pacts.

An AP article and accompanying photo published on August 3 said it all. It reported that Karzai 'dismissed allegations yesterday that the United States tried to cover up a deadly airstrike [which Afghan officials claimed occurred south of Kabul on August 1] and said a continued American presence was crucial to Afghanistan's future. Flanked by US special forces bodyguards, Karzai said he visited one of the villages attacked in the July 1 air raid and when asked if he believed there had been a cover-up, said, "I don't think so. People would have told me."'

Reporters were asking about a UN report leaked to the *Times* of London stating that US forces may have removed evidence after the attack and violated human rights. Now, the UN, once a site of contestation between the US bloc and the Third World (and frequently the object of Washington's scorn), has since the collapse of the Soviet Union been more or less tucked under Washington's armpit. The New World Order in international diplomacy has been especially evident since December 1991, when the Security Council revoked Resolution 3379 (passed in November 1975) describing Zionism as a form of racism. Many nations' delegates changed their votes under extreme pressure from the Bush administration. In December 1996 the US vetoed a second term for Boutros Boutros-Ghali (of Egypt) as United Nations Secretary-General; the 14 to 1 vote in the Security Council outraged the Arab world. Under the leadership of Kofi Annan, the UN has avoided confrontation with the US (and with Israel), as indicated by Annan's report on the Israeli invasion of Jenin in April, which Human Rights Watch has called 'fundamentally flawed.'

That even this lapdog UN secretary-general alleges US misconduct in the Uruzgan province incident of July 1 lends particular credence to the allegation. And for the President of Afghanistan to dismiss the report out of hand is to confirm that he is a lapdog of even more abject status than Mr Annan. The AP photo shows Karzai walking towards a shrine, fingering prayer-beads, with (as the caption states) 'US bodyguards clearing the way.' There are well-armed US forces to the fore, one peering forward, the other walking sideways, gun in hand, scrutinizing the rear.

Way back in 1857, Friedrich Engels (who made some very interesting observations about Afghanistan, then pivotal to 'the Great Game' played out in Central Asia between Britain and Russia) described 'the attempt of the British to set up a prince of their own making in Afghanistan' in 1842, linking its failure to the Afghans' 'indomitable hatred of rule, and their love of independence.' (This was published in the *New American Cyclopedia* in 1858.) Like most of Marx and Engels's stuff, it's probably on the Net now; in his leisure time, in his Kabul office, surrounded by his Swiss Guard, Mr Karzai might want to peruse it.

Gary Leupp is a professor in the Department of History at Tufts University and coordinator of the Asian Studies Program.

September 7, 2002

THE TENTH CRUSADE
by Alexander Cockburn

Amid the elegies for the dead and the ceremonies of remembrance, seditious questions intrude: Is there really a war on terror; and if one is indeed being waged, what are its objectives?

The Taliban are out of power. *Papaver somniferum*, the opium poppy, blooms once more in Afghan pastures. The military budget is up. The bluster war on Iraq blares from every headline. On the home front the war on the Bill of Rights is set at full throttle, though getting less popular with each day as judges thunder their indignation at the unconstitutional diktats of Attorney General John Ashcroft, a man low in public esteem.

On this latter point we can turn to Merle Haggard, the bard of blue-collar America, the man who saluted the American flag more than a generation ago in songs such as 'The Fighting Side of Me' and 'Okie from Muskogee.' Haggard addressed a concert crowd in Kansas City a few days ago in the following terms: 'I think we should give John Ashcroft a big hand … (pause) … right in the mouth!' Haggard went on to say: 'The way things are going I'll probably be thrown in jail tomorrow for saying that, so I hope y'all will bail me out.'

It will take generations to roll back the constitutional damage done in the wake of the attacks. Emergency laws lie around for decades like rattlesnakes in summer grass. As Joanne Mariner of Human Rights Watch pointed out to me, one of the main legal precedents that the government is using to justify detaining 'enemy combatants' without trial or access to a lawyer is an old strike-breaking decision. The government's August 27 legal brief in the Padilla 'enemy combatant' case relies heavily on *Moyer v. Peabody*, a Supreme Court case that dates back to 1909.

The case involved Charles Moyer, president of the Western Federation of Miners, a feisty Colorado trade union that fought for such radical reforms as safe working conditions, an end to child labor, and payment in money rather than in company scrip. As part of a concerted effort to crush the union, the governor of Colorado had declared a state of insurrection, called out the state militia, and detained Moyer for two and a half months without probable cause or due process of law.

In an opinion that deferred obsequiously to executive power (using the 'captain of the ship' metaphor), the US Supreme Court upheld Moyer's detention. It reasoned that since the militia could even have fired upon the strikers (or, in the Court's words, the 'mob in insurrection'), how could Moyer complain of a mere detention? The government now cites the case in its Padilla brief to argue that whatever a state governor can do, the president can do better. As Mariner remarks, next thing you know they'll be citing the Japanese internment precedents.

September 7, 2002

THE TROUBLE WITH NORMAL
by Jeffrey St. Clair

We are told that we are different. That things have changed, changed irrevocably. That it's a strange new world now. And there's no going back. Some pundits even appropriated the language of Stephen Jay Gould (though he would never have done so), calling the leveling of the towers a kind of historical punctuated equilibrium, a great leap forward in the evolution of the nation.

The collapse of the towers became a metaphor for the shedding of a tarnished exoskeleton, a tale right out of Ovid directed by Roger Corman. In Jerry Falwell's words, 9/11 was a preview of the Apocalypse, which expurgated the Sixties, humanism, cultural tolerance, and all of that jazz. Suddenly, everybody espoused an eschatology.

By and large, out here in Oregon, people just wanted to get back to normal, slide back into a daily routine of work, family and play. After all, Oregon's economy had bottomed out prior to 9/11. There wasn't any time for extended periods of cross-continental grief, and there wasn't money to 'buy a car to demonstrate our patriotism,' even with Greenspan quashing interest rates. But the media refused to go along, they force-fed us patriotism through the cable lines as if we were all hooked up to a collective IV. Even so, the ubiquitous

American flags didn't start going up in our little mill-town until two or three weeks after the attacks on the WTC and the Pentagon. These raisings didn't seem like genuflections of patriotism so much as symbols of surrender to the imprecations of CNN diva Paula Zahn.

The 3,000 victims at 'ground zero,' especially the firemen and cops who rushed into the towers only to have them collapse on top of them, were swiftly turned into sacrificial heroes, national martyrs in the cause of the revenge tragedy that is now being played out on a global scale. Bruce Springsteen roused himself out of hibernation to sing the soundtrack, for $20 a pop. Suddenly there were martyrs everywhere, from Mohammed Atta to Todd Beamer, whose last words were trademarked by his wife, Lisa – it's the American way. Is the thirst for virgins in the afterlife so inexhaustible?

Every aspect of American society continues to be drenched in this sticky and unrelenting patriotism. You get the sense that even our serial killers are uniquely American. Something to be proud about. And perhaps so it should be. Those Special Forces troops who came back from the hunting grounds of Afghanistan to kill their wives at Fort Bragg are the most pampered and 'understood' killers since William Calley.

Looking back, it's hard to see any fundamental change in the character of life in America. The events of 9/11 and their aftermath merely solidified the status quo. The economy remains in a rut. Environmental laws are being peeled back day by day. The Sharon war machine tramples Palestinians with impunity. The unemployment rolls grow daily by the thousands. More and more are going without food stamps or welfare checks. It's all blotted out by the manufactured trauma of 9/11.

Of course, some things were clarified. The fragility of the Constitution. The supine nature of the environmental groups and big labor, which stood down as the Bush administration cravenly pursued its post-9/11 domestic agenda. And, of course, the complicit character of the Democratic Party, which green-lighted Bush's war without debate and helped enact some of the most oppressive domestic policing laws in the history of the Republic with only two or three voices of dissent. Now one of those, Cynthia McKinney, has been driven from the Congress for her impertinence. And the beat goes on.

I opened the paper this morning. More indications of a double-dip recession. Boeing stiff-armed the machinist union, again. The number of Americans ensnared by the criminal justice system topped 6 million. The US-armed death squads in Colombia slaughtered more peasants. More than 90 per cent of Native Americans live without access to adequate health care. GE's Jack Welch got a severance package that pays him $17,000 a day. The spotted owl population has declined by 50 per cent in the last ten years and seems headed inevitably toward the black hole of extinction.

It all seems so familiar. Same direction, faster pace. The trouble with normal, Bruce Cockburn sings, is that it always gets worse.

September 12, 2002

THE MOST DANGEROUS MAN IN WASHINGTON
by Alexander Cockburn

At 2.40 pm, September 11, 2001, Defense Secretary Donald Rumsfeld was commanding his aides to get 'best info fast. Judge whether good enough hit S. H.' – meaning Saddam Hussein – 'at same time. Not only U.B.L.' – the initials used to identify Osama bin Laden. 'Go massive.' Notes taken by these aides quote him as saying: 'Sweep it all up. Things related and not.' We can thank David Martin of CBS for getting hold of these notes and disclosing them last Wednesday.

This was our Donald, thinking fast as he paced about the National Military Command Center, seeking to turn the attack into a rationale for all sorts of unrelated revenges and settlings of accounts. For Rumsfeld, as for his boss, as for so many, it was a turning point in his career as a cabinet member in the Bush II presidency. In the wake of the attacks Rumsfeld swiftly learned to revel in his role as America's top exponent of bully-boy bluster. And he's kept it up, running rings around Colin Powell, whose pals are now leaking stories that Powell may throw in the towel at the end of Bush's present term. Small wonder. Rumsfeld has humiliated Powell, reaching a peak in effrontery when, a few weeks ago, he contradicted decades-worth of formal US foreign policy and declared that Israel had every right and every reason to occupy the West Bank and have settlements there.

The specter of military government here in the US lurks eternally in the imagination of fearful constitutionalists, right or left. There's a lot more reason for these fears today, particularly after the Patriot Act shot through Congress. Today the FBI can spy on political and religious meetings even when there's no suspicion that a crime has been committed. Dissidents can get labeled 'domestic terrorists' and be the target of every form of snooping.

The Patriot Act allows 'black bag' searches for every sort of record that might shed light on suspects, including the books they get out of a library. Computers and personal papers can be confiscated and not returned even if an indictment is never lodged against the suspect. Such secret searches can take place even in cases unrelated to terrorism. The Justice Department argued in two federal cases that the president has the power to indefinitely detain without any charges any person, including any US citizen, designated as an 'enemy combatant.' Furthermore the administration argues that the president's conduct of the war on terrorism can't be challenged and that civilian courts have no authority over the detentions.

The Justice Department argues that people designated 'enemy combatants' can be put behind bars, held incommunicado and denied counsel. If the detainee does get a lawyer, their conversations can be bugged.

In such manner we are saying goodbye to the First, Fourth and Sixth Amendments. Back to Rumsfeld. The Defense Secretary is currently trying to get the Pentagon greater authority to carry out covert ops. He also wants Congress to agree to have a new undersecretary of defense, responsible for all intelligence matters. Now blend these proposals in with the erosions of the Posse Comitatus Act, which forbids the US military to have any role in domestic law enforcement, shake the blender vigorously, and you have the Rumsfeld cocktail with an Ashcroft cherry. A defense undersecretary may soon be able to target YOU (or the antiwar couple in the apartment next door), bug your phone and computer, burglarize the place, grab you, stick you in prison and let you rot.

All legally. That's what we call military government, the way we teach the Latin American officers mustered for training at Fort Benning to do things in their countries, plus hanging electrodes on the testicles and nipples of those slow to confide who their team-mates were in the antiwar group mentioned above. Remember, there's a strong lobby here for torture too.

Try holding a placard up when George Bush is driving by. Kevin O'Neill had a good column last Thursday in the *Pittsburgh Post Gazette* describing what happened when demonstrators against

President Bush were herded inside a fence at Neville Island for his Labor Day visit.

Police called this enclosure the designated free-speech area, though anyone who had signs praising the president was evidently OK to line the island's main street for the motorcade.

The mini-Guantanamo on the Ohio was set up strictly for security reasons, of course. Those who pose a genuine threat to the president are expected to carry signs identifying themselves as such, as a courtesy. Hence the erection of the Not-OK Corral.

Bill Neel of Butler just doesn't get it, though. He's 65 and can remember a time when our entire country was a free-speech zone. So when he refused to get inside the fence with his sign, he was arrested, cuffed and detained in the best place for inflammatory rhetoric, the fire hall.

Neel's confiscated sign said, 'The Bushes must truly love the poor – they've made so many of us.' For holding this contrary opinion in the censored speech zone, Neel was given a summons for disorderly conduct.

September 25, 2002

THE DOGS OF WAR, THE BEARS OF WALL STREET
by Alexander Cockburn

The higher Bush tries to loft himself with war talk, the darker grow the economy's dire responses. On Tuesday the Dow-Jones industrials dropped nearly 190 points to hit a four-year low. The broader market also finished down. The Nasdaq composite index, homeport for the New Economy, set a new six-year low. The Standard & Poor's 500 index was down 14.45, or 1.7 per cent, at 819.25.

The Fed's Open Market Committee chose to leave rates at forty-year lows at its meeting on Tuesday, saying bravely that consumer and business demand is 'growing at a moderate pace.' But it also noted that considerable uncertainty remains about the timing and strength of an economic recovery. Meanwhile, leading economic indicators and housing starts have fallen for three months in a row. Oil prices are up 40 per cent since the start of the year.

We've now seen seven straight quarters of declining investment on plant and equipment and a sharp drop of the growth of consumer spending over the past four or five months. Suppose, we asked, there's another drop in equity prices, reflecting dawning awareness that the performance of many of America's mightiest corporate names has been based entirely on fraudulent numbers.

So now equity prices have dropped again and federal prosecutors have announced they're opening a criminal probe into Xerox's accounting practices. Xerox stock promptly fell 71 cents to $5.96 after the company said federal prosecutors were opening a criminal inquiry into the company's accounting practices. WorldCom revealed that it probably misreported $9 billion in revenue, not $7 billion. The official rate of profit on capital stock in the non-financial corporate sector as a whole is now at its lowest level of the postwar period (except for 1980 and 1982).

If this was Bill Clinton, the commentators would be flaying him alive for wag-the-dog attempts to use war talk as a way to distract attention from economic bad news. Thus far Bush has remained aloft on his magic carpet, but he's losing altitude steadily while Wall Street chews its lip, foreign denunciations pour in, and the German

Social Democrats and Greens exult in the way Bush handed them an entirely unexpected victory last weekend. America no longer has Senior Reps of the Ruling Class like John McCoy or 'Wise Old Men' like the infinitely tacky Clark Clifford. At moments like this, such Senior Reps would step forth with measured warnings to Bush about his reckless path. These days we're left with Henry Kissinger.

Probably the nearest thing we have to a senior statesman is that brilliant Democratic politician Senator Bobby Byrd, whose monuments strew West Virginia. The only opponent Senator Byrd has to fear is death itself, so in Congress he speaks with a frankness rivaled only by the Texan libertarian, Rep. Ron Paul. In the last week Byrd has excelled himself in speeches on the Senate floor. He denounced Bush's proposed Homeland Security Agency as a ramshackle, hastily conceived outrage to constitutional protections, a way of undercutting the hard rights of federal workers, all in a mission thus far entirely undefined. Byrd made particular reference to Bush's contemptuous dismissal of criticism of the proposed Agency as Lilliputian. The venerable but frisky senator riposted by deriding Bush as a Caesarist Gulliver impatient with the restraints of democratic constitutional government. In another speech Byrd gave Bush some derisive whacks on the topic of his warmongering against Iraq: 'The president was dropping in the polls and the domestic situation was such that the administration was appearing to be much like the emperor who had no clothes.' Byrd described the coming of 'war fervor, the drums of war, the bugles of war, the clouds of war.'

'I sat in on some of the secret briefings,' Byrd said, 'and nobody from the administration has been able to answer the question: Why now?'

A few days later in San Francisco another prominent Democrat, Al Gore, lacked Byrd's fizz but still wagged an admonitory finger at Bush. Gore's weekend speech to the Commonwealth Club was widely billed as antiwar. Gore did issue some strong language denouncing Bush's onslaught on the freedoms guaranteed by the Constitution. Beyond that the speech was in fact a measured, fairly well written advisory on the pretenses and postures appropriate to the world's premier imperial power. Gore echoed Henry Kissinger in saying that an attack on Iraq had to be properly justified, not by bluster about a 'regime change,' and by hot talk about America's right to wage 'preemptive war,' but by traditional rhetorical escalation within the grand tradition of such rationales, stretching back to the dawn of the Cold War.

There's probably not been a president since World War Two held in such low international esteem as Bush. Mark how Gore felt it safe to play on this theme in his San Francisco speech. Six, even three months ago, Gore would never have taken such a risk: 'In just one year,' he said, 'the President has somehow squandered the international outpouring of sympathy, good will and solidarity that followed the attacks of September 11 and converted it into anger and apprehension aimed much more at the United States than at the terrorist network.'

If the economy continues to slide, Bush and his circle will face a truly desperate gamble, trying to figure whether a $200 billion war on Iraq will save them, or just plunge them into the mother of all messes.

October 9, 2002

DWARF-THROWING AND THE UN
by Alexander Cockburn

Here's why I'm against the UN as promoter of federalism and world guv'mint. This just in from Geneva, Switzerland, via the Reuters wire: 'UN upholds French ban on "dwarf throwing."' It turns out that a diminutive stuntman who had protested against a French ban on the practice of 'dwarf throwing' has lost his case before some sort of a UN human rights judicial body. The tribunal issued some typically pious UN claptrap about the need to protect human dignity being paramount.

The dwarf, a fellow called Manuel Wackenheim, argued that a 1995 ban by France's highest administrative court was discriminatory and deprived him of a job being tossed around discos and similar venues. The UN Human Rights Committee said it was satisfied 'the ban on dwarf-tossing was not abusive but necessary in order to protect public order, including considerations of human dignity.' It also said the ban 'did not amount to prohibited discrimination.'

Dwarfs and their throwers will have to search out venues, like prizefighters in eighteenth-century England. Soon some place like Iceland will be the only venue. No doubt a UN embargo will then ensue, with draconian sanctions, appointment of inspector/spies, followed by the inevitable intervention and occupation.

So here's a bunch of UN administrators, each of them probably hauling down an annual salary hefty enough to keep a troupe of dwarfs in caviare for life, dooming poor little Wackenheim to the unemployment lines before going home to scream at their underpaid Romanian maidservants or to get a blowjob from a thirteen-year-old girl from Kiev in the local whorehouse. (UN guys would do that, you ask? Oh yes they would. Remember the nasty little sex scandal about UN observers in Kosovo?)

In the old days dwarfs could stand proud, strutting down the boulevards, around circus rings, or forming part of some amusing display, or matching themselves against pitbulls (a popular nineteenth-century English pastime). I can remember plenty of dwarfs from my childhood in Ireland, along with other bodies remote from conventional anatomy. Walking down the mainstreet of any Irish town reminded one of Breughel. Not any more. I guess even in Catholic Ireland the doc takes a look and chokes nature's sports before they've got out of the starting gate.

If the UN had been around at the time, the hunchbacks of Philip IV of Spain would have been forbidden to pose for Velázquez, and Jeffrey Hudson (18 inches at the age of nine, albeit gracefully proportioned) would never have been permitted to step out of a pie on the dining-room table of his boss, George Villiers, first duke of Buckingham. Having emerged from the pastry, Hudson saluted Villiers's guests, King Charles I and his queen, Henrietta Maria, who promptly adopted him.

Spared a UN-sponsored abortion to save him from an existence incompatible with human dignity, Hudson led an adventurous life and survived two duels, one against a turkey cock and the other in combat with a certain Mr Crofts. The arrogant Crofts turned up for the duel with a water pistol, but Hudson stood on his dignity and insisted that the engagement be for real. They put Hudson up on a horse to get him level with Crofts and he promptly shot the man dead. Captured by Turkish pirates, Hudson said his tribulations made him grow, and having held steady at 18 inches from nine to thirty, he shot up to 3 feet 9 inches.

Another dwarf, Charles Stratton (aka General Tom Thumb), killed one of my favorite painters, Benjamin Haydon, who was exhibiting his vast work *The Banishment of Aristides*, in the Egyptian Hall in London. But the crowds preferred to gawp at General Thumb, on display in the same hall. Thumb drew £600 sterling in his first week, while Haydon got only a measly £7 13 shillings. Haydon went off home to his studio and killed himself.

Dwarf tossing? The job came with the stature. William Beckford, the eccentric millionaire who wrote *Vathek* and built the famous folly at Fonthill, was one of the last to have a dwarf in private service, though E. J. Woods, author of the useful *Giants and Dwarfs* (1860) says Beckford's dwarf was 'rather too big to be flung from one guest to another, as was the custom at dinners in earlier days.'

As the repellent harbinger of world guv'mint the UN holds scant allure. Its kangaroo tribunal, the International Criminal Court (rightly denounced by the Bush administration), bears all the same features as the International Criminal Tribunals on Yugoslavia and Rwanda (heartily endorsed by the Bush administration). To quote a fine recent piece on the *CounterPunch* site by George Szamuely, addressing US hypocrisy on this issue, 'The prosecutor is out of control. Prosecutor and court are one and the same. Appellate court and trial court are also one and the same. The court is answerable to no one. There is no jury. Prosecutors may appeal an acquittal and insist on continued detention of a defendant.'

Perhaps the most grotesque recent display of UN Kulchur at full stretch was the carrying of a cheesy 'Ark of Hope' containing the Earth Charter from the US to the Earth Summit in Johannesburg last month. This same charter is the spawn of Steven C. Rockefeller, Canadian eco-mogul Maurice Strong and Mikhail Gorbachev, who has said of it: 'My hope is that this charter will be a kind of Ten Commandments, a Sermon on the Mount, that provides a guide for human behavior toward the environment in the next century and beyond.'

The portage of the Charter at the end of last year began at an Earth Ceremony in Vermont, where Rockefeller (chairman of the Rockefeller Brothers Fund and the Earth Charter International Drafting Committee) is professor emeritus of religion at Middlebury College. Present was Jane Goodall, of chimpanzee fame. (One of her thumbtips was once nipped off by a chimp asserting its dignity when Goodall tried to cosy up to it at the Laboratory for Experimental Medicine and Surgery in Primates, part of NYU and located in Sterling Forest. Goodall tried to cover up by saying she'd caught her thumb in a car door.) The Charter was housed and transported to Johannesburg its cheesy Ark of Hope, furiously described on the *New American Patriot* website as 'a blasphemous mimicry of the biblical Ark of the Covenant, which held the two tablets containing the Ten Commandments that God gave to Moses.' Accompanying Charter and Ark are the 'Temenos Books,' containing aboriginal Earth Masks and 'visual prayers/affirmations for global healing, peace, and gratitude,' created by 3,000 artists, teachers, students, and mystics. 'Temenos' is the word for the precincts of a temple, and accurately reflects the ersatz religiosity of UN ritualism.

According to the Charter, we must: 'Recognize that all beings are interdependent and every form of life has value ...' (except of course for human foetuses, which are not included in the UN's definition of 'every form of life,' rating merely as disposable protoplasm). There's the predictable affirmation of faith in the 'inherent dignity of all human beings,' excluding those who are finished off by euthanasia or haled before the ICC or required to give blowjobs or clean the bathrooms of overpaid UN bureaucrats.

Now comes the jackboot. The Earth must 'adopt at all levels sustainable development plans and regulations. Prevent pollution of any part of the environment. Internalize the full environmental and social costs of goods and services in the selling price. Ensure universal access to health care that fosters reproductive health and responsible reproduction.' In other words, population control, as promoted through the century by the Rockefellers, who of course assigned the Manhattan real estate to the UN for its HQ.

October 12, 2002

THE ANATOMY OF FEAR
by Carol Norris

The first time I heard the now famous, overused slogan 'Either you're with us or against us' I thought it was one of the most inane, xenophobic lines I'd ever heard. Frankly, as an American, I was embarrassed. I had an incredible urge to write a blanket apology to the people the world over. This oversimplification utterly dismisses the complexities of people, societies and their relationships. Of course I can be 'with' my country and still not agree with many of its policies, just as I can remain completely loyal to my friends, family and clients even when I think they make incredibly foolish choices, as they do for me.

But as I thought more about it, I realized it was an absolutely brilliant line, exactly because it was meant to encourage people to overlook the complexities of life and think in oversimplified terms, tapping into deep-seated fears. Someone paid attention in psychology class and I'm thinking it wasn't C-student Bush.

It is no coincidence that Ted Geisel, aka Dr Seuss, the hugely successful children's author, was once a writer of war propaganda. Both genres of writing get in touch with the same concrete, childlike (not to be confused with childish) thought processes like 'You bad, me good.' Young children think like this because of where they are in their cognitive development.

Adults whose lives have been seriously threatened – or perceive that their lives are seriously threatened – sometimes think similarly. They move from a healthy balance of operating from all areas of the brain (including the rational neocortex) to operating primarily from the limbic system (the primitive brain and the intermediate brain), which, among other things, is responsible for self-preservation.

The limbic system is where fear and its physiological responses are born, and they function to help us mobilize and defend ourselves against the woolly mammoth or the saber-toothed tiger. This is also where the mechanisms of aggression are developed. The neocortex is responsible, among other things, for rational thought, abstract thinking and the ability to consider complexities. And during such fearful times, as the neocortex is overridden by the limbic system, we find ourselves with fear-based, reactive, jingoistic and seemingly intractable pro-war reactions in much of the American people. It's about self-preservation. (As this isn't a neuropsychology class this is an oversimplification and certainly a spotty explanation, but you get the drift.)

Coupled with this fact, I've come to realize that many Americans have parentified our government – not in the literal sense, but in the psychological one. I do not say this in a condescending or judgemental way, but in a factual one. We've all done it in one arena of our life or another.

Carol Norris is a psychotherapist and freelance writer.

October 15, 2002

IRAQ AS PRISON STATE
by Jeffrey St. Clair

Iraq isn't a rogue state; it's a captive nation, the world's first prison state, kept under a level of microscopic control and surveillance that would have made Jeremy Bentham tremble with envy.

All the recent chatter in the media about a forthcoming war on Iraq conveniently ignores the fact that the US and Britain have been waging war against Saddam since 1990 – although it's been a decidedly one-sided affair, too one-sided to mention, apparently. Since the accords that brought an end to the Gulf War Round One, Iraq has been remorselessly bombed about once every three days. Its feeble air defense system is shattered and its radars are jammed; its air force is grounded, the runways cratered; its primitive navy is destroyed. The nation's northern and southern territories are occupied by hostile forces armed, funded and overseen by the CIA.

Every bit of new construction in the country is scrutinized for any possible military function by satellite cameras capable of zooming down to a square meter. Truck and tank convoys are zealously monitored. Troop locations are pinpointed with a lethal certainty. Bunkers are mapped, the coordinates programmed into the targeting software for bunker-busting bombs.

This once wealthy and secular nation is bankrupt, its financial reserves crippled by the sanctions that have blocked not only the export of Iraqi oil but also the import of medical and food supplies, leading to the deaths of millions of Iraqi civilians. Now along comes mini-Bush to proclaim to the world that this emaciated nation, shackled in the political equivalent of an isolation tank inside a maximum-security prison for these past twelve years, is the greatest threat to world peace on the planet.

The case against Saddam boils down to the following allegations: Iraq is in league with Al Qaeda; Iraq is rebuilding its chemical and biological weapons capability; Iraq is close to developing a nuclear bomb or radiological weapon; Iraq is exporting weapons of mass destruction to other nations or terrorist groups. Most of these allegations are accepted as fact by the US press, but Milan Rai proves there's precious little substance to the charges.

Rai, a founder of the London-based antiwar group ARROW, doesn't spare Tony Blair. It's only natural. Bush has, of course, left Blair to do much of the heavy lifting – or at least the elocution. Blair serves as a kind of Minister of Rhetoric for the Bush crowd. He was assigned the task of assembling the dossier against bin Laden. And later he was given the task of presenting the case against Iraq.

Blair's bin Laden indictment was frail on facts and speculative in the extreme. But his dossier against Saddam, his litany of 'killer facts,' was vaporous by comparison. The Iraq dossier was written by John Scarlett, a former MI6 officer presiding over the Joint Intelligence Committee, the British equivalent of the National Security Council. Scarlett submitted his report in April, but it fell far short of what had been demanded by Blair and Bush. In fact, British Foreign Secretary Jack Straw was so infuriated by the lack of evidence that he sent the six-page document back to Scarlett with instructions to amp up the allegations against Saddam.

In the end, the Blair dossier didn't disclose much that was new. Indeed, all of the hard evidence regarding Iraq's bio-weapons capacity stems largely from reports by UN inspectors prior to 1999. British intelligence concluded that there wasn't any evidence that Saddam was any greater a threat than he was in 1991 at the conclusion of the Gulf War.

Some of the new claims are tenuous at best.

Take the peregrinations of Dr Khidir Hamza, the self-professed former head of the Iraqi nuclear program, who defected in 1994. The US-educated Hamza retired from the Iraqi nuke program in 1987, but has been put forth to the media by US intelligence to make a number of wild claims, including: that Iraq was behind the anthrax attacks in the US; that Iraq gave technical and financial aid to the Al Qaeda operatives behind the 9/11 attacks; that Iraq is developing a 'dirty bomb' and is close to assembling a nuclear weapon capable of striking Israel. Hamza hasn't been in a position to know about any of these matters in over a decade, and former UN weapons inspector Scott Ritter labels him a 'fraud' who concocts information to curry favor with his backers in the CIA.

On the crucial issue of Iraqi weapons of mass destruction (the top reason cited by the Bush–Blair tag team for overthrowing Saddam), Rai concludes that there's been no new evidence produced since December 1998 and there's no evidence at all that they've provided such weapons to other nations or to terrorist groups.

The second argument advanced for invading Iraq is that Saddam was somehow behind the attacks of 9/11. This conspiracy was first promoted by former CIA director James Woolsey, Al Gore's tutor in intelligence matters. Recall that Woolsey helped script Gore's craven speech on the floor of the Senate justifying his vote for war against Iraq in 1990. Then in 1998 Woolsey helped peddle through Congress the Clinton/Gore-crafted Iraq Liberation Bill, authorizing funds for the overthrow of Saddam. 'Regime change' isn't a new coinage.

Within days of 9/11, the ghastly Woolsey was front and center before the cameras asserting, with the knowing look of a Langley insider, that the attacks had been carried out by a 'state-sponsored' group of terrorists. The culpable state? Iraq, naturally. Woolsey's main piece of evidence consisted of a rumor that Osama bin Laden had sent an emissary to Saddam's birthday party in Baghdad in April of 1988. That's right, 1988.

After the initial allegations promoted by Woolsey fell flat, a new charge surfaced. Supposedly, hijacker Mohammed Atta met with Iraqi agents in Prague a few months before the 9/11 attacks, the implication being that here Atta received his final instructions from Saddam. The evolution of the story is a textbook case of media inflation. Within days the allegation had mushroomed from Atta huddling with a 'low-level' Iraqi agent, to a secret meeting with a 'mid-level' Iraqi intelligence agent, to a session with a 'senior' Iraqi official to, finally, a pow-wow with the 'head of Iraq's intelligence service.' One report played up in the German press even had Atta 'obtaining a flask of anthrax' at this assignation.

While the US press ran wild with speculation over Atta's ties to Saddam, a Czech police investigation revealed that Atta had not visited Prague in 2001, although a Mohammed Atta (not necessarily *the* M.A.) apparently had been to the city twice in the previous year. But this Atta didn't meet with an Iraqi diplomat/intelligence operative. The man who met with the Iraqi agent (identified as the ambassador to the Czech Republic) was actually another Iraqi named Saleh, who is now a used-car dealer living in Nuremberg, Germany.

At the time Atta was supposed to be getting his murderous instructions in Prague, he was actually living just down the road from the FBI HQ in Virginia Beach, Virginia.

October 22, 2002

IRAQ: WHEN THE GOING WAS GOOD
by Vanessa Jones

The interview takes place impromptu, in a café in the exclusive diplomatic suburb of 'Manuka' in Canberra, the capital of Australia. The suburb, pronounced Mar-nik-a by locals, reads phonetically to out-of-towners as Ma-nu-ka, which is Arabic slang for (female) 'slut'; pronounced ma-nuke, its masculine form is used for a gay (receiving) male. Not quite polite to mention, I know, but an interesting choice for a Western diplomatic suburb, considering that 25 per cent of Australia's food exports are bought by Arabic countries. It is an extremely offensive and derogatory label to use or to receive.

Sitting in Manuka, at an Italian café, I meet a handsome man smoking Drum and drinking a flat white. We start to chat slowly, and we comment on current politics – Afghanistan, Sept. 11, the likelihood of things spreading to Iraq. He tells me he's been to Iraq, after minimally completing his compulsory Egyptian military service. A friend of his had refused to do military service, and had paid for it dearly – he was imprisoned in putrid conditions for three years in Cairo.

His own military service was cut short by him paying a military officer three hundred Egyptian pounds in 1987 (equal to a couple of months' wages) and doing some carpentry work in the man's house, in exchange for his freedom. Not a bribe at the normal level of bribes, normal being at the thousands of pounds level, to escape compulsory military service. It was more an illegal, compassionate release from duty. The military officer was aware of the horrendous situation for young men of being in the military, and probably released many others in a similar fashion.

He was twenty, and wanted to 'piss off' anywhere. Visas to get to the West were impossible to obtain, so he ended up in Iraq. He left Cairo by bus – over the Suez Canal – the bus went inside a ship, through the Aqaba Gulf, across the Sinai desert and into Jordan. From Jordan another bus to Iraq. A three- or four-day journey. A long trip. Memory fades. Speaking his native Arabic all the way. Everything new. Different cultures and different food. He felt like a refugee in a way.

Iraq was the only place it was easy to enter and get a visa to work in. At the time, in 1987, it was a wealthy and prosperous country. The liquor shops he saw there he'd never seen in such amounts in Europe or Australia. If he wanted to go to work in the Gulf, he had to buy a work contract, which is dear for the average man, and a good contract even dearer. And when you get there you are as a slave, you cannot leave the country or travel to another city before the employer signs your papers. He didn't like the idea of being a slave to another. He chose, instead, Iraq. A country at that time at war with Iran.

He arrived after three or four days, by coach, in Baghdad. There was not a sign of poverty. In 1987 the population in Baghdad was just under 4 million people. Food was very cheap and plentiful. There were many foreign nationals, Thais, Filipinos, operating businesses. Unlike Gulf countries, foreigners could open and operate businesses of their own. East Europeans, Russians, Europeans. He moved in to a cheap hotel, and found work making furniture, sofa frames, cinema chairs, parliament chairs, furniture work in Saddam Hussein's relative's house – his cousin or sister's palace home. His Egyptian co-worker was petrified of making a mistake for fear of being shot. Most government men seemed to carry guns. The Iran–Iraq war was going on. You could hear the rockets nearby and a school was bombed by an Iranian rocket during his stay.

Everything in Iraq was running fine, as long as you didn't speak of politics, dissent or critique the powers that were. There used to be prostitutes visiting the carpentry workshop. You could go to a prostitute bar anywhere in Baghdad. Iraq was the first Arabic nation to legislate equal property inheritance rights for men and women. It happened in 1969, after the July 17, 1968 Revolution. Women were also given the vote, the right to divorce and to own land, the option to be a politician or to go for top jobs. Food was plentiful. The average wage was adequate to cover living expenses comfortably. It was a socialist system, so the government was responsible for food, health and education, and there were adequate government family payments to cover the well-being of each child.

He noticed young women were really into their own education, unlike some other Arabic nations. It was a civilized, plentiful and prosperous country, comparable to US and UK standards. No one appeared homeless, starving or medically neglected. Free healthcare was for anyone, Iraqi or foreign, unlike the current US private health system, refusing to freely treat even its own citizens. During 1987 he saw the Iraqi men killed in the war carried home to their families in coffins, wrapped in the Iraqi flag, on top of taxis, tied to the roof racks. On the streets, each day, many taxis could regularly be seen driving at normal speed, taking the dead men home to their families.

In the hotel where he stayed, military men were openly, actively gay and the whole society seemed very liberal and open. People were free to go to church, or to the mosque, or to a liquor store, or to university, or to a prostitute, or to their gay lover. Without any moral or political interference. The only thing disallowed was political agitation/meeting. Healthcare, education, food and housing were readily available. This is what the West's sanctions have wrecked in many ways.

The hidden agenda of the Gulf War and the sanctions has been to shove the Iraqi people, their economic prosperity, free healthcare, education, back into the basement of the Third World. Now Iraq has been crippled and frozen. Within fourteen years of his visit to Iraq, the Egyptian man has migrated out of Egypt, to the West. In fourteen years from now, how will a young Egyptian find Iraq?

Vanessa Jones lives in Melbourne, Australia.

PART THREE

WAR ON IRAQ

November 11, 2002

FROM MARINE TO ANTIWAR ORGANIZER: TO SERVE OR NOT TO SERVE?
by Scott Cossette

Being an activist for social justice is not an easy task. You seldom get paid and often lose partners, family, friends or your job when it is discovered that you equate the welfare of others with your own. This somehow makes you a pariah, a target for derision.

So why do it, you ask?

I believe that if you see injustice and fail to act, then you are just as guilty as the perpetrators of the injustice. I bring this up now because our nation's 'volunteer' armed services are being forced, not asked, to continue the perpetration of injustice on the people of Iraq. An injustice all the more rank because it has nothing to do with liberation of people but aims to liberate natural resources for exploitation. US servicepersons are forbidden to choose whether or not they will facilitate or actively engage in this slaughter of innocent civilians for the interests of the oil barons, I mean national security. They – mostly poor African-American, Latino and White enlisted men and women enticed by the promises of education, medical benefits and 'job' training – are bound by oath to obey the orders of their arbitrarily appointed superiors and 'elected' officials even when those orders result in the commission of war crimes that they and not their chain of command or political masters can be charged with and convicted of. Our refusal to join the World Court ensured this. My recruiter never revealed that information to me. To be fair I never asked, because I never thought that I could be in such a situation.

Having recently read *Up Against the Brass*, the story of Private Andy Stapp, who founded the American Servicemen's Union in 1967 to support GIs in opposition to the war in Vietnam and to fight the hypocrisy of the military in general, I decided to try and carry on this endeavor in a small way by relaying my own experiences and offering reasons why our men and women in uniform and those pondering enlistment should oppose this war and resist serving in it by all means necessary.

In August 1999, at the ripe 'old' age of twenty-nine, I enlisted in the United States Marine Corps. Why? The truth is, to this day I really do not know the answer to that loaded question. Maybe I was deluded into thinking that I was championing the cause of freedom and democracy. Perhaps I felt I was serving my fellow Americans by ensuring their safety. The heroic deeds of General Smedley Butler and many other war 'heroes' are methodically drilled into your head during Marine recruit training. Their names and accomplishments are recited by boots while waiting in the endless lines for haircuts, toiletries, forced vaccinations, urination and chow. This is done to ensure that each and every Marine feels pressure to aspire to greatness in battle and bring honor to their country and themselves.

Sadly, I came across General Butler's enlightening 'War Is Just A Racket' speech after being discharged from the Corps. This, the most important of the General's accomplishments, is conveniently left out during 'indoctrination,' even though it was delivered in 1933!

Being the police protection for big business in the Third World is neither honorable nor just. If the rank–and–file service members knew whom they really represented, I have no doubt that they would refuse to do so. Boot camp is like the first day at a new school, with all the fear and anxiety of being alone in a foreign place except that in this school the teachers control your every waking moment. You are admonished never to call the drill instructor a drill 'sergeant' (that's the nasty Army terminology and Marines are superior to all other branches), or to look them in the eye for any reason. You do not speak unless spoken to and if you need to urinate, permission must be requested in the proper military manner. I witnessed more than one boot piss on himself at the position of attention because he failed repeatedly to request permission in the proper military manner. This is truly a proud moment in someone's life.

It doesn't pay to have a stammer or nervously mix up your words. It also doesn't behoove you to stand too close to a drill instructor. It is made clear to you at the beginning of training that if an instructor feels 'threatened' by a recruit he or she may respond with extreme force in 'self-defense.' Let's say that some kids never heard this, because I saw a few black eyes while I was there.

The only words that make the loneliness, the physical torture, the verbal abuse, the humiliation, the gas chamber, the group punishment for individual mistakes, the endless hours of make your bunk, unmake your bunk worthwhile are: 'It gets much better at your next duty station.' The School of Infantry – I assume from the word 'infantile' – was my next duty station.

It does not get any better. When in formation you must stand at attention and keep your eyes straight. One of our sergeants used to take great pleasure in walking up to a Marine and asking him: 'Do you know what my favorite city in Thailand is?' When the Marine, without moving, answered No, the sergeant would slap him in the genitals and exclaim: 'Bangkok!' After a few rounds of this we learned to answer correctly while shielding our groins.

I still am not sure what this sort of 'training' was preparing us for. After three months of learning how to kill 'Luke the gook,' 'Jackie the Iraqi,' and 'Joe rag-head' with all means available and reciting chants like 'Napalm sticks to kids' and 'We're gonna rape, kill, pillage and burn' while we ran on the streets of the base, I began to really question what the hell I was doing in the Marine Corps. Why were we dehumanizing these people? Does racism make the job of killing them easier? That certainly couldn't be what this was all about. Could it?

The most sobering experience, even for the hard-core would-be killers in my class, was Urban Combat training. When it was learned that a 30 per cent casualty rate was expected in house-to-house fighting more than a few of them regretted signing the 'contract'! Imagine that: at least three out of ten GIs will DIE when they invade Iraqi towns and cities. Haven't we learned from Vietnam that people will fight furiously to defend their homes? Wouldn't you?

Another duty station and nothing changed. This time I was enrolled in electronics school at 29 Palms. My career in Infantry had thankfully been scrapped after an injury during Reconnaissance training and due to much pleading on my own behalf to be out of the combat 'arts.' Who knows, I might have gone on to protect former Unocal Oil spokesman and now President of Afghanistan, Hamid Karzai, from his own brethren. More than likely, I would still be in the brig for refusing to crash wedding parties.

Marine Corps Base 29 Palms is just about the most desolate and bizarre piece of real estate in the country. Located in the high desert outside Palm Springs, it is hard to believe you are not on Mars. Morale here is said to be the lowest of any duty station in the Corps. If my new superiors were any indication, the reason is clear. Every morning before class the platoon would get into formation for inspection. They look at your uniform, your haircut and most importantly, your shave. One of the young corporals in charge of our class liked to pace up and down the ranks and indiscriminately swat an unsuspecting Marine in the crotch. Non-commissioned officers seem to have an affinity for this in the Marine Corps. Was this the secret to defeating your enemy? Why do they fight so hard to exclude homosexuals from military service?

One particular morning stands out in my memory. A few Marines had been found to have, in the class sergeant's opinion, unsatisfactory shaves. Protests and verbal abuse, including threats of bodily harm and death, over the situation caught the attention of our instructors, two staff sergeants. One of them produced a pink Lady Bic shaver and handed it to Corporal 'Slaps Your Nuts.' Brimming with satisfaction he ordered the offending parties to dry-shave right there on the spot. I was pissed. After a few moments one of the instructors ordered them into the head so as not to attract attention. Death threats and sharing a lady's razor because of poor hygiene? I could see that the only battles we were being trained for were among ourselves. When one human being believes they are above another then they become their own enemy. I vowed then and there to get out any way I could.

I was losing weight. I was unable to eat without severe stomach cramps and diarrhea. I missed almost all of my physical training sessions due to weakness and the frequent visits to the hospital for rehydration. More than once I needed IV fluids. Their solution to 'my' problem was not the discharge that I sought but the idea that I buck up and get with the program. They even suggested putting me on antidepressants! I told them under no circumstances was I going to medicate myself in order to put up with this shitty existence. And I certainly wasn't going to engage in the universal military pastime of drunkenness in order to deal with it.

After seeing a shrink on base it was determined that I was suffering from a 'personality disorder' and should be let go. It was the best news I had heard in a long time.

My master sergeant, however, was not going to let me go. 'My wife has been bipolar for twenty-two years. We are all depressed. Get over it,' he shouted. I wasn't quite sure how his unhappiness with his wife or her illness had anything to do with me.

My memory flashed back to Recon training. I had witnessed three Marines attempt suicide because they felt they had no other way out. They requested discharges and were denied and given orders to fleet combat units. This had so devastated their morale that they traveled to Mexico and bought a large amount of Valium in their desperation. Lucky for them Valium is a poor choice for poisoning. The dose one would have to take is almost impossible to swallow. They were groggy as hell for the first few days and spent at least a week in the psych ward for observation. I won't forget having overheard one of their instructor's remark that they should have died because they were pussies. *Semper fidelis!*

I can only imagine what the parents of these young men must have gone through. I was just glad that they had survived and would be on their way home in a few short weeks.

In truth I was jealous. I could not bring myself to even think about taking my life. After all, I had so much to live for. But I knew I had to get away from this demoralizing machine.

I decided, after a letter I wrote to my commanding officer failed to get the ball rolling, to go UA. That's the Marine Corps version of AWOL.

After five days, in which my mother was pressured and frightened to divulge my whereabouts, I contacted legal counsel and turned myself in.

There are some good people in the Marine Corps. One of them spoke up on my behalf at my adjudication proceeding. My master sergeant, on the other hand, advised punishment to the fullest extent allowed. My commanding officer agreed. I received forty-five days' restriction to barracks and thirty days' extra duty to run concurrent. I was also fined half a month's pay for two months. More importantly, and as I greatly desired, they were processing me for discharge.

During this period I came into contact with all the 'malcontents' that were in various stages of separation or legal limbo. I found them on the whole to be decent, hard-working individuals and we all had one thing in common; we were not going to be broken and used to propagate the degradation and cruelty of militarism.

Some take to military life very well. Especially senior NCOs and officers. The enlisted however live in constant anxiety. The pay is low, racism and sexual harassment are rampant, and domestic violence is a harsh reality. Fort Bragg has recently come to everyone's attention because of the number of murder/suicides that have taken place there. Vaccinations that are FDA-approved for experimentation only are routinely given to US soldiers with the threat of court martial for refusal. Ground troops are in constant danger from 'friendly fire' by USAF pilots. These pilots are given amphetamines to increase their stamina for longer missions and downers when they land to allow them to sleep. Could the Canadian unit in Afghanistan have been bombed as a result of this criminally negligent policy?

Times have changed little. Soldiers in Vietnam were given speed to increase their killing efficiency. This gives a new meaning to the 'war' on drugs. Not only do troops have to be wary of their own forces, but now civilian contractors almost outnumber them on the battlefield. According to a recent report, the army does not have any idea how many contractors they employ! Many new combat systems are totally dependent on civilian maintenance. What's more, they are upset because in their words, 'You can shoot a soldier when he fails to show up, but you can't shoot a civilian contractor.'

A soldier is expendable. Remember that. 167,000 veterans of the last war in Iraq are being denied benefits because the government refuses to acknowledge Gulf War Syndrome. They also deny that depleted uranium is hazardous. Many US and allied soldiers still pass uranium in their urine! Still others deliver hideously deformed children or watch as seemingly normal ones die of rare cancers. Be all that you can be: Do Not Go To Iraq.

I guess the reason why I joined the Marine Corps was so that I could speak to others on this subject and have them listen. My work, as an activist with ANSWER, Act Now to Stop War and End Racism, and the International Action Center, afforded me the opportunity to be in Washington DC on October 26th with the rest of the over 200,000 civilians and veterans of previous wars who came to show their opposition to this unjust military aggression.

Helping to organize this important event will always be one of the greatest achievements of my life. I spoke with veterans from Korea, Vietnam and the first Gulf War. They all had the same thing to say: 'No War On Iraq.' To those who are currently enlisted and those thinking about it I say this. Iraq is not a threat to this country. There is no proof that Iraq sponsors terrorism or has any connections to those that do. They are barely able to feed themselves or treat their sick. Why would they provoke even more devastation than has already been visited upon them?

The US government used Saddam while he was capable of 'punishing' Iran. Donald Rumsfeld was present in Iraq when the

Kurds were being gassed with technology that the US government provided and said nothing! Our ambassador to Iraq told Saddam we would not interfere in Iraq's conflict with Kuwait. A conflict that was about territorial integrity and the illegal pumping of oil from Iraqi fields.

The first Gulf War reduced Iraq from the most industrialized, educated and progressively secular nation in the Middle East to beggar status. Sanctions and daily bombing for nearly eleven years have killed over a million innocent people without one loss of an American life. Now that Saudi Arabia is becoming more and more non-cooperative with the US, the oil companies need to gain access somewhere else. Iraq just happens to possess the second-largest oil reserves in the world and by coincidence is a militarily weak and ostracized country.

If they could defend themselves effectively, say like China, then would the US be so bold? The US corporate media thoroughly demonizes Iraq and grossly misreports the demonstrations against this war that are taking place daily in this country and around the world. George Bush is using fear and patriotism to justify the restriction of civil liberties, racial profiling and imperial aggression on behalf of corporations. Save yourselves.

Don't become thugs for big business. Instead use your talents to help alleviate the conditions that breed terrorism in the first place. Stand up and be counted among the majority that say: 'Money for Jobs, Education, Healthcare and Housing, Not for War!'

Scott Cossette, a former marine, is now an organizer with the International Action Center in San Diego.

November 14, 2002

THE ANTIWAR MOVEMENT AND ITS CRITICS
by Alexander Cockburn

Do we have an antiwar movement? We're getting there. We must be, because we're catching flak from the anti-antiwar movement, Light Infantry division, staffed by Marc Cooper, Todd Gitlin, David Corn and Christopher Hitchens.

Marc Cooper, like Gitlin, has carved out a pleasant niche for himself, belaboring various left causes from a position purporting to represent robust common sense. It's a posture endearing to op-ed editors, particularly if there's an insinuation that somewhere, way back, the author had left credentials. It's fair to raise the issue of credentials, since the prime line of attack by the Light Infantry is to rubbish the credentials of the antiwar left as dumbos, cat's-paws, dictator-lovers, cultists, practitioners of unmentionable vices.

Back at the start of 2000 Cooper publicly prayed to God to make that same year 'free of Mumia.' How precisely the year would be liberated from this man on Death Row he tastefully left unstated. In the jibes at the Mumia cult that followed, Cooper hiccuped bashfully that Mumia Abu Jamal 'probably' didn't get a fair trial, then suppressed important facts about the fatal encounter between Mumia and the police officer, or even that the Mumia 'cult' probably saved his life by drawing attention to Mumia's situation in the mid-Eighties when no one cared a whit.

In a recent *Los Angeles Times* column Cooper prays once more, this time for 'an effective, attractive and moral opposition.' And how can the antiwar opposition become effective, attractive and moral? Cooper's recipe: condone the US rationale for continuing sanctions; accept as framework for discussion of the war and military action the rationales offered by George Bush and his associates. Cooper derides Ramsey Clark for calling the sanctions 'genocidal.' Would you march with Clark or Cooper? If you are hesitating read Joy Gordon's chilling description in the November *Harper's* of how the US has been applying sanctions designed to kill children in Iraq, then make up your mind.

Todd Gitlin has made a career out of issuing advisories about the 'hard left,' the 'Old Left' and others. Though Gitlin usually pretends that he's trying to counsel the left towards improved conduct under the Gitlin Seal of Approval, I don't think he has much interest in the left as anything other than raw material for his unctuous punditry. In a recent *Mother Jones* Gitlin reports that at a rally outside the UN he spotted placards saying 'No Sanctions, No Bombing.' Snappy, you say. Exactly the message a peace movement might want to get across. Gitlin disagrees. His preferred placard would be the most heavily footnoted text since Lynn White Jr's history of the stirrup. Like Cooper, Gitlin craves for respectability, which means that he wants the placard to make it clear that (a) Saddam bears responsibility for his country's plight, (b) the bombings of Iraq since 1991 by the US (tactfully described by Gitlin, echoing the DoD, as 'no fly zone sorties') are okay. Tough placard to design, and pretty heavy, if you factor in the square footage required for Gitlin's text.

David Corn's most substantial piece of work to date is *The Blonde Ghost*, which could be described as a not unsympathetic account of Ted Shackley, a CIA supervisor of one bloodbath after another, most notably the Phoenix program. Corn has now taken to issuing cop-style intelligence reports, reminiscent of FBI field advisories to Hoover, on the Workers World Party, stigmatizing the party for its nefarious role in the DC and Bay Area antiwar demonstrations.

No need to dwell any longer on Hitchens, at least as a 'left' commentator, speaking in good activist faith. When Hitchens libels the left (in modes excellently pilloried by Katha Pollitt) he now does so as one who has forsworn any left credential, and who is new-born as a neocon, dispensing to the *Washington Post* anti-left prose whose frothing crudity eerily echoes that of his erstwhile butt, Norman Podhoretz.

A recent Hitchens piece in *Slate* attacks the term 'chicken hawks,' while carefully avoiding the main point of its use now, which is to indicate that many of the current civilian war-whoopers like Bush or Cheney shirked the call to duty back in the Vietnam period but are mustard keen on deploying others to the front lines. It now seems that G. Bush was an actual deserter from the National Guard. It's well documented on www.awolbush.com: that George W. Bush never showed up for National Guard duty for a period of approximately one year, possibly more, in 1972–73. Some definitions: AWOL, absent for thirty days or less. Desertion, absent for more than thirty days with evidence of no intent to return to duty.

General Hitchens invokes the 'fairly good pay' of the armed forces, a view he should impart personally on his next tour of inspection at Fort Bragg, where members of the Special Forces get $25,000 a year, which is probably less than Hitchens's annual bar bill. As with Poddy, Hitchens's mind appears to have become clouded by the fog of war-whooping. He reviles his old chum Bob Kerrey, seemingly unaware that this particular war criminal favors attacking Iraq, then states flatly that 'Lincoln became the first and last president to hear shots fired in anger.' While president? What about Madison, fleeing the advancing troops commanded by Admiral Sir George Cockburn? TR too if you count the angers and joys of the chase. Hitchens invokes the 'glorious Douglas McArthur.' Is this written with a straight face? Hard to know these days with General Hitchens. He's offended that chicken hawk's original meaning was that of preyer on young people. Reading the above-mentioned article on sanctions, this seems appropriate.

So, having scouted out the anti-antiwar movement, now we can ask, What sort of an antiwar movement do we have?

Look back to the early 1960s. In 1962, a full eight years after President Eisenhower had decreed secretly that Ho Chi Minh could not be permitted to triumph in open elections, the left was just beginning to educate itself about Vietnam. When President Kennedy was sending the first detachments of US troops to South Vietnam and setting the stage for the assassination of South Vietnamese president Ngo Dinh Diem there was scarcely the semblance of an antiwar movement. In Oxford in 1962 I remember being incredulous when one of my radical mentors, the historian Thomas Hodgkin, remarked to me that the next big anti-imperial battleground would be Vietnam. It wasn't until 1966 and 1967 that the left, particularly the Socialist Workers Party, managed to stage the big anti-war rallies that broke for ever the pro-war consensus and set the stage for more radical actions. And by then there was that potent fuel for an antiwar movement, the draft, which prompted Stop the Draft Week.

By 1968 we had a worldwide anti-imperial movement; we had the May–June upheavals in Paris; we very definitely thought history was on our side. Not any more.

Today? We have the premonition of a big antiwar movement. Like the SWP forty years ago, the Workers World Party did much of the organizing of the recent demonstrations, which doesn't mean the 150,000 or so who marched in the Bay Area and in Washington DC are dupes of Karl Marx, Ramsey Clark and Saddam Hussein, but merely that organizing big demonstrations takes a lot of dedication, energy and experience. I have a dream, said Martin Luther King, and so he did, but the Communists in the south helped him put flesh on that dream as they did the dreams of Rosa Parks.

Will there be a war with Iraq? To judge by the amended US resolution rubber-stamped by the UN Security Council, we can have one any time the Commander-in-Chief decrees it, with February/March 2003 as probably the earliest practical slot. A draft? No time soon. A calling up of the National Guard? More likely, and already there are tens of thousands of reservists on duty, many of them no doubt chafing at their condition.

And if George Bush lets slip the dogs of war on the grounds that Saddam wouldn't submit to a full personal cavity search, will we see a new age of protest? Certainly, if the war goes on long enough and Americans get killed in large numbers. There's a slab of the right that's denouncing America's imperial wars. That wasn't happening in the early Sixties. If the left could ever reach out to this right, which it's almost constitutionally incapable of doing, we'll have something.

Merle Haggard on Ashcroft's colonoscopy. The night after the Democrats nosedived I drove fifty miles through the first storm of the fall to my local town of Eureka, for a concert by Merle Haggard. Merle has a rap sheet for no-shows and there'd been worrying talk about him canceling on this tour because of a herniated disk. But at 9 pm there he was on the stage with his band, The Strangers, walking a bit stiffly but looking and sounding good.

When it comes to the big themes of love and war and history nothing concentrates the mind like a few songs by Merle, whose 1969 pro-war country anthem 'Okie from Muskogee' lambasted the dope-smoking hippie peaceniks and earned the former resident of San Quentin a full pardon from Governor Ronald Reagan.

Sitting there in a white, mostly working-class audience even a tad older than the equally white crowd listening to Bob Dylan in the Greek amphitheater in Berkeley a few weeks ago, an obvious question bulked as large as the Stars and Stripes hanging above Merle: had Merle changed since the time when he riposted to the antiwar movement of the Sixties with 'Muskogee' and 'The Fighting Side of Me'? Back to Merle.

Yes he has, as we already knew. Cheryl Burns reported this to *CounterPunch* a few weeks ago from Kansas City: 'I saw Merle Haggard tonight in KC – great show. He said something about "so now we're in another war" and went on to say he was still proud to be an American and all that, so I was wondering just where he was headed. But then he said there was nothing good about any war except the soldiers, sailors, etc.

'Then he says, "I think we should give John Ashcroft a big hand ... (pause) ... right in the mouth!" Went on to say, "the way things are going I'll probably be thrown in jail tomorrow for saying that, so I hope ya'll will bail me out."'

Merle wasn't in this ripe form in Eureka, but he dropped some hints. 'Friends and conservatives,' he began, then he made a joke about George Bush's colonoscopy, and the search for Osama bin Laden. 'He's up there somewhere,' Merle said somewhat cryptically, and the crowd wasn't quite sure how to take it. Then he said offhandedly, without enthusiasm: 'Looks like we're in another war,' and sang 'The Fighting Side of Me.'

At another concert, June a year ago, he was quoted by John Derbyshire in *National Review* online as saying: 'Look at the past 25 years we went downhill, and if people don't realize it, they don't have their fucking eyes on ... In 1960, when I came out of prison as an ex-convict, I had more freedom under parolee supervision than there's available to an average citizen in America right now ... God almighty, what have we done to each other?'

★

Coming from inside the Beltway in Washington DC is Sam Smith's on-line *Progressive Review*. In the wake of Hitchens's departure from *The Nation* and his foolish denunciations of the left, Sam had some interesting reflections on what exactly 'the left' consists of, contrasting the 'elite' or old Marxist left with the colloquial, informal, spontaneous left:

> I have always been far closer to the idiomatic, colloquial left than to the more elite varieties. I have never gotten on that well with Hitchens' former pals in the elite left because I never could find the time to straighten out my paradigm. It turns out it wasn't all that important anyway, because the people who made the difference were not the famous talkers but the little known doers, ordinary people who, in Conrad's phrase, for one brief moment did something out of the ordinary.
>
> They were people who had not studied Marx and Hegel and couldn't tell a Trotskyite from a troll. But they knew, in Pogo's words, when to 'stand on the piano and demand outrage action.' These are the people of whom Carl Sandburg wrote: 'I am the people – the mob – the crowd – the mass. Do you know that all the great work of this world is done through me? I am the workingman, the inventor, the maker of the world's food and clothes. I am the audience that witnesses history. The Napoleons come from me and the Lincolns. They die. and then I send forth more Napoleons and Lincolns ... Sometimes I growl, shake myself and spatter a few red drops for history to remember. Then – I forget. When I, the people, learn to remember, when I, the People use the lessons of yesterday and no longer forget who robbed me last year, who played me for a fool – then there will be no speaker in all the world to say the name: "The People", with any fleck of a sneer in his voice or any far-off smile of derision. The mob – The crowd – The mass – will arrive then.

Consistently, the East Coast shuttle left from which Hitchens has departed has been indifferent about, ignorant of, or even in opposition to the issues of the idiomatic, colloquial left. The people who are changing the way other people think about things are found scattered around the nation. And when some of them came together in the most effective progressive political organization of modern times – the Green Party – they were not only not welcomed into the club, they were frequently excoriated. And as for the critics of an Iraqi invasion, they are typically just ordinary citizens who have learned without the help of Ramsey Clark to be scared to death of what their leaders are about to do to them.

Hitchens and his ilk will continue to have their little debates, all carefully framed in a manner that excludes most of the people they claim to care about and most of the people who actually produce change. It worked at university and it works now. But it has little to do with either America or the left as it really is.

I liked some of what Smith said about the left and non-left, but I think his contrasting of the doctrinaire sterility of failed 'old left' with creative, non-doctrinaire spirited 'real left' left a lot of the story untold.

In my years of going around the country doing anti-intervention talks, fund-raisers, book tours etc, etc, the first thing to notice is that there's a truly vast left that is invisible to almost all East Coast commentators. Church people, labor people, public defenders, Lawyers Guild, faculty people, farm people, radical greens, World Federalist types, red-diapered middle-agers, in almost every town. (And in every town the left will tell you with gloomy pride how conservative their town is.)

And in meeting after meeting you can look at the audience and see older folk who were labor commies in the Fifties and who have certainly had their share of doctrinal struggle and who have read Marx etc, and Sixties vintage people who might have fought their way through the RCP and out the other side, and then younger people still who might have come aboard in WTO wars and who read *CounterPunch*.

It's a rich geology that varies from place to place. For example in one town in Wisconsin the two most bustling left activists and organizers were both kind of ex Revolutionary Communist Party. In the Deep South I've met radical lawyers who are still the organizing backbone of their communities who came down as Maoists in the Seventies. In for the long haul and lively and not deserving of Smith's misprision. A lot of good organizers are still in left groups mainstreamers might instinctively deride as fossilized Trots or Maoists or whatever. Red-baiters like Corn may write long articles on the *Nation* site about how the Workers World Party stage-managed the DC demo, but so what? Corn's ideological forebears were redbaiting the Commies for being behind the civil rights movement, which often they were. Sectarians know how to organize. Someone has to do it.

Sam was right in one thing: many of these, especially the younger lot, couldn't give a toss about Hitchens. I was reminded of this when I gave a speech in SF a few months ago and derided Hitchens's positions and a lively young woman in a left group asked me impatiently what was all the talk about this 'Clifford Hutchins.' As for Hitchens, he parted ways with anything decently radical long, long ago, as I occasionally point out. My hope of course, which Jeffrey and I try to push along in *CounterPunch*, is that the left should understand that common cause can be made with many in the populist right who take the Bill of Rights seriously. Attorney General Ashcroft is doing his best to help.

December 12, 2002

TORQUEMADAS IN BIRKENSTOCKS
by Jeffrey St. Clair

My dear old friend David Brower must be fuming in his grave. The Sierra Club, the organization he almost single-handedly built into a global green powerhouse, has become so cowardly since his death two years ago that now it refuses even to take a stand against war, which Brower believed to be the ultimate environmental nightmare.

Even worse, its bosses – like petty enforcers from the McCarthy era – are now threatening to exile from the Club any leaders who step forward to voice their opposition to the looming bombing and subsequent invasion and occupation of Iraq.

It is a telltale sign of the enervated condition of the big greens that there's precious little dissent in the Sierra Club on the prospect of another war in the Persian Gulf. Indeed, it took four activists from Utah, of all places, to light the fire. Let them be known as the Glen Canyon Group Four: John Weisheit, Tori Woodard, Patrick Diehl and Dan Kent. Last week they announced that they opposed the war. They identified themselves as leaders of the Sierra Club's Glen Canyon Group, based in Moab, Utah, former stomping grounds of Edward Abbey.

'The present administration has declared its intention to achieve total military dominance of the world,' says Patrick Diehl, vice-chair of the Glen Canyon Group. 'We believe that such ambitions will produce a state of perpetual war, undoing whatever protection of the environment that conservation groups may have so far achieved.'

This noble stand was soon followed by a similarly principled anti-war resolution enacted by the Club's San Francisco Bay Chapter.

Then: slam! The long arm of Sierra Club HQ came down on them – clumsily as usual. There's apparently scant room for free speech inside the Sierra Club these days, even when the topic is of paramount concern to the health of the planet. Especially then.

The Club's executive director, Carl Pope, and his gang of glowering enforcers blustered that the Glen Canyon Four had impertinently violated Club rules. They threatened to level sanctions against the activists, ranging from expelling them from their positions to dissolving the rebellious group entirely. Angry phone calls and nasty emails flew back and forth. The Glen Canyon Four were threatened with a BOLT action – BOLT is the acronym for a Breach of Leadership Trust.

'For the board to compel our silence plays right into Bush's mad world, where a nation of police, prisons, bombs, bunkers is better than lowering oneself to diplomacy to save lives,' says Dan Kent.

The Sierra Club's Breach of Leadership Trust rule functions as a kind of prototype for Ashcroft's Patriot Act, designed to stigmatize, intimidate and muzzle internal dissenters. As a result, the Club is rife with snoops, snitches, and would-be Torquemadas in Birkenstocks.

In this case, the intimidation isn't likely to work. John Weisheit is perhaps the most accomplished river guide on the Colorado. He's stared down Cataract Canyon and Lava Falls in their most violent incarnations without flinching. Tori Woodard and Patrick Diehl live in the outback of Escalante, Utah, where they routinely receive death threats for their environmental activism. A couple of years ago, a band of local yahoos vandalized their home, threw bottles of beer through two front windows, kicked in the front door, trashed the garden, and cut the phone line to the house. They're still there – the only enviros in that distant belly of the beast. Pompous chest-thumping by the likes of Carl Pope won't scare off these people.

Peculiarly, the Club has chosen to invoke its internal policing power mainly against members who have pushed for the Club to adopt more robust environmental policies: ending livestock grazing, mining and logging on public lands; backing Ralph Nader and the Green Party; or opposing the sell-out of Yosemite National Park to a corrupt firm linked to Bruce Babbitt. The most disgusting internal crackdown came last year in a spiteful attack on Moisha Blechman, a Sierra Club activist in New York City, who was smeared with accusations of the most scurrilous kind, mainly because she was too green for the cautious twerps who run the Club.

Meanwhile, the Sierra Club turns a blind eye to renegade chapters in New Mexico and other places that attack and ridicule its current policies, such as the No Commercial Logging plank, as being too radical. Even worse, the Club leadership stands mute as a gang of Malthusian brigands infiltrate its ranks seeking to hijack the organization as a vehicle to carry forward a racist anti-immigration agenda that would make Pat Buchanan cringe.

All of this would seem mighty strange, if you remain naïve enough to believe that the Sierra Club is an organization principally (or even parenthetically) devoted to the preservation of the planet. It's not, of course. Like any other corporation, the Sierra Club's managers are obsessively preoccupied with beefing up the Club's bottom line and solidifying its access to power, the bloodstream of most nonprofits. (Read: a snuggling relationship to the Democratic National Committee, supine though it may be.)

So here's a warning: When you join the Sierra Club and affix your signature to that membership card you are also signing a loyalty oath. Loyalty to what? Certainly not the environment. These days it's loyalty to the image of the Club that matters. And increasingly the desired image of the Club is manufactured by its bosses, not its members.

How important is 'image' to the Sierra Club? Well, it spends more than $2 million a year and employs twenty-five people to work full-time in its Communication and Information Services unit – the outfit's largest single amalgamation of funds.

It's not as if the environmental ruin caused by the first Gulf War is unknown. In January 2000 Green Cross International, a Christian environmental group, released its detailed investigation of the war's environmental consequences. Their findings were grim: more than 60 million gallons of crude spilled into the desert, forming 246 oil lakes; 1,500 miles of the Gulf Coast was saturated with oil; Kuwait's only freshwater aquifer, source of more than 40 per cent of the country's drinking water, was heavily contaminated with benzenes and other toxins; 33,000 landmines remain scattered across the desert; incidences of birth defects, childhood illnesses and cancers climbed dramatically after the war.

Cruise missiles targeted Iraqi oil refineries, pipelines, chemical plants and water treatment systems. Ten years later, many of these facilities remained destroyed, unremediated and hazardous. Months of bombing of Iraq by US and British planes and cruise missiles also left behind an even more deadly and insidious legacy: tons of shell casings, bullets and bomb fragments laced with depleted uranium. In all, the US hit Iraqi targets with more than 970 radioactive bombs and missiles.

More than ten years later, the health consequences from this radioactive bombing campaign are beginning to come into focus. And they are dire, indeed. Iraqi physicians call it 'the white death' – leukemia. Since 1990, the incidence of leukemia in Iraq has grown by more than 600 per cent. The situation is compounded by Iraq's forced isolation and the sadistic sanctions regime, recently described by UN secretary-general Kofi Annan as 'a humanitarian crisis,' that makes detection and treatment of the cancers all the more difficult.

The return engagement promises to be just as grim, if not worse.

Compared to a titan like Brower, timid little people run the Sierra Club these days. In her two years as president, Jennifer Ferenstein has gone from being the bubbly Katie Couric of the environmental movement to its Margaret Thatcher. In the process, she may have set back the cause of eco-feminism by twenty years. But Ferenstein is largely just a figurehead, the hand puppet of executive director Carl Pope. Pope has never had much of a reputation as an environmental activist. He's a wheeler-dealer, who keeps the Club's policies in lockstep with its big funders and political patrons. Where Dave Brower scaled mountains, nearly all of Pope's climbing has been up organizational ladders.

This limp state of affairs has been coming for some time. After 9/11, the Club leadership was so cowed by the events that they publicly announced that they were putting their environmental campaigns on hold and pledged not to criticize Bush, who at that very moment was seeking to exploit the tragedy in order to expand oil drilling in some of the most fragile and imperiled lands on the continent.

To date only two board members have stood up against the war: Marcia Hanscom from Los Angeles and Michael Dorsey, the Club's only black board member and a man with a true passion for social and environmental justice. That's two out of fifteen. There's more vigorous dissent inside Bush's National Security Council.

All this would have disgusted Brower, who was a veteran of the famous 10th Mountain Division in World War Two but a peacenik at heart. I first met Brower in 1980. He'd already been booted out of the Sierra Club for being too militant and had gone on to found Friends of the Earth, where he was about to meet the same fate. He asked me to do some writing for him on what he thought was the great environmental issue of our time: war. At the time, Brower was helping jump-start the nuclear freeze movement and I was honored to join him.

'If we greens don't broaden our thinking to tackle war,' he told me, 'we may save some wilderness, but lose the world.' He was a master at aphorisms like that. Especially after a couple of martinis – heavily charged with Tanqueray.

He was right, of course. A century of wars have ravaged the environment as brutally as the timber giants and the chemical companies. And the nuclear industry, headquartered in DC and Moscow, threatened the whole shebang with what Jonathan Schell in *The Fate of the Earth*, a book Brower ceaselessly plugged, called 'the second death': the extinction of all life on Earth.

Brower also knew what most contemporary enviros don't: that the day-to-day operations of the military complex itself – weapons production and testing – amount to the most toxic industry on the planet, as a trip to the poisoned wastelands of Hanford, Fallon, Nevada or Rocky Flats will readily reveal.

Back in 1990, Brower and his beautiful and courageous wife Anne came to Portland, just as the bombing of Iraq had gotten into high gear. There were demonstrations on the streets nearly every night over the course of that war. Together we joined a crowd of several hundred activists gathered in the December rain. We stood shoulder-to-shoulder on the old Hawthorne Bridge for an hour, shutting down rush-hour traffic out of downtown. We sang 'We Shall Overcome,' the Browers' unmistakable voices sailing above it all.

Those days are gone. Both Dave and Anne are dead. But a new peace movement is rising and Brower helped give it life and meaning.

The spirit of the new peace (and environmental) movement won't be found within the confines of any club. It's out on the streets and in the woods, where it's always been. Hurry. It's not too late to join. No membership card required.

January 6, 2003

DECEPTIONS IN MILITARY RECRUITING: AN EX-INSIDER SPEAKS OUT
by Chris White

I condemn my past Marine identity, and therefore I proudly call myself an 'ex-Marine' who is against any offensive use of the US military.

I am not against the men and women serving in the military per se; I am against the way in which they are used by the government to promote the interests of its richest constituents. Which is why I work hard to dissuade anyone from joining the military. Military recruiters are the first line of offense in this machinery that serves the interests of the power elite at the expense of the less fortunate. Recruiters creep into the civilian world touting slogans to make an otherwise dismal job seem appealing. Their training is largely oriented toward marketing and sales techniques: on the first day at recruiting school, a recruiter friend of mine was told to come up with a gimmick for selling a pen. What business does the military have teaching recruiters to sell anything? Are the lives of America's youth just another commodity for the government to exploit? If the war is justified, then why do recruiters have to exist at all? Why do they even have to sell the military to young people? Why do they have to use manipulative sales techniques to convince young, uneducated minds to carry out the dirty work of war? As an assistant recruiter, I witnessed first-hand how recruiters manipulate the poor and young into fighting for the rich.

First, recruiters have every incentive to be dishonest. Speaking for the Marine Corps only, recruiters have monthly quotas and, once filled, they can slack off for the rest of the month. However, the more people they sign up, the better their chances for promotion. So the incentive for dishonesty is high indeed. Recruiters lie about college benefits, duty station assignments, veterans' benefits, and countless other aspects of the military in order to convince their clients to sign. Once you are in boot camp, it is too late to change anything.

How do they lie about college benefits? They fail to tell you that you must pay $1,200 in your first year of the military in order to get the GI Bill, which is quite a chunk of money when your salary is only $700 a month. You will be lucky if you get your monthly GI Bill check in your first three months of college anyway, as the bureaucracy is so inept that you had better hope to have enough money saved up before you arrive. Another point recruiters leave out is that most students who are independent and over twenty-five, civilians and veterans alike, are eligible for enormous amounts of financial aid anyway. That is, unless you already receive the GI Bill.

Wait a minute. Back up. So, if I earned the GI Bill for serving 'my country,' then I may not be eligible for any financial aid? Yep, ask any veteran over twenty-five working in college, and they will tell you that the financial aid office determines one's eligibility for grants and fellowships (free money) according to one's income, and then deletes one's income from the amount of aid one is eligible for. Therefore, if one were eligible for $9,000 in grants, but received $9,000 from the GI Bill, well, one gets no grants. One can get loans though. All the loans one desires. This may seem like a petty argument, but remember, recruiters use the GI Bill to lure civilians into joining the military. So, if the GI Bill is not necessarily a benefit, then why should one join for the college money?

How do recruiters lie about duty station assignments? Recruiters tell potential reservists that they can go to college and serve one weekend a month, with very little chance of being called back to active duty. However, the current administration wants to call up to 300,000 reservists to the Gulf alone. I can further illustrate this with the story of my neighbor's daughter who had considered joining the National Guard. As an incentive to get her to sign, her recruiter told her that she would be stationed in Kansas, but luckily I persuaded her not to join. Her friend was not so lucky. Shortly after joining the Guard, he was called to active duty and sent to Bosnia for two years. Thousands of National Guard and other reservists have been called back to active duty since 9/11, and thousands more will be called to go to Iraq.

How do recruiters deceive us about veterans' benefits? I can use VA medical facilities if I want to wait five months for an appointment, but my wife cannot use them (at least in Kansas). We are both veterans, but I am 30 per cent disabled, and she is not at all. Of course, who would want to use the VA hospital in Kansas City anyway? According to an AP report in March 2002, the infestation of mice, maggots, and flies in the years leading up to 2001 created such a scandal as to pressure VA Secretary Anthony Principi to remove 'the director and deputy director for the regional network, which includes Missouri, Kansas, and southern Illinois.' The janitorial staff did not touch the food storage areas or cafeteria for a year, and maggots had nested in two of the comatose patients' noses! This is not necessarily the fault of the VA because the federal government decides how much money will be allotted to our disabled veterans.

Ron Kovic exposed the horrible conditions of the VA hospitals during the Vietnam era in his book, *Born on the Fourth of July*. As a wounded Vietnam veteran, Kovic was outraged at the outdated equipment, under-qualified and uncaring staffs and the unsanitary conditions that disabled veterans were forced to endure. Therefore, not much has changed since 1970s, and any hope of future change is diminished by Dubya's slashing of the VA's healthcare budget by $275 million in 2002, and further cuts all around to the VA. Of course, recruiters never mention this in their deceit-filled speeches about the benefits of the military, which is why more veterans need to speak to high-school students and parents about the realities of military life.

Although the lies are bad enough, interactions with recruiters can be hazardous to one's health. One poolee (person waiting to go to boot camp who has already enlisted) wrote me that my first essay had helped him to decide to leave the Marines. The recruiter lied to the poolee by saying that it was too late, that he had already enlisted and therefore he was obligated for the next four years. During my recruiting days, I learned that any poolee can get out before boot camp, and after several more emails, the poolee told me that he had finally received his discharge after pushing the matter a little more. His recruiter responded to him with a physical threat by saying: 'If I was in front of you right now I'd knock you out.' Great example of the quality of leadership instilled by military service.

My recruiter in 1994 was a Marine sniper who had served in El Salvador and Somalia among other places. He actually admitted to me with excitement that he had killed noncombatants in Somalia with a .50 caliber sniper rifle, a weapon only to be used on vehicles, and that he had taken pictures of his victims afterward. His story was semi-confirmed for me seven years later, once I read Scott Peterson's *Me against My Brother*. Peterson wrote: 'the snipers killed more than 14 Somalis, some of them children who were found later to have a toy pistol, or nothing.' UN spokesperson George Bennet later told Peterson: 'They were shooting at anything by the time they left,' and this statement only further confirms my recruiter's story.

Unfortunately, I too am guilty of following an unlawful order from that same recruiter, but of a much lesser magnitude. While assisting him for two weeks just after I graduated from boot camp, part of my job was to make poolees lose weight before they shipped out. One poolee was still 12 pounds overweight the day before boot camp, so naturally my recruiter ordered me to force the poolee to eat an entire box of Ex-lax, after which I had to make him do calisthenics until he lost the 12 pounds. Needless to say, he was admitted to boot camp the next day, but I am still ashamed that I made him do that. The business of recruiting is dark indeed.

Recruiters now have even more access to the young minds of America, with the No Child Left Behind Act of 2001 and the National Defense Authorization Act for Fiscal Year 2002. These Acts require every high school receiving federal education funds to hand over the names, addresses, and phone numbers of every junior and senior to local recruiters upon request. That means that even fifteen-year-olds, with no idea whatsoever about the real world, let alone the military, are now vulnerable to the manipulation and deception of recruiters in their own homes. If a school refuses to hand the information over, the Department of Defense steps in and pressures the school, after which federal funding may be withdrawn. According to Secretary of Education Rod Paige and Secretary of Defense Donald Rumsfeld, the Acts give students more access to college, but we need to ask why it is that the government does not offer any alternative to the military for unskilled high school graduates who wish to go to college but are unqualified for college.

Our Commander-in-Chief himself took the opportunity to join the military, then took a Bush prerogative and failed to return to his duty station for a year and a half. Of course, he did not have to serve the prison sentences that others who left for that long did. Nevertheless, it makes perfect sense. After all, the president is not any different from half of Americans, who support our impending war on Iraq. While over 50 per cent support an invasion, approximately 1 per cent serves in the military. Therefore, only 1 per cent of us is willing to fight a battle that over 50 per cent of us favor, which makes it much more palatable to start a war. As long as the majority faces no direct military consequences, I guess anything, including deceptive measures in recruiting, goes. Thus, the cycle of historical amnesia is allowed to continue, and future US military action will surely bring about more 9/11s.

Chris White is an ex-Marine infantryman with experience as a recruiter-assistant. He is currently working on his doctorate in history at the University of Kansas, Lawrence. He served from 1994 to 1996, in Diego Garcia, Camp Pendleton, CA, Okinawa, Japan, and Doha, Qatar. He is also a member of Veterans for Peace.

January 30, 2003

BOMBING IRAQ: THEY'VE BEEN DOING IT FOR EIGHTY YEARS
by Alexander Cockburn

The word 'new,' as in 'new US doctrine' or 'new imperial role,' has no place in any discussion of the latest Western plans for Iraq. Western bombing strategies in Iraq stretch back as far as 1920, when the Royal Air Force ventured into the 'Shock and Awe' business in the earliest moment of Iraq's existence as a mandate of the League of Nations after World War One.

As with Palestine and Transjordan, the newly conceived entity of Iraq, created by the imperious drafting pencils of Gertrude Bell and

T. E. Lawrence, was under British supervision. As the Turks were evicted there was brave talk of an independent Iraq, but soon came the familiar vista of colonial supervisors and occupying troops from British garrisons in India. Though Iraq was, as it is today, an essay in enforced multiculturalism – Kurds, Sunnis, and Shi'a – British stupidity soon wrought the near-miracle of the unified revolt of 1920.

At a cost of some 8,000 Iraqi lives the revolt was finally suppressed, but the British government reeled at the expense of rushing large numbers of troops to the scene. The bill exceeded the entire cost of financing the Arab rising against the Ottomans in World War One.

At this point the Royal Air Force, desperately seeking rationales for independent existence, stepped forward and offered itself as a thrifty guarantor of the 'security' of Iraq. Air Marshall Hugh Trenchard promised that the RAF would cheaply police the former Ottoman provinces of Mesopotamia. The RAF took over its new duties in 1922. Only four years old as an independent arm of the British military, it had already formulated a prototype of Shock and Awe. Here's what Wing Commander J. A. Chamier wrote in the *Journal of the Royal United Services Institute* in 1921, under the boastful title 'The Use of Air Power for Replacing Military Garrisons':

> To establish a tradition, therefore, which will prove effective, if only a threat of what is to follow afterwards is displayed, the Air Force must, if called upon to administer punishment, do it with all its might and in the proper manner. One objective must be selected – preferably the most inaccessible village of the most prominent tribe which it is desired to punish. All available aircraft must be collected … The attack with bombs and machine guns must be relentless and unremitting and

carried on continuously by day and night, on houses, inhabitants, crops and cattle … This sounds brutal, I know, but it must be made brutal to start with. The threat alone in the future will prove efficacious if the lesson is once properly learnt.

Citing Chamier's prescriptions in a highly informative and witty essay on 'The Myth of Air Control' in *Aerospace Power Journal* (winter 2000), the military historian James Corum cites the RAF's *Notes on the Method of Employment of the Air Arm in Iraq* as proudly pointing out that 'within 45 minutes a full-sized village … can be practically wiped out and a third of its inhabitants killed or injured by four or five planes which offer them no real target and no opportunity for glory or avarice.'

But just as Tony Blair today faces dissent in the ranks of the British Labour Party, so too did dissent ascend from the same ranks three-quarters of a century ago, after the first Labour government came to power in 1924. Displaying far more moral fiber than his remote political descendant in the Foreign Office, the repellent Jack Straw, Colonial Secretary James Thomas wrote to the high commissioner in Iraq stating flatly that reports of heavy civilian casualties in Iraq, consequent on the RAF's raids, 'will not be easily explained or defended in Parliament by me.' The RAF fine-tuned its PR about collateral damage. Henceforth there would be early warnings of Shock and Awe forays, leaving time for the villagers to run away. Then the bombs would rain down, though not, so the RAF insisted, with the aim of actually destroying the village, but merely of disrupting daily life.

Out in the field, such niceties were swiftly discarded. Corum quotes an RAF flight commander based in India's Northwest Frontier in the 1930s as recalling the fairly constant action against tribes in that part of the empire:

If they went on being troublesome, we would warn them that we would bomb an assembly of people. An assembly was normally defined as ten people … Indeed, in my case I can remember actually finding nine people and saying 'That's within ten per cent and that's good enough,' so I blew them up.

This was before the days when oil become the prime objective of Western plunder in Iraq and throughout the Middle East, but time-honored methods of imperial extortion from subject peoples required the collection of taxes, and the RAF was placed in charge of Levies and Collections, bombing to extort money. Nothing has changed, the 'tax' in its modern guise being recapture and control of Iraq's oil. (Corum notes that while 'the French, under their air-control doctrine, regularly bombed tribes and villages, no evidence exists that they ever bombed the natives as a means of revenue enforcement, as did the British in Iraq. This difference in air-control doctrines between the French and British may indicate deep cultural differences between the two nations. A likely explanation is that the French are culturally more tolerant of and sympathetic to tax evasion than are the British.')

Naturally enough, the RAF was at great pains to suppress in its reports and histories of campaigns in Iraq the role of the army, thus giving the entirely false impression that air power alone could maintain imperial control. But in fact RAF bombing accuracy in the interwar period was mostly awful, and there were all the usual unfortunate mistakes, familiar today to those following US bombing mishaps in Afghanistan.

Bombing remote Kurdish villages was one thing, but dropping bombs on Palestinian villages quite another. The outbreak of the Arab revolt in Palestine from 1936 to 1939 elicited eager suggestions from RAF commanders, such as Air Commodore Arthur Harris, commanding officer of the RAF in Palestine and later chief of Bomber Command in World War Two, and hence one of the major war criminals of the twentieth century. Harris offered his recipe to halt Arab unrest. Drop 'one 250-pound or 500-pound bomb in each village that speaks out of turn ... The only thing the Arab understands is the heavy hand, and sooner or later it will have to be applied.' The British army saw this as folly, and certain to make a bad situation worse. Harris's advice was rejected, and the world had to wait till later years to see Israeli bombers dropping US-supplied explosives on Palestinian villages and camps.

In the years after World War Two the US Air Force prowled eagerly through the RAF's mendacious accounts of its prewar triumphs in Iraq. Corum reports that among these enthusiasts Colonel Raymond Sleeper, a member of the Air War College faculty, developed 'Project Control,' an air-control doctrine to deal with the Soviet Union. In an article in *Air University Review* in 1983, Lt Col. David Dean, USAF, issued a fervent but misleading testimonial of the RAF's experience with air control. Dean saw air control as a cheap and effective way of policing the empire. The airpower theorist Carl Builder discussed British air control in an *Airpower Journal* article in 1995, arguing that it provided an excellent model for 'constabulary missions' in support of the United Nations or 'peace operations.' But as Corum concludes, 'the idealized air-control system described by US Air Force writers never really existed ... Basically, one could barely justify air control as a doctrine 80 years ago, and people who advocate an updated version of such doctrine for current US Air Force operations have misread history.'

So much for 'new strategies' and 'revolutions in military affairs.' The punitive expedition pressed by Bush and his circle remains squarely within the tradition of similar punitive expeditions launched, with aerial bombardments, nearly eighty years ago over the same terrain.

February 9, 2003

CONDITION ORANGE AS A WAY OF LIFE
by Alexander Cockburn

The day Ashcroft and Ridge announced that the entire nation had joined New York at Level Orange, four fugitive Cubans from the military made landfall on the Homeland, passing undetected by southern Florida's vast flotillas of Coast Guard and Navy vessels, plus Fat Albert, the blimp panopticon tethered above the lower Keys. The four tied up their 32-foot fiberglass cigarette boat (sporting the Cuban flag and containing two AK-47s, eight loaded magazines and a GPS finder tuned to the coordinates of the US Coast Guard station) on the southern shore of Key West, at the Hyatt Resort dock. Then, clad in their Cuban army fatigues (one had a Chinese-made handgun strapped to his hip) they wandered about, marveling at the serene emptiness of the evening streets, looking for a police station where they could turn themselves in. Had they been terrorists there were plenty of rewarding targets within strolling distance, including a major surveillance center for the Caribbean and Latin America, run by US Southern Command, also a US Navy base, plus of course Key West's extensive literary colony.

February 16, 2003

COLIN POWELL AND THE GREAT 'INTELLIGENCE' FRAUD

by Alexander Cockburn

Events do rush by us in a blur, I know, but let's not abandon Secretary of State Colin Powell's Feb. 5 speech to the UN in the graveyard of history without one last backward glance. It was, after all, billed by the President as a conclusive intelligence briefing on exactly how Saddam Hussein has been concealing his weapons of mass destruction, and how he's hand-in-glove with Al Qaeda.

Now, when the Commander-in-Chief states publicly that his Secretary of State will deliver the goods, we can be safe in assuming that he's been assured that Yes, the US intelligence 'community' has indeed got the goods. But barely more than a week after Powell's speech it now looks as though its major claims were at best speculative, and at worst outright distortions, some of them derided in advance by UN Chief Inspector Hans Blix.

There was the supposed transporter of biotoxins that turned out to be a truck from the Baghdad health department; the sinisterly enlarged test ramp for long-distance missiles that was nothing of the sort; the suspect facility that had recently been cleared by the UN inspection teams; the strange eavesdropped conversations that could as well have been Iraqi officers discussing how to hide stills for making bootleg whisky. The promoter of the Iraq/Al Qaeda link, Abu Musab Zarqawi, turns out to be an imaginative liar trying to get a prison sentence commuted, and the terror cell Ansar al-Islam a bunch of Islamic fundamentalists violently opposed to Saddam and operating out of Kurdish territory. (A few days later Powell cited Osama bin Laden's latest tape as confirming that

Saddam and Al Qaeda are in cahoots. Actually it's mostly a vivid account, which has the ring of truth, of how he and his men in their Tora Bora foxholes survived ferocious US bombing with minimal casualties. Bin Laden concludes by urging all Muslims 'to pull up your pant legs for jihad' against the forces of darkness. Of Saddam and the Ba'ath he says: 'The Socialists are infidels wherever they are, either in Baghdad or Aden. Such war which may take place these days is similar to the war between Muslims and Romans when the interests of the Muslims came along with the interests of the Persians who both fought against the Romans.')

And of course there was the British intelligence report sent by Tony Blair to Powell, who commended it in his UN speech as particularly 'fine.' The report turned out to be a series of plagiarisms from old articles from *Jane's*, and from a paper on Iraqi politics written by a student called Ibrahim al Marashi, at the Monterey Institute for International Studies. The Marashi plagiarism represents an intrusive parable on how 'intelligence' reports actually get put together, to fulfill a political agenda. From some enterprising work by freelance reporter Kenneth Raposa, who worked on the Iraqi Dossier story for the *Boston Globe*, it emerges that Marashi himself comes from a Shi'a family in Baltimore, Md. He's never visited Iraq and is keen to see Saddam toppled by US invasion.

Marashi's essay was published in September 2002, in the *Middle East Review of International Affairs*, a scholarly magazine run by the GLORIA (acronym for Global Research in International Affairs) Center in Herzliya, Israel. Its director is Barry Rubin, who has also been a senior fellow at the Washington Institute for Near East Policy – an Israel policy think tank. Rubin is part of the coterie – which includes Daniel Pipes, Michael Ledeen, and the arch conspirator Richard Perle – who have been pressing for a US attack on Iraq.

Marashi told Raposa that the documents on which he had based his paper had been given him by Kenaan Makiya, a well-known Iraqi exile, and proponent of invasion, much favored by Powell's own State Department. Makiya claims to have some 4 million pages of documents seized from northern Iraq after Operation Desert Storm.

So here we have a politically inspired document, spliced together by a Shi'a student, published by an Israeli-based think tank hot for war, swiped off the web by Blair's harried minions and served up to Powell as a masterpiece of British intelligence collection from MI6.

Quite aside from the welcome damage done to Powell's credibility and to the war party in general, the Marashi saga vividly reminds us of just how much rubbish has been served up to the American people in the guise of reliable 'intelligence.' Remember how back amid the build-up to the last Iraqi war, the Pentagon invoked satellite photos of 265,000 Iraqi troops massed to invade Saudi Arabia? Jean Heller, a journalist from the *St. Petersburg Times* in Florida, persuaded her newspaper to buy two photos at $1,600 each from the Russian commercial satellite, the Soyuz Karta. No troops showed up on the photos. 'You could see the planes sitting wing tip to wing tip in Riyadh airport,' Ms Heller says, 'but there wasn't was any sign of a quarter of a million Iraqi troops sitting in the middle of the desert.'

The ridicule now being showered on Powell's Iraq Dossier won't slow up the production of these ridiculous documents or hinder the endless flourishing of supposedly conclusive satellite photography or communications intercepts. If war does come, we can be sure there will be repetitions of the 'misinterpretations' and 'tragic errors' of the 1991 onslaught.

When my brother Patrick drove from Amman to Baghdad back

at the end of the 1991 onslaught he passed the hulks of oil tankers bombed to bits under the claim they were mobile Scud launchers. The single biggest atrocity of that war was the US bombing of the Almariya shelter in Baghdad. The Pentagon claimed it was a top-secret military command center. It wasn't. In the absence of its intended occupants, university professors and technocrats, ordinary Iraqi mothers and children had taken shelter there. Just another intelligence screw-up, with several hundred dead mothers and kids as the price.

And yes, we are in the wake of the greatest intelligence failure in American history, for which not one intelligence head rolled. Instead they gave the CIA even more money, and yes, its grateful chief George Tenet is sitting beside Powell in the UN Security Council. He should have been too ashamed to show his face in public.

February 23, 2003

RUMSFELD'S ACCOUNT BOOK: WHO ARMED SADDAM?
by Stephen Green

You have to give Defense Secretary Rumsfeld this much credit: he's a risk taker and he's damned brassy about it.

Both were in evidence last week when he testified before the Senate Armed Services Committee. Under criticism for his prior characterizations of France and Germany as 'old Europe,' Rumsfeld fumed: 'We would not be facing the problems in Iraq today if the technologically advanced countries of the world had seen the danger and strictly enforced the economic sanctions against Iraq.'

The Defense Secretary knew well, naturally, his audience in the Senate Armed Services Committee. As Senator Robert Byrd recently said from the Senate floor, 'this Chamber is, for the most part, silent – ominously, dreadfully silent. There is no debate, no discussion, no attempt to lay out for the nation the pros and cons of this particular war. There is nothing.'

Still, Rumsfeld's statement was some chutspa! He was well aware that it was the US Senate itself (Committee on Banking, Housing and Urban Affairs) which had conducted extensive hearings in 1992 and 1994 on 'United States Dual-Use Exports to Iraq and Their Impact on the Health of Persian Gulf War Veterans.' And he'd probably read the front-page *Washington Post* story ('US Had Key Role in Iraq Buildup,' December 30, 2002) based upon recently declassified documents, which revealed that it was Rumsfeld himself who, as President Reagan's Middle East Envoy, had traveled to the region to meet with Saddam Hussein in December 1983 to normalize, particularly, security relations.

At the time of the visit, Iraq had already been removed from the State Department's list of terrorist countries in 1982; and in the previous month, November, President Reagan had approved National Security Decision Directive 114, on expansion of US–Iraq relations generally. But it was Donald Rumsfeld's trip to Baghdad which opened up the floodgates during 1985–90 for lucrative US weapons exports – some $1.5 billion worth – including chemical/biological and nuclear weapons equipment and technology, along with critical components for missile delivery systems for all of the above. According to a 1994 GAO letter report (GAO/NSIAD-94-98) some 771 weapons export licenses for Iraq were approved during this six-year period ... not by our European allies, but by the US Department of Commerce.

To be sure, many of these weapons were expended in the latter phases of the Iran–Iraq War. Others were destroyed by Coalition forces in the Persian Gulf War, or by UN weapons inspectors in the control regime established by the UN Security Council following that conflict. But a great many undoubtedly remain, and pose grave risks to the 150,000 US troops deployed in Kuwait, and 100,000 on the way. Imagine the embarrassment to Defense Secretary Rumsfeld before the Armed Services Committee last week if one or more senators had had the awareness AND the courage to raise the matter of Iraq's secret supplier.

And in this case, the devil is quite literally in the details.

There were few if any reservations evident in the range of weapons which President Ronald Reagan and his successor George W. H. Bush were willing to sell Saddam Hussein. Under the Arms Export Control Act of 1976, the foreign sale of munitions and other defense equipment and technology is controlled by the Department of State. During the 1980s, such items could not be sold or diverted to Communist states, nor to those on the US list of terrorist-supporting countries. When Iraq came off that list in 1982, however, some $48 million of items such as data privacy devices, voice scramblers, communication and navigation equipment, electronic components, image intensifiers and pistols (to protect Saddam) were approved for sale during 1985–90. But it was through the purchase of $1.5 billion of American 'dual-use items,' having, sometimes arguably, both military and civilian functions, that Iraq obtained the bulk of its weapons of mass destruction in the late Eighties. 'Dual-use items' are controlled and licensed by the Department of Commerce under the Export Administration Act of 1979. This is where the real damage was done.

In 1992 and again in 1994, hearings were conducted by the Senate Banking, Housing and Urban Affairs Committee, which has Senate oversight responsibility for the Export Administration Act. The purpose of the hearings was the Committee's concern that 'tens of thousands' of Gulf War veterans were suffering from symptoms associated with the 'Gulf War Syndrome,' possibly due to their exposure to chemical and biological agents that had been exported from the US during that brief period of 'normalization' of relations with Iraq in 1985–90.

At the opening of the second round of hearings on May 25, 1994, Chairman Donald Riegle and Ranking Member Alphonse D'Amato released a detailed staff report which constituted a searing indictment of US arms export policies during the Reagan/Bush administrations, linking those exports to the health problems of Gulf War veterans, and excoriating the then current (Clinton) administration for denying that such a link existed.

According to the hearing reports (which are available on a current website: www.chronicillnet.org/PGWS/tuite/default.htm), among the chemical weapons which had been sold to Iraq were some of the very most lethal available: Sarin, Soman, Tabun, VX, lewisite, cyanogen chloride, hydrogen cyanide, blister agents and mustard gas. Some of the powerful biological agents sold included anthrax, *Clostridium botulinum*, *Histoplasma capsulatum* (causes a tuberculosis-like disease), *Brucella melitensis*, *Clostridium perfringens* and *Escherichia coli*.

Witnesses on the first day of the hearings included Under-Secretary of Defense for Personnel and Readiness, Edwin Dorn, and the officials in both the Defense Department and the CIA responsible for non-proliferation policy. Interestingly, in what was often an adversarial exchange between the Committee and these officials, the latter admitted in sworn testimony that while no chemical/biological weapons had been found to have been 'stored or used' by the Iraqi army during the conflict, American troops had nevertheless been exposed to airborne traces of C/B agents from having been downwind of storage facilities that were bombed by US planes.

Simply put, while Saddam Hussein had shown restraint in the Gulf War by not deploying his most lethal weapons, the US government had, a) sold chemical/biological agents and shipped them directly to Iraqi military installations, including some just months before Iraq's invasion of Kuwait, b) distributed faulty chemical/biological agent detection sensors and protection gear such as gasmasks to US troops, and, c) caused the exposure of these troops by the bombing of military storage areas upwind of them.

It got worse. Dr Gordon Oehler, Director of the Central Intelligence Agency's Non-Proliferation Center, testified that, between 1984 and 1990, the CIA's Office of Scientific and Weapons Research had issued five alert memos 'covering Iraqi's dealings with United States firms on purchases, discussions, or visits that appeared to be related to weapons of mass destruction programs.' Such memos, Oehler explained, were sent to Commerce, Justice, Treasury and the FBI when collected intelligence indicated that US firms had been targeted by foreign governments of concern, or were involved in possible violations of US law.

At another point in the hearings, Dr Oehler indicated that the CIA's concerns about Iraqi weapons programs, in particular 'a Samarra chemical plant, including six separate chemical weapons lines between 1983 and 1986,' had been reported 'directly to our customers.' Under questioning from Chairman Riegle, he identified these as the President and the Secretaries of Defense and State. Perhaps the most surprising testimony taken by the Senate Committee on Banking, Housing and Urban Affairs was that given in the earlier 1992 hearings on the matter of US assistance to the Iraqi ballistic missile and nuclear weapons programs. Gary Milhollin, Director of the Wisconsin Project on Nuclear Arms Control, testified that US companies were being licensed by the Commerce Department to ship such items directly to the Al-Qaqaa and Badr facilities, which the Pentagon had formally identified as part of the Iraqi nuclear weapons production program, and to Salah al Din, known to be the center of its ballistic missile development efforts.

In all, Milhollin identified forty US companies involved in such sales. And it was critical equipment – vacuum pumps, electron beam welders, mass spectrometers, accelerometers, missile guidance systems, navigational radar, high-speed computers and filling systems to load C/B agents in missiles, among many other items. Such 'stuff' was being sent to Iraq until late 1989, less than a year before Iraq's invasion of Kuwait!

Through the mid and late 1980s, said Milhollin, the Pentagon, the CIA and the Office of Naval Intelligence, among others, continued to warn the White House that Iraq's nuclear, chemical and biological weapons were maturing at a rapid pace, as was work on the ballistic missiles to deliver them. The warnings were falling on deaf ears: in October 1989, ten months before the Kuwait invasion, President George Bush signed NSD 26, updating NSDD 114, and again committing the US to normal relations with Saddam Hussein's government. As had been the case with chemical and biological weapons, the list of American and European companies which sold the nuclear equipment and technology to Iraq was a virtual pantheon of industry names: Hewlett Packard, International Computer Systems, Siemens, TI Coating, Carl Zeiss, Rockwell Collins International, Spectra Physics, Unisys, Tektronix, Scientific Atlanta and Semetex, among many, many others. With such assistance, Iraq became a regional power during 1984–90, and developed regional ambitions.

But these companies were not, per se, Saddam Hussein's main weapons suppliers: that designation should properly go to Ronald

Reagan and George W. H. Bush, the signers, respectively, of NSDD 114 and NSD 26, both of which remain classified. As the primary recipients and ultimate 'customers' of the alert memos from the CIA and the US intelligence community, they were currently and fully aware of the use to which the equipment and technology were being put, and of the security policy implications of the process.

And the instrument, the person, the envoy, who negotiated the process in the first instance is the current US Secretary of Defense, Donald Rumsfeld.

Stephen Green lives in Berlin, Vermont.

February 25, 2003

THE WEEKEND THE WORLD SAID NO TO WAR
by Gary Leupp

At least 10 million people demonstrated in major cities against an Iraq attack, in open-air rallies and marches. If we include smaller demonstrations, the figure will be larger; in Greece, for example, between 100,000 and 150,000 are reported to have rallied in Athens, but another 60,000 rallied in 52 other communities.

The demonstrations occurred on all continents (including Antarctica, where 50–55 scientists staged a half-hour rally), indicating extremely widespread opposition to Bush policy, and effective lines of communication linking the US and European antiwar movements, and also international links between anti-globalization activists in the Western countries, Latin America, Asia and Africa.

News reports indicate that there were at least 60 demonstrations of over 10,000 people. Almost 40 of these occurred in Europe, the greatest center of economic power outside the US and the likely focus of contention for years to come.

Five of the demonstrations probably exceeded 500,000: Barcelona, Rome, London, Madrid and Berlin. There is a big gap between the Madrid and Berlin figures, so the first four are especially conspicuous. And notice: the top four demos all occurred in nations with governments pledged to support the Bush–Blair Terror War on Iraq.

Five Top Antiwar Demos, Feb. 15: Barcelona 1.3 million; Rome 1–2 million; London 750,000 (police), 1.5 million (organizers); Madrid 660,000–800,000; Berlin 300,000–600,000. Spain, Italy and Britain are all members of the 'gang of eight' pieced together as the relationship between the US and France and Germany deteriorated, to reassure the US public that Bush has international backing. Their heads of state all signed a letter circulated last month indicating their intention to cooperate in a future US-led attack on Iraq. (Other gang members include Portugal, Denmark, and the former Soviet-camp members Poland, Czech Republic and Hungary.)

Within the 'gang of eight' governments, Spain's meets with particularly widespread opposition in supporting the US war plans. Of the four largest demonstrations, two occurred in Spain, in widely separate regions; there were also several other demonstrations of over 100,000 in the country. It appears likely that between 2.5 and 3 million Spaniards (out of 40 million total) took a stand against war on Saturday.

There appears to be strong support in the vilified European nations of France, Germany and Belgium for the antiwar stands currently assumed by their regimes. The demonstration in Berlin was complemented by large gatherings in Stuttgart (50,000) and

Gottenberg (30,000). Paris heads the list of venues of the thirteen demonstrations I've found so far estimated to involve 100,000 to half a million.

There were huge demonstrations in Australia around February 15, including two in this next category of rallies between 100,000 and half a million. Australia is another key ally in the US war effort.

Demos of 100,000–500,000

Paris 400,000; Sydney 250,000 (Feb. 16); Damascus 200,000; Ovidio (Spain) 200,000; San Francisco 150,000 (police), 250,000 (organizers) (Feb. 16); Las Palmas (Spain) 100,000; Cadiz (Spain) 100,000; Melbourne 100,000–200,000 (Feb. 14); New York 100,000 (police), 375,000–500,000 (organizers); Los Angeles 100,000; Montreal 100,000; Dublin 100,000; Athens 100,000 (police), 150,000 (organizers).

Demos of 50,000–100,000

Lisbon 80,000; Amsterdam 70,000; Seattle 60,000–75,000; Oslo 60,000; Seville 60,000; Brussels 50,000; Montevideo 50,000; Buenos Aires 50,000; Stuttgart 50,000.

There was significant participation in antiwar organizing in Latin American cities, especially Montevideo (Uruguay) and Buenos Aires (Argentina), but also in Mexico City and São Paulo (Brazil). There were demonstrations in Havana, San Juan (Puerto Rico) and Santo Domingo.

The only demonstrations of around 10,000 to take place in Southeast Asia were in (predominantly Muslim) Pattani, in Thailand, and in Manila. Twice that number rallied in Pattani on February 16. There were smaller demonstrations in Djakarta (following one of between 10,000 and 50,000 a week earlier), Kuala Lumpur (3,000 despite a police ban) and Bangkok. Largely, one supposes, because of government repression, the antiwar movement remains low-key in the region.

In South Asia, 10,000 rallied in Calcutta, India, and smaller numbers in Dhaka, Bangladesh, and Karachi, Pakistan. In this region, too, the movement faces organizational difficulties. In Africa, protest against the war has been largely confined to the large cities of South Africa. There were demonstrations of 4,000–5,000 in Durban, Cape Town and Johannesburg.

The 200,000-strong rally in Damascus, Syria, was among the top ten demonstrations on February 15, but (like the pro-Saddam rally in Baghdad the same day) this was a government-sponsored event. In Beirut, perhaps 10,000 protested; in Amman, 3,000. Riot police attacked a rally of 3,000 in Sfax, in Tunisia. Palestinians demonstrated in Ramallah and Jews and Palestinians marched together two or three thousand strong in Tel Aviv. A few hundred protested in Bahrain, as if to test the monarch's commitment to democratic reform. But in Cairo, greatest city in the contemporary Arab world, only a few hundred rallied, some suffering arrest and torture for violating security regulations. (This is the third time this has happened since the Cairo Conference helped launch the Egyptian antiwar campaign in December.) The fear of repression restrains a potentially mighty anti-imperialist movement in the Arab world.

Demos of 20,000–50,000

Berne (Switzerland) 40,000; Stockholm 35,000; Glasgow 30,000– 50,000; Gottenberg 30,000; Girona 30,000; Toronto 25,000– 80,000; Tokyo 25,000; Copenhagen 25,000; Vancouver 20,000; Budapest 20,000; Trondheim (Norway) 20,000; Brisbane 20,000; Vienna 15,000–30,000; Montpelier 15,000–20,000.

Demos of 10,000–20,000

Canberra 16,000; Helsinki 15,000; Newcastle (Australia) 15,000; Bergen (Norway) 15,000; Munich 14,000–20,000 (Feb. 8); Mexico City 13,500; São Paolo 10,000–20,000; Toulouse 10,000; Calcutta 10,000; Porto (Portugal) 10,000; Copenhagen 10,000; Thessaloniki 10,000; Zagreb 10,000; Philadelphia 10,000; Leipzig 10,000 (Feb. 10); Hobart 10,000; Warsaw 10,000; Perth (Australia) 10,000; Manila 10,000 (Feb. 14); Pattani 10,000; Auckland 8,000–10,000; Seoul 2,000–10,000; Beirut 10,000.

February 26, 2003

MEET THE *NEW YORKER'S* GOLDBERG
by Alexander Cockburn

Who's the hack? I nominate the *New Yorker's* Jeffrey Goldberg. He's the new Remington, though without the artistic talent. Back in 1898, William Randolph Hearst was trying to fan war fever between the United States and Spain. He dispatched a reporter and the artist Frederic Remington to Cuba to send back blood-roiling depictions of Spanish beastliness to Cuban insurgents. Remington wired to say he could find nothing sensational to draw and could he come home. Famously, Hearst wired him: 'Please remain. You furnish the pictures and I'll furnish the war.' Remington duly did so.

I wouldn't set the *New Yorker's* editor, David Remnick, in the shoes of a Kong-sized monster like Hearst. Remnick is a third-tier talent who has always got ahead by singing the correct career-enhancing tunes, as witness his awful reporting from Russia in the

1990s. Art Spiegelman recently quit the *New Yorker*, remarking that these dangerous times require courage and the ability to be provocative, but alas, 'Remnick does not feel up to the challenge.'

That's putting it far too politely. Remnick's watch has been lackluster and cowardly. He is also the current sponsor (Marty Peretz of the *New Republic* was an earlier one) of Goldberg, whose first major chunk of agitprop for the *New Yorker* was published on March 25 of last year. Titled 'The Great Terror,' it was billed as containing disclosures of 'Saddam Hussein's possible ties to Al Qaeda.' This was at a moment when the FBI and CIA had just shot down the war party's claim of a meeting between Mohammed Atta and an Iraqi intelligence agent in Prague before the 9/11 attacks. Goldberg saved the day for the Bush crowd.

At the core of his rambling 16,000-word piece was an interview in the Kurdish-held Iraqi town of Sulaimaniya with Mohammed Mansour Shahab, who offered the eager Goldberg a wealth of detail about his activities as a link between Osama bin Laden and the Iraqis, shuttling arms and other equipment. The piece was gratefully seized upon by the administration as proof of The Link. The coup de grâce to Goldberg's credibility fell on February 9 of this year in the London *Observer*, administered by Jason Burke, its chief reporter. Burke visited the same prison in Sulaimaniya, talked to Shahab and established beyond doubt that Goldberg's great source is a clumsy liar, not even knowing the physical appearance of Kandahar, whither he had claimed to have journeyed to deal with bin Laden; and confecting his fantasies in the hope of a shorter prison sentence.

Another experienced European journalist, whom I reached on the Continent, who visited the prison last year agrees with Burke's findings. 'I talked to prisoners without someone present. The director of the prison seemed surprised at my request. With a prison authority present the interview would be worthless. As soon as we talked to this particular one a colleague said after thirty seconds: "This is worthless. The guy was just a story teller."' The European journalist, who doesn't want to be identified, said to me charitably that Goldberg's credulity about Shahab 'could have been a matter of misjudgement but my even stronger criticism is that if you talked, as we did and as I gather Goldberg did, to anybody in the PUK [the Kurdish group controlling this area of northern Iraq] about this particular Islamic group all of them would tell you they are backed by Iran, as common sense would tell you. Look where they are located. It's 200 meters across one river to Iran. That's what I find upsetting. Misjudging a source can happen to all of us, but Goldberg did talk to generals in the PUK. I think it's outrageous that the *New Yorker* ran that story.'

Finally, I hear that a *New York Times* reporter also concluded after talking to the prisoners that there was one who was obviously lying and who would say anything anyone would like to hear about Al Ansar and Saddam, Saddam and Al Qaeda. I have not been able to talk to this reporter, though it would not have been surprising for the *Times* to have tried to check up on Goldberg's 'scoop.' An American with a lot of experience in interviewing in prisons adds: 'It's tricky interviewing prisoners in the first place – their vulnerability, etc – and responsible journalists make some sort of minimal credibility assessment before they report someone's statements. But the prisoner said exactly what Jeffrey Goldberg wanted to hear, so Goldberg didn't feel that he needed to mention that the prisoner was nuts.'

On February 10, amid widespread cynicism about the administration's rationales for war, Remnick published another Goldberg special, 'The Unknown: The CIA and the Pentagon take another look at Al Qaeda and Iraq.' This 6,000-word screed had no pretensions to being anything other than a servile rendition of Donald

Rumsfeld's theory of intelligence: 'Build a hypothesis, and then see if the data supported the hypothesis, rather than the reverse.' In other words, decide what you want to hear, then torture the data until the data confess.

This last piece of Goldberg's was a truly disgraceful piece of brown-nosing (of Rumsfeld, Tenet *et al.*), devoid of even the pretensions of independent journalism. 'Reporter at Large'? Remnick should retire the rubric, at least for Goldberg, and advertise his work as 'White House Handout.' I should note that Goldberg once served in Israel's armed forces, which may or may not be a guide to his political agenda.

March 4, 2003

WHY LET FACTS STOP A GOOD WAR?
by Alexander Cockburn

CounterPunch hears that the top 2,500 Iraqis have been getting calls on their cellphones from US intelligence officers telling them that if they lay down their arms when D-day comes they may escape trial for war crimes. One seasoned Iraqi hand tells us the US did the same thing in 1991, but that often the calls got screwed up. Few predict prolonged resistance. Estimates of the duration of any war range from five minutes to three weeks.

To our mind the most significant story of the season was the one by John Barry in a recent *Newsweek*. On February 24, *Newsweek*'s issue dated March 3 reported that the Iraqi weapons chief who defected from the regime in 1995 told UN inspectors that Iraq had destroyed its entire stockpile of chemical and biological weapons and banned missiles, exactly as Iraq claims. Gen. Hussein Kamel, Saddam Hussein's former son-in-law who defected and who was killed shortly after returning to Iraq in 1996, was debriefed by officials from the International Atomic Energy Agency (IAEA) and the UN inspections team, UNSCOM. Barry got hold of the transcript of that debriefing. Kemal told the inspectors, in Barry's words in *Newsweek*, 'that after the Gulf War, Iraq destroyed all its chemical and biological weapons stocks and the missiles to deliver them.' All that remained were 'hidden blueprints, computer disks, microfiches and production molds.' The weapons were destroyed secretly, in order to hide their existence from inspectors, in the hopes of someday resuming production after inspections had finished. The CIA and MI6 were told the same story, Barry reported, and 'a military aide who defected with Kamel ... backed Kamel's assertions about the destruction of WMD stocks.' But these statements were 'hushed up by the UN inspectors' in order to 'bluff Saddam into disclosing still more.'

On February 26, the media watchdog FAIR reports, a complete copy of the Kamel transcript – an internal UNSCOM/IAEA document stamped 'sensitive' – was obtained by Glen Rangwala, the Cambridge University analyst who in early February revealed that Tony Blair's 'intelligence dossier' was plagiarized from a student thesis. Rangwala has posted the Kamel transcript on the Web:

http://casi.org.uk/info/unscom950822.pdf.

In other words Bush, Blair and the rest of them have known perfectly well all along that there are no chemical and biological war stocks to be found. No one seriously maintains that Iraq has any nuclear capability. Barry's tremendous scoop in *Newsweek* was ignored by the mainstream press.

March 7, 2003

WHEN JEFFREY GOLDBERG DID BRAZIL
by Alexander Cockburn

Jeffrey Goldberg is the *New Yorker* fantasist whose work on Al Qaeda, so succulent to the Bush crowd, I discussed here last week. No continent is safe from his inventive pen. On October 28, 2002, the *New Yorker* published a Goldberg piece called 'The Party of God: Hezbollah Sets Up Operations in South America and the United States.' It 'confirmed' – in his mind, National Public Radio's mind, and all of the right-wing pundits' minds that Hezbollah had long set up shop in the 'Triple Frontier' of Argentina, Paraguay and Paraná state, Brazil.

A journalist and friend of *CounterPunch* who lives in that region part of the year, who read Goldberg's story at the time and wrote a letter of protest to the *New Yorker*, recalls:

> It is incredible that one journalist, who has as his mainstay the theme that Arabs are plotting to kill Jews and destroy America's 'interests,' could come and visit Brazil just to see if Hezbollah is operating here, and voilà, he found 'em running rampant. It was an impressive feat of research actually. Not only did Goldberg come up with what many here thought was a far-fetched hypothesis – could the Hezbollah be funding anti-Israel/US operations from the Triple Frontier? – but he proved that they are doing just that, all by himself. No reporter in this part of the world has been able to find the slightest bit of evidence along those lines. I'm fairly convinced that his claim is irresponsible, and a slap in the face to the peaceful communities that exist here. Even the police, who monitor narco-trafficking, don't see the link.

The CounterPuncher phoned the Ministry of Justice in Brasilia in November and talked to the Justice Minister's assistant, who confirmed that joint Brazilian, Paraguayan and Argentine federal police, including undercover forces, had not found any evidence that Arabs involved in narco-trafficking were laundering money into terrorist operations. There WERE some arrests made in these Arab communities along the triple frontier, for CD piracy. But all of the arrests that were made post-September 11 were minor charges, and the Arabs that were held were let go.

March 10, 2003

A CIA ANALYST ON FORGING INTELLIGENCE: WHOSE DELIBERATE DISINFORMATION?
by Ray Close

There was a small but very important passage in Mohammad Elbaradei's testimony on behalf of the UN's International Atomic Energy Agency before the UN Security Council last week that cries out for further investigation:

> With regard to uranium acquisition, the I.A.E.A. has made progress in its investigation into reports that Iraq sought to buy uranium from Niger in recent years. This investigation was centered on documents provided by a number of states that pointed to an agreement between Niger and Iraq for the sale of uranium between 1999 and 2001.
>
> The I.A.E.A. has discussed these reports with the governments of Iraq and Niger, both of which have denied that any such activity took place. For its part, Iraq has provided the I.A.E.A. with a comprehensive

explanation of its relations with Niger and has described a visit by an Iraqi official to a number of African countries, including Niger, in February 1999, which Iraq thought might have given rise to the reports.

The I.A.E.A. was able to review correspondence coming from various bodies of the government of Niger and to compare the form, format, contents and signature of that correspondence with those of the alleged procurement-related documentation. Based on thorough analysis, the I.A.E.A. has concluded, with the concurrence of outside experts, that these documents, which formed the basis for the reports of recent uranium transaction between Iraq and Niger, are in fact not authentic. We have therefore concluded that these specific allegations are unfounded.

On Saturday, March 8, the *Washington Post* reported under the headline 'Some Evidence on Iraq Called Fake' that the documents in question had been given to the UN inspectors by the British government and 'reviewed extensively by US intelligence.' The documents were then forwarded to the IAEA by the US government, an action clearly implying that in Washington's opinion they constituted reliable intelligence. A similar stamp of authenticity must have been implied in the case of the British government's actions. Such is certainly the impression that would be gained by the United Nations recipients, knowing that the documents had been 'reviewed extensively' by US intelligence experts.

However, after the IAEA determined through its own 'outside experts' that the documents were bogus, the US and British governments were reluctantly compelled to acknowledge that they had both been the victims of an elaborate deception operation. One unnamed (but hopefully red-faced) US official was honest enough to admit to *Washington Post* reporter Joby Warrick that 'We fell for it.' In a curious display of unwarranted courtesy, an IAEA spokesman graciously informed the *Washington Post* that his agency did not blame either Britain or the United States for the forgery. The documents 'were shared with us in good faith,' he said.

The following questions immediately occur to anyone with experience in the area of covert technical operations ('Department of Dirty Tricks'), and to everyone else with a modicum of common sense:

The fabrication of false documentation, especially what purports to be official correspondence between the agencies of two different governments, is a major undertaking for any professional intelligence service or criminal enterprise. This is obviously most true when the perpetrator intends to accomplish an extremely important purpose and so anticipates that his work will be carefully scrutinized by competent experts. The job requires extensive and time-consuming research, reasonably advanced technical skills, and a high level of motivation. It would not be attempted by anyone whose intentions were frivolous. All of these factors would be accentuated in a case such as this, where the political costs of exposure of deliberate fraud would be very high.

Unless accomplished with a high degree of skill, the counterfeit quality of the documents in this case should have been quickly obvious to the British and American intelligence services, and the contents dismissed immediately as a trivial diversion. Surprisingly, however, according to the *Washington Post* story, the forgeries contained 'relatively crude errors' that gave them away. This clearly points to one or the other of two possible conclusions:

a. The technical services departments of MI6 and CIA (historically reputed to be credible rivals to the KGB and Israel's Mossad for technical sophistication) are in fact incompetent. If they manufactured the forgeries themselves, they did a careless and clumsy job. On the other hand, if they merely evaluated the authenticity of the documents as a means of determining whether the information contained therein was valuable intelligence for their own governments, they obviously showed an equally appalling lack of professional skill. They 'fell for it,' we are informed.

b. The only other explanation that I can think of is that the British and American intelligence services, despite having figured out that the documents were crude forgeries, nevertheless decided to pass the information to the UN inspectors anyway, knowing that they would serve conveniently to mislead the IAEA into thinking that this was documentary evidence supporting US–UK claims that Iraq has made illegal attempts to acquire nuclear resources. (Of course, intelligence services can be incredibly obtuse sometimes. Note the recent public admission by the British that the famous 'dossier' of evidence against Iraq, glowingly praised by Colin Powell in his testimony to the Security Council, consisted mainly of hearsay plagiarized from the work of a California graduate student.)

Somebody has engaged in the criminal act of manufacturing false evidence. If it has been done once, it may well have been done before. The issues under consideration are matters of war and peace, life and death for perhaps thousands of people. How much more despicable could a crime be? And yet our government and that of Great Britain seem more bemused than concerned. Shouldn't Congress be alarmed that our intelligence service, on which we are so dependent these days, is so incompetent or so inured to the corruption of the national intelligence process as to tolerate the deliberate or careless introduction of false evidence into a process so critically important to our national security and to the credibility of the United States? Those responsible for this humiliating fiasco should be exposed and discredited – for the good of our country.

The *Washington Post* story is also a testament to the flaccid quality of American investigative journalism these days. It apparently never occurred to any reporter how important it would be to know exactly who it was that forged the documents in the first place. Here was an organized effort to spread extremely significant disinformation to at least two governments, and through them to the Security Council of the United Nations, that might have a direct influence on a momentous decision about war and peace.

Immediately, a host of other specific questions come to mind. Who were the 'outside experts' consulted by the IAEA who correctly spotted the falsity of the Iraq–Niger correspondence (and exposed the incompetence of MI6 and the CIA in the process)? Were they governments, or private agencies? Where located? By whom controlled?

Elbaradei reported that these documents were provided to the IAEA by 'a number of states.' Very interesting. Any other government besides the British and American? Did 'a number of states' provide identical counterfeit documents to the UN inspectors, representing those documents as reliable 'intelligence'? Did each of those states originally obtain the documents from the same source? When the information was passed by the British and Americans to the United Nations, was the original source identified? Or did MI6 and the CIA claim the necessity to protect 'sensitive sources and methods'? (Wouldn't it be interesting to learn that in this case that same familiar claim was made? What would that do to the credibility of other intelligence provided by us to the United Nations? This is not a trivial question. If the United States is accused of either careless indifference or deliberate corruption in matters of this import, what does that do to our reputation and to our image as 'leader of the free world'? Or is Brady Kiesling right – it only matters that others fear our power?)

It would make no sense to suppose that a neutral or non-governmental entity would go to the trouble and expense of falsifying documentation and then convincing 'a number of states' to deliver that evidence to the IAEA. Quite clearly, the more one thinks about this intrigue, the more obvious it becomes that someone was responsible for a deliberate intelligence disinformation campaign targeting the United Nations with an aim toward padding the evidence supporting an American–British invasion of Iraq. That is a world-class criminal act, a felony of historic proportions, by any definition. We should not let it be swept under the carpet.

Ray Close was a CIA analyst in the Near East division.

March 21, 2003

FOURTH-GENERATION PROTESTING: SHUTTING DOWN SAN FRANCISCO'S DOWNTOWN
by Scott Handleman

Thursday, the day after the start of bombing, was the long-anticipated day of direct-action protest in San Francisco. For weeks, the flyers were circulating from Direct Action to Stop the War, and weekly spokescouncil meetings were held, alternating between San Francisco and Oakland. The decentralized planning paid off: Thursday morning seemed like Sunday morning in large parts of San Francisco's financial district.

The most noteworthy thing about this day of protest, I think, was the effectiveness of the new strategy of protest by small, autonomous clusters. A little after midnight yesterday, I got a call to report at 7 am to 9th and Bryant for legal observation. Arriving a few minutes late, I saw a freeway off-ramp blocked by debris and large objects (old sofas, etc). California Highway Patrol officers were pushing back protesters and hauling the obstacles aside, while rush-hour traffic honked in irritation. I understand why some might question the nobility of blocking drivers from getting to work, far from the seats of power that are the true targets, but what was surprising was that, here in Police State America, a group of twenty to thirty openly created a fairly serious (though brief) disruption, and not a single one got arrested. As the cops cleared the ramp and things started looking hot, the crowd started shambling up 9th Street toward Market, taking the wide street and chanting. This bunch, incidentally, was Queers Against Capitalism, marching under a giant pink flag.

Upon reaching Market, the militant queers took over the intersection, still unbothered by cops. Meanwhile, a block away at the intersection of Van Ness and Fell, a small group had occupied the intersection, linking arms in lock-boxes. Van Ness was silent as Market. A block further on, a similar group had the intersection of Franklin and Fell occupied. I fed a banana to a supine young woman in a lock-box, and felt a stirring in my subconscious. Upon returning to Market, the perambulating homosexuals had somehow taken over the major intersection of Van Ness and Market, and the cops had still made no move to arrest. 'Move aimlessly,' a woman on bullhorn directed, and the group moved on.

Bear in mind that there were small numbers at each of these sites. The Queers had perhaps grown to fifty by this point, and the lock-down sites, counting the surrounding supporters, probably had less. Dispersal, and the simultaneity of many happenings, meant the cops' resources were spread thin; they were too busy clearing the sit-down intersections to deal with the troublemakers on foot.

Riding my bike down Market Street, empty of cars, I encountered similar scenes. A sparse crowd, around twenty people, had taken over 6th and Market. This was a guerrilla-theater group in costume, called Dead Against War. Scary horse cops approached, and the group walked off.

At Montgomery and Sutter, in front of the Schwab building, another tiny cluster had taken the intersection, including a core group locked down. A couple of fellows sat in lawn chairs in the middle of the street. This group included a hippyish contingent, joined in a soothing hum. But argument broke out between protesters and an angry driver, a scene that I saw repeated several times today.

At Montgomery and Pine, a group of only seven persons in lock-boxes closed Pine on one side; on the other side, protesters sat on overturned newspaper bins. At Montgomery and California, another tiny group held the intersection. I waited while two bus-loads of cops arrived. The cop's leader came and said: 'You are in violation of the traffic law. I am ordering you to move to the side-walk,' etc etc. The mystery is why this group did not take advantage of their warning and walk around awhile to another intersection, in conformity with the emerging principles of fourth-generation protest. This group sat there and let themselves get arrested.

Montgomery and Clay, the corner of the Transamerica Pyramid, saw another blockading group, some in lock-boxes. Hay was myste-riously scattered in the street, a warm pastoral touch. A firetruck showed up and menacingly took out its hose, but only used it to fill plastic trench plates with water. They drove away, protesters dry. I talked to two white-collar onlookers, mildly sympathetic.

Back to Market, where a group was locked down in boxes, surrounded by a fairly large crowd of protester onlookers (maybe

100). Sparks flew copiously as the firemen cut through a lock-box. It was here that I first saw ugliness on both sides. Someone threw a glass bottle which hit a cop square on the helmet. (He didn't even flinch.) Protesters booed. A line of cops marched briskly into the crowd, and looked around. From my perch high in a tree, I saw the cops' body language. They walked around for a while acting unconvincingly like they were in pursuit of some-body, then the victim-cop pointed at a fellow standing on a bench, and the cops went and grabbed him. I did not see who threw the bottle, but a legal observer later told me it was not the young man who got arrested. It stands to reason that the fellow who threw the thing would try to blend away and not stand in high view. I think the cops just decided they had to punish and deter, so better to arrest an innocent person and show eye-for-an-eye retribution.

(As they were pulling away their unfortunate victim, one of these cops backed into the misplaced bicycle of yrs truly and fell over; another cop somehow fell with him. This severely warped my back tire and broke three spokes. Safe in my tree, I declined to request compensation.)

Meanwhile, the lock-box extractions had been continuing – but the firemen did not break open the box linking the last two protesters. The cops dragged them off, still linked together. This was a piggish move on their part, for it was causing those arrested visibly to shout out in pain, and looked like the sort of thing that might do them lasting physical damage.

I continued down Market, where Christmas trees in big cement planters had been dragged to the middle of the street, and many newspaper vending boxes were overturned. At this point, I stopped taking regular notes. It was probably around 10 in the morning, and anarchy reigned downtown. Unwarping my tire, I rode to the

Federal Building; protesters had shut it down. Red, white and blue vomit puddles all over the sidewalks.

Back downtown, Market remained in chaos; I hooked up with a large and rowdy bunch on Mission Street, around a thousand or so rejoicing in their numbers, Spearhead blasting from bike-ferried speakers. We went back to Market for more intersection facedowns with riot-ready cops. It was 11.45 and I noticed, strangely, that Old Navy was open for business. I went to Civic Center for the noon rally; there was plenty of room and no one listened to the speaker. Ready for home, I headed back down Market. At around 5th Street was a confrontation noteworthy because the cluster of perhaps 100 protesters consisted almost entirely of youth of color (many of high-school age).

From my observations today, I think that small, mobile clusters are a good way to go to make numbers have their maximum effect. The linger-then-escape method of blocking intersections seems ideal in that it frustrates cops and minimizes risk of arrest. It creates thrills and a sense of defiance that a permit-obeying march does not. On the other hand, the cat-and-mouse confrontations of the fourth generation lack a certain dignity and moral high ground associated with the sit-downs. Hard to picture Rosa Parks pull a sofa onto an off-ramp and scram.

I saw a lot of graffiti and overturned newspaper racks, but no smashed windows; I had a feeling the hard-core vandals were planning to let loose at another time, perhaps after the 5 pm convergence at Powell and Market.

By 1.00 I had had enough of the noise and chaos. Our government is still bombing Baghdad, and reflecting on that, I wonder what it all means. None of this is going to Stop the War. Of course, but what will? The day of protest didn't have to stop the war to be a good in itself. Not freedom, but defiance was in the air. People were starring in their own movies, circumstances were revealing the blend of human nature: people honorable and craven, among cops and protesters alike. People got a chance to get together and blow off steam. Last but not least, they sent a strong signal that business will not be tolerated, not if that business is war.

Scott Handleman is a law student at Berkeley. He can be reached at: scotthandle@yahoo.com

March 28, 2003

A ROAD TRIP IN WARTIME
by Daniel Wolff

My thirteen-year-old son and I drove from New York to Memphis and back during the first week of the war.

Thursday, March 20 We will see almost no TV, get most of our news from local papers in the towns we pass through and from the radio. We can bring in National Public Radio stations almost wherever we go, including the long stretch of Highway 81 that cuts south through Pennsylvania Dutch country. NPR's coverage of the war is intelligent, exhaustive, and very carefully modulated. It reminds me of the prose in the higher-end garden catalogues or on the packaging of gourmet foods. The overwhelming impression is that a smart person is talking; so much so that you forget, sometimes, that they're trying to sell you something.

This first day, the news is mostly about the war not going according to plan. There's been tactical bombing of Baghdad instead of 'shock and awe.' The NPR journalists keep repeating that the military is not following the script; isn't it odd they're not following the script; what does it mean that they're not following the script? It's raining hard and the landscape is brown and gray, except for the hex signs painted on the barns.

In Roanoke, Virginia, there's a peace vigil at the downtown war monument. Most of the people holding candles are gray-haired, but there are some teenagers, too. It's the twenty- to forty-year-olds who seem to be missing. A woman tells us that, yes, the city is probably mostly pro-war. Still, about but one out of five cars honks or waves their support. There are no hecklers, no police, and none of the tingling sensation I'm used to at a demonstration about to get dangerous – just thirty or so people standing among the marble slabs engraved with the names of Roanoke's war dead.

Our motel clerk is a black woman in her twenties. She checks us in with a cellphone cradled by her ear; someone's on hold. The war comes up as she hands us our key, and she is adamant. 'We should get out of there. We got no business there.' Does she have friends serving? 'Friends of friends. And we got no business there.' It's not only clear to her, but it's a position she's ready and willing to volunteer to strangers.

Friday, March 21 We're below the Mason-Dixon line and climbing through the mountains of West Virginia to Tennessee. My prejudice is to expect the South to be adamantly and visibly pro-war. On empty hilltops over the fields where cows graze, the owners have often erected three plain wooden crosses, the middle one painted white. And there are military bases all through this area. But the American flags are few and far between, much fewer than after 9/11. There are 'Support Our Troops' signs here and there and yellow ribbons, but not many.

Bristol is where the famous Bristol sessions took place: the first commercial recordings of country music including the Carter Family and the singing brakeman, Jimmie Rodgers. If you cross Main Street from the side with the antique shops filled with Confederate flags to the side with the amateur geek show that includes a chick with two heads in formaldehyde, you're crossing from West Virginia to Tennessee. Today, the streets are busy with trailers and motorcycles pulling into town for the NASCAR race on Sunday.

On the Tennessee side of the street, there's a repair shop with a line of antique jukeboxes, pinball machines, and some video games in the window. The owner's a lanky man with gray hair and glasses, probably in his seventies. He asks how things are in New York. I'm cautiously non-committal: folks are worried. 'I'm worried we're going to end up looking like Hitler,' he volunteers. I can't quite believe he's said that – not on this sunny Main Street in this quiet store. He goes on that he served in World War Two: 1943 in Italy, 1945 in France.

He can't understand why France isn't supporting us: 'We spilled more blood there than they got red wine.' But he also doesn't understand what we're doing there, and he's most worried about what's going to happen after we win. 'Everyone's going to be blaming us, they're gonna want to get back at us, and what'll we have gained?' He shakes his head. We get to Nashville at dusk, and it's packed with tourists for the NCAA basketball game. Here, among the well-fed and slightly tipsy crowd, there are some 'These Colors Don't Run' T-shirts. We overhear a middle-aged man with a shaved head tell his friend: 'Just because I have this haircut doesn't mean I'm a bigot.'

The radio tells us that the first strikes may not have killed Saddam Hussein. On the other hand, the video of him on Iraqi TV doesn't prove he's alive. The local paper profiles families with sons and daughters in the military and editorializes for supporting the troops. There are also good-sized articles covering the antiwar protests both here and overseas. Nashville has the largest Kuwaiti population in the US.

Saturday, March 22 We've been stopping at little towns all along the way, wandering through flea markets where folks are selling their children's toys, used clothes, old records. Now, we drop into Jackson, Tennessee, and the main street is empty but clean. It's hard to judge the economy from the outside, but there are lots of trailer parks and small factories, and the car washes are busy. The downtown pawnshop is full of stereo equipment, guitars, toolboxes and power drills.

NPR interviews various experts, from retired generals to people from think tanks, and they all agree on the good news that the troops are progressing faster than expected towards Baghdad. We are progressing to Memphis and arrive there early enough in the afternoon to tour Graceland. It's a small house.

Tonight, outdoors, to a crowd of some 1,200, George Clinton and P-Funk play a long and inspired concert. The Memphis crowd comes ready to party. There are young white professionals, drunk and feeling each other up; middle-aged black couples doing the funky two-step; here and there a blitzed freak jumping up and down in place. Clinton wanders out an hour into the set. He's a big, gray-haired man who lets his dreadlocks grow down to his shoulders.

As well as singing, cueing the band, and signaling for solos from the fifteen or sixteen musicians and singers who drop in and out, he seems most interested in the crowd's hand clapping. He calls for it, sets the beat, and then listens attentively, his sunglasses pushed up on his head. It's as if the clapping were the true measure of the music. Among his many chants is 'Free your mind and your ass will follow.' The power of the groove to do that – to free people – is apparently best gauged by hand clapping.

We don't know how long the concert eventually lasts, but as we get ready to leave – three and a half hours into the music – the band bumps into 'One Nation Under A Groove,' and it really does seem that way. P-Funk's crazy-ass dream to unite us around James Brown riffs, throaty girl singers and wailing guitar seems to have worked. The open-air space just off Beale Street moves as one kinky, thousand-piston machine. Clinton announces, 'This is America,' and we believe.

Sunday, March 23 West Memphis, Arkansas, at noon is the exact physical manifestation of a hangover. It's sleepy and flat with boarded-up yellow-brick buildings and hand-painted signs announcing barber shops and discount meat. The radio says we're experiencing setbacks. Again, NPR's experts seem mostly shocked, almost angry, that the assault isn't going forward according to plan. One of our own, a black Muslim sergeant, has apparently fragged a tent full of his fellow officers. Iraqis capture an army maintenance unit with twelve missing or captured, and citizens in the southern cities instead of welcoming our troops are resisting.

As we cross the Mississippi, headed back east, NPR runs a long piece on the history of Iraq. Asked what most surprised her in doing the research, the reporter says she wasn't aware how much Saddam Hussein was created and supported by the US.

We drive up through Tennessee and into Kentucky. It sounds like many of the captured and the dead are either from around here or were stationed nearby. The parents of a missing woman soldier explain that she joined the army after high school because she couldn't find any work in her small Kentucky hometown.

In a motel run by a Pakistani couple (their daughter practices cricket out on the driveway), we watch the Oscars. We count the number of celebrities who speak either against the war or for peace. Then Michael Moore wins and begins his speech denouncing the election results, shaking his finger into the camera, and shouting 'Shame on you, Mr Bush' as the music rises to drown him out.

It's offensive. I'm a little surprised at my reaction, but it's offensive. Moore looks big and soft and self-involved: a man who is always talking about himself no matter what. Part of it is the contrast to what we've been seeing. From town to town, most of the people we've talked to seem thoughtful and quietly concerned. They want the country to be a decent place, believe it is, and can't quite fit this war into that picture. They aren't 'radicals' or liberals; they're worried. And everywhere there seems to be a sadness. There's no sadness in Michael Moore's speech, only Michael Moore.

Monday, March 24 A long day's drive through Kentucky and West Virginia to Maryland. At some point in the dry hills, we switch over to AM radio and get G. Gordon Liddy's program. He is lecturing his listeners on the right way of dealing with the antiwar protesters in San Francisco. He recalls with approval how, during the Vietnam War, the Justice Department was prepared to defend its building with machine guns. His rant seems as out of place as Michael Moore's was. The Kentucky Folk Art Center in Morehead features a lot of Judgment Day scenarios: bright red devils pitchforking sinners into hell (a brightly painted tire rim). But fierce and absolute as much of the art is, it's filled with humor. Now, the radio says that the cities we had captured in southern Iraq aren't actually secure. A sandstorm has slowed troops outside of Baghdad. Instead of the single news event – a war – it has become a series of complicated stories. The experts are still eager to give their opinions, but you can almost hear them running out of certainty. It hasn't been a week yet, and the war's gone on too long.

In a bar in Frostburg, Maryland, CNN is playing on one television set while a sit-com plays on another. A thin, unsmiling girl tends bar. All of her customers are men. They talk about the pickup they're selling, the motorcycle they're racing, the loan they're trying to take out on the house. One guy keeps feeding quarters into the pool table, playing by himself and rolling his eyes at the ceiling: 'I ain't been able to shoot anything since yesterday.' Every once in a while, when the announcer's voice gets more insistent, people will look up at the news. It's mostly a clip of two American prisoners of war, repeated over and over.

Occasionally, there's a tank on a desert, lights flaring over a city, a woman in a veil. But nobody's bleeding, nobody's dead. The men look for a moment, then go back to talking and drinking. Draft beer is fifty cents.

Tuesday, March 25 It's stifling in the Pennsylvania Dutch family restaurant, and we leave before ordering. 'Smells like old people,' my son says. Instead, we eat sandwiches by the bank of a stream in Bloomsbury, New Jersey. We've stopped listening to the news much, shifting to a books-on-tape 'Spoon River Anthology.' My son's favorite part is where an old woman goes crazy and burns down their house, dancing on the lawn as the flames leap up.

At home, we're road-numb and glad to be back. We've covered something close to 2,500 miles.

Six days' worth of emails includes lots of denunciations of George Bush: pictures of him looking simple, jokes, messages from friends saying he's various kinds of idiotic. Maybe I'm just tired, but I skip over a lot. The president seems mostly beside the point: a face on which to hang a policy. It's the country we're talking about.

Daniel Wolff lives in New York. He is the author of You Send Me, *the acclaimed biography of the great Sam Cooke, and* Memphis Blues Again, *an exquisite collection of Ernest Withers photographs of Memphis and its streets, people and musicians.*

PART FOUR

THE THIRTEEN YEARS' WAR

March 31, 2003

US PROPAGANDA DURING THE FIRST
TEN DAYS OF THE IRAQ WAR
by Paul de Rooij

It has become much more difficult to sell wars these days, and the propagandists are remarkably inept. Watching CNN or BBC reveals jarring shoddy propaganda that is immediately transparent. Marines 'discovered' a camouflaged chemical weapons factory, but then both CNN and BBC revealed the source of the story: the *Jerusalem Post*. It was then distributed by Fox News. This was the fastest way to discredit the story, which only lasted two days – later exposed as a fabrication by the March 25 *Financial Times*. In the meantime, one of the warmongering neocons appeared on CNN, repeating the story, elaborating the details and saying that there was now proof of the existence of weapons of mass destruction (WMD).

A day later CNN mentioned finding a Scud missile inside a factory – another story with a half-life of a day. On March 26, they were talking about finding 3,000 chemical protection suits, as if this proved something. It is like smelling manure, and then claiming you have found a horse. This story also is destined for the trashcan, if only because Hans Blix, the ex-UN weapons inspector, mustered a pixel of backbone to state that it didn't prove anything. Finally, the first few missiles shot by the Iraqis on Kuwait were intimated to be Scud missiles (illegal under UN resolutions), but this turned out to be false too.

Jacques Ellul, in his book *Propaganda*, states that for propaganda to be effective it must have monopoly and drown out everything else. One of the reasons that propaganda doesn't stick at present is that there are so many alternative information channels. CNN doesn't have a monopoly by any means; at an Amsterdam airport lounge recently, the waiting passengers rebelled and forced the attendants to change the channel! The Internet has also become a very important alternative news source. Robert Fisk's reports on DemocracyNow or his columns in London's *Independent* prove that he is a one-man propaganda demolition machine. Listening to his reports from Baghdad allows one to peer through the fog, and obtain a clearer view of what is happening on the ground. Every other paragraph of Fisk's comments demolishes yet another nonsense statement uttered by Ari Fleischer and his ilk. The hard task of selling or justifying the war has given way to a barrage of lies or semi-lies that only last a few days – thereafter they are immediately forgotten. The next lies follow directly.

On March 26, a missile killed scores of civilians at a Baghdad market and wounded even more. Houses and shops were demolished. The subsequent stream of propaganda is very instructive. It went from: 'Must check what happened,' to 'Inevitably collateral damage occurs,' to 'Likely that an Iraqi missile was the cause of the explosion,' and finally, on March 28 it was: 'It was a missile fired by the enemy.' Another market bombing on March 29 killing sixty-two-plus civilians was immediately denied and blamed on the Iraqis themselves. Some historical background may reveal the real reason for these explosions. During the bombing of Serbia over the Kosovo situation, both the Americans and the general staff were surprised because they expected a quick capitulation. Serious dissension grew within the ranks of the then 'coalition of the willing,' and it was necessary to increase the pressure on the Serbs to obtain their surrender. This was achieved by hitting more military targets, then bridges, railroads, factories, and even the TV station (with some lame justification). After the war, it was revealed that most Serbian factories had been bombed! Even with this bombing intensity, the Serbians didn't yield, and at this point the laptop bombardiers started targeting the civilian population, i.e., plain and simple terrorism in the true sense of the word.

Propaganda also entails censoring things. Most Americans remember the TV scenes where dead US soldiers were dragged through the streets of Mogadishu. Within a week the US's appetite for that intervention collapsed. Americans only accept clean wars, only the ones that appear like a video game. All the blood and gore must be excised, especially if there is blood of American soldiers, and Americans will not see this on TV. When Al Jazeera showed dead Americans it elicited a vicious reply from the censors shutting down websites and hindering Al Jazeera from broadcasting in the US. If the US finds out the coordinates of the Al Jazeera journalist in Basra, then this could be bombed. During the attack on Afghanistan, the Al Jazeera offices in Kabul were bombed when their reporting proved awkward to the media spinners.

Bush's practice session for his 'war ultimatum' speech was shown to Portuguese and Italian TV audiences, but it was never shown on American TV stations. Perhaps the unflattering appearance didn't portray the monosyllabic president as a 'statesman.' The media spinmeisters prefer to have the president with his mouth firmly shut, and at a safe distance from the media. On the eve of the impending war, they chose to film the dear president from a distance on the White House lawn. The burden of worrying about the impending deaths and destruction required some light distraction by throwing some balls for his dogs. But wait, even his dogs ignored him, and they didn't run after the balls he threw! Maybe it is time for a pet change.

The most important propaganda topic deserving some discussion is the reason to go to war and its evolution over time. Months earlier, the warmongers uttered 'regime change' as a justification for the war. This was considered too crass, and it briefly made way for 'Iraq has links to terrorism,' a very short-lived justification. This gave way to 'Rid Iraq of WMD.' A UN inspection team was set up, and it was clear from the beginning that this was meant to fail. Once the UN didn't lend its imprimatur to justify the war, and given the fact that many Europeans sought to continue the inspections regime, then another justification was necessary. Now, 'Let's liberate Iraq' – in other words, a euphemism for 'regime change' – was concocted without much reflection.

There is only one antidote against propaganda, and that is a relevant sense of history and a strong collective memory. When we remember the lessons from the past, and when we remember what happened even a few days ago, then the job of the propagandists and their warmongering bosses becomes much more difficult. It is ultimately when their message is challenged that war can be stopped; bloated armament budgets can be pared; international law can be upheld; and shallow mean-spirited politicians with blood-soaked hands can be put on trial in an international war crimes tribunal.

Paul de Rooij is an economist living in London. He does not spend the whole day glued to the TV – this would have a detrimental effect on anyone's mental health. He is grateful for all the snippets forwarded by many folks.

April 2, 2003

HATING WOLF BLITZER'S VOICE
by Bruce Jackson

I have recently come to hate Wolf Blitzer's voice. I didn't used to hate it, but now I do. Before I came to hate Wolf Blitzer's voice the only TV performer's voice I really hated was George Bush's.

I didn't hate George Bush's voice all the time. When he read speeches crafted for him by Karen Hughes I hated what he was saying, but not so much how he was saying it. That's because Karen Hughes is one of the few speechwriters who could get him to utter words and phrases the way people normally utter them in English – stopping briefly where the text has a comma or semicolon and a little longer where it has a period.

When he's speaking without Karen Hughes's script, Bush usually talks in four- or five-syllable bursts, with the caesurae coming at points where there's no reason for a pause. There is no link between phrase and content, but he hits those dead stops and his eyes dart left and right over that smug born-again grin as if there were. It drives me nuts, that dissonance between George Bush's content and phrases. Watching and listening to unscripted Bush is like being the victim of some mad disco DJ who keeps stopping the disk when everybody is still moving and then starts it again before anybody has figured out where to go next. Neither Bush nor the mad disco DJ give a damn where you are. It's all in terms of some inner beat only they can hear, one that wouldn't make sense to you even if they told you about it.

Wolf Blitzer's voice is a lot like that, only with him it's the punch rather than the pause. Unlike Bush, Blitzer can utter an unscripted and unrehearsed complex sentence. He can utter an unscripted and unrehearsed paragraph. Wolf Blitzer is a very intelligent, informed and articulate man.

But, when he's on camera, all of his sentences have the same number of punches, no matter what the substance. Bush has irrelevant silence; Blitzer has irrelevant punch. It's like they went to the same elocution school but reversed the polarity.

Blitzer has the same velocity, the same hysteria, the same triple stress in every phrase. If I were a musician scoring his voice, the bars would be perfectly regular, the tempo allegro or presto, and I would have at least one fortissimo notation in every single measure. Bam! bam! bam! bam! bam!

Wolf Blitzer is not like that in conversation. In conversation he's like you or me, with ordinary major and minor stresses, inflected and uninflected syllables, and with phrases of varying duration. I've listened to him take a few cellphone calls: there too his voice is like anyone else's on a cellphone. The driving relentless voice is Wolf Blitzer's on-camera television voice. That voice and velocity and stress pattern belongs to his on-camera persona.

You're maybe thinking: 'Well, Jackson, if you don't like Wolf Blitzer's voice you don't have to turn on the TV.' I hardly ever turn on the TV. Most of the time I have the experience of Wolf Blitzer's voice only when I go to the kitchen to get coffee or take a break from working at my desk elsewhere in the house. My wife likes to work in the kitchen. She is capable of sitting at the kitchen table and reading the newspapers, grading exams, or getting ready for class while the TV is on. I am incapable of ignoring the images and voices. When I come into that kitchen from the other part of the house I hear the punch punch punch in Wolf Blitzer's voice before I get close enough to make any sense at all of his words. For Diane, I suppose it's like elevator music; for me it's like somebody doing angry carpentry in the next apartment or someone working with a pneumatic jack down the block.

I became aware of the newsreaders' punching technique at the movies. William Hurt's character Tom Grunick tries unsuccessfully to teach it to Albert Brooks's neurotic Aaron Altman in James L. Brook's *Broadcast News* (1987).

'And try to punch one word or phrase in every sentence,' Grunick tells his hapless friend. 'Punch one idea a story. Punch!'

When he's on camera, Wolf Blitzer is punching all the time. It matters not one iota what the story is. Sometimes the subject deserves punching: major awful things are indeed happening out there, halfway around the world, where the holy war, the terrible jihad of George Bush and Donald Rumsfeld, is being executed. But just as often the subject could have been dealt with in an uninflected aside. It matters not: Wolf Blitzer will fill the time segment with the same number of words, the same number of punches, the same passionate intensity.

A humvee went off the road? a Huey went down killing everyone aboard? bombs destroyed a market where civilians were shopping for food? Rumsfeld and the generals say the war is going well? food and water are being offloaded at an Iraqi port? the Brits have something to say? It's all punched exactly the same, it's all of equivalent value.

Cut for a few minutes to the commercials (a huge portion of which seem to be for garden or pharmaceutical products) or to the guy back in CNN stateside HQ with a tabletop mockup of the war zone, a pointer, and a general as his foil or respondent, or cut to Donald Rumsfeld at a press conference doing his Claude Rains imitation ('You ask me THAT? I'm shocked! SHOCKED!'), and then cut back to Wolf Blitzer with those slightly-out-of-focus Kuwait City minarets over his shoulder and it's as if the camera had never cut away. No matter what the subject: bam! bam! bam! bam! bam!

While Blitzer's voice punches away, headlines of disasters on the battlefield and elsewhere crawl telegraphically across the bottom of the screen, along with the single constant in the CNN universe, the phrase 'CNN the most trusted name in news.' It appears down there in the telegraphic crawl, as if it were the same order of fact and deserved the same kind of belief as the number of dead reported just before and the number of bomber sorties flown against Baghdad reported just after.

And when there is no new news for a minute or so? Then Blitzer asks the 'CNN Web question of the day,' which on Sunday was 'What's the biggest threat to Coalition forces in Iraq? Friendly fire? Weapons of mass destruction?' There was a third alternative I didn't write down and forgot. In what world of sane journalism is such a question subject to a vote by members of a television audience every one of whom is ignorant of every fact at play? Why would 'the most trusted name in news' waste time pooling such ignorance, processing it in its computers, making charts and graphs of the results? Why would 'the most trusted name in news' give currency to the idiotic notion that people of good will can vote on facts?

Before we got any answers, there was another cut to commercials for pharmaceuticals or garden products, after which Blitzer read questions and emails from the audience with exactly the same stresses, same velocity, same implication of significance he earlier reported battlefield casualties and statements by presidents of nations and leaders of armies.

There is no difference, no discrimination. CNN is a world of equal-opportunity information. Facts and pooled ignorance, off-the-wall opinion, all are equal in the carnival of 24/7 reporting.

Anyone who has ever taken high-school physics can recognize what is going on. It's all about gas. A gas will always expand to fill whatever container it occupies. Put the same amount of gas in a little container and a big container and the gas will fill either. The only difference is the distance between gas molecules and pressure in the container. The gas couldn't care less. It has no shape, no form, no structural identity of its own. The only shape comes from the container, the space available to be filled.

Jim Lehrer, in his three- or four-minute summary at the top of *Newshour*, provides just about everything you might have learned in a full day watching CNN or any of its less competent clones. A few minutes spent reading the day's briefs on the *Guardian*'s website will give you a wider range of far more accurate information and a much wider range of informed opinion.

When I was carrying on about this a little while ago in the kitchen, where the TV was on and Wolf Blitzer was talking about something, Diane said: 'You don't get it. For you, TV is information. You're thinking the wrong generation. For Blitzer and CNN, it's entertainment. CNN isn't news; it's entertainment. Get it?'

I got it, and she's right. This is war as entertainment, as titillation. It's war as computer game, only it's more passive because you don't even get to fondle the joystick. Facts don't matter except as things with which to fill space between commercials. One fact is exactly as good as another, one bit of videotape exactly as important as another. CNN is a medium in which there is no difference between noise and information. All that matters is that ever-changing eye-candy appears on the screen, voices you cannot ignore are heard, and you're awake for the lawn product and pharmaceutical commercials.

I hate Wolf Blitzer's voice not because of what he's saying, but because everything he's saying is exactly the same, everything has exactly the same value. All those things are not exactly the same and they do not have exactly the same value. Some are awful, some are unspeakably horrible, none is simple – and not one of the

terrible facts in dispute will be resolved or even clarified by a vote
of the well-meaning ignorant.

*Bruce Jackson is SUNY Distinguished Professor and Samuel P. Capen
Professor of American Culture at University at Buffalo. He edits* Buffalo
Report.

April 3, 2003

BAGHDAD: FAREWELL TO A CITY UNDER SIEGE
by Jo Wilding

I started crying this morning. I thought I was leaving at 8 am in a
convoy for Jordan and I said goodbye to the staff in the Andalus.
Many's the evening I've spent setting the world to rights over tea
and cake round the desk on the ground floor or, in the last week
and a bit, leaning against a post on the roof with Ahmed, looking
out at the city lights, or sometimes the lack of them, and the flashes
and the jets of flame.

It got worse when I said goodbye to the young soldiers on the
street outside, who share their tea with us and tell jokes in mime.
'Ma'assalama,' I said, and added, as a reflex, 'Good luck.' And then
I couldn't bear the thought of them having to face those overwhelmingly powerful tanks and guns and ammunition that can
pierce body armour, with nothing but an aging rifle and a hard hat
to protect them.

Then when all the bags were in the car, there was a mix-up and
the rest of the convoy left without us and I wasn't leaving after all,
and leaving was the last thing in the world I wanted to do, but by

then my defences had lapsed and the crater of sorrow inside me had filled to the top and it overflowed with the tears of Akael's mother for her boy, writhing in pain, with metal in his head, and Nahda's husband for his new wife, crushed in the rubble of the farmhouse, and all the unbelievable, intolerable, uncontainable sadness in this place.

Missing the convoy meant I got to say goodbye to Zaid, at least, because he arrived here at the Service Centre just after I did. He looks tired – he said he hasn't been sleeping, because there's nothing to do all day: no work, no money, nowhere open to go to, not even the kids to play with because they're staying somewhere else.

There's been no chance today to go and catch up with the people we met yesterday in the hospital and find out how they're doing. Akael's mother rebounds around my thoughts. Please let his head wound be shallow.

The bombing is a constant background noise today, a rhythm in stereo with no visible source.

Ali is playing a game on the computer involving tanks firing missiles at things in a city. Wasn't that a bit too close for comfort, I asked, or was it simulator practice in case he needed those skills in the coming weeks? He thought that was funny.

The kids in the Fanar Hotel were playing Risk the other day – basically a war board game, where players invade each other's countries and try to take over the entire world with small plastic pieces. War is deeply strange.

It will probably be a while before any of my friends in Iraq are able to read this, but when you do, this is what I wanted to say. I'm so glad I've met you and had time to hang out with you. Thank you for your friendship, for glasses of tea and numi basra and coffees and nargilehs and songs and chat and gossip and tours of the city and evenings by the river and rollercoaster rides and shared secrets and everything.

I hope you make it safely through this war and I hope you find your freedom, from the bullying of the US/UK and the Iraqi government; I hope you are allowed your peace. Your courage, your dignity, your kindness and humor inspire me. Ma'assalama.

Jo Wilding is a British peace activist from Bristol.

April 5, 2003

WAR MEANS (ALMOST) NEVER HAVING TO SAY YOU'RE SORRY
by Joanne Mariner

It may reflect a purely humanitarian concern for civilian life, or perhaps a more calculated apprehension of what commentators have dubbed the 'Al-Jazeera effect' – the fact that images of civilian death and suffering in Iraq will further inflame an already angry Muslim world. Whether for altruistic or strategic reasons, or a combination of both, President George W. Bush has repeatedly promised that US military forces will take all necessary steps to minimize the number of civilian casualties in the Iraq war. 'I want Americans and all the world to know,' Bush declared in a radio address on Saturday, that US and allied forces 'will make every effort to spare innocent civilians from harm.'

But President Bush and his top military brass have also acknowledged that civilian deaths are inevitable. Baghdad, currently under heavy bombardment, is a city of some 5 million people. Even with careful reliance on precision-guided weapons, any mistakes made during the ongoing 'shock and awe' bombing campaign could be lethal.

Questioned about possible civilian deaths not long before the start of hostilities in Iraq, White House spokesman Ari Fleischer explained that they are an inevitable consequence of war. But, he affirmed, 'The President will regret any action that is taken that does lead to loss of innocent life.'

Fleischer's note of sympathetic regret is worth examining, for it is a telling and accurate indicator of the US government's approach to civilian deaths during armed conflict. Unquestionably, the government would prefer to minimize the number of civilians killed during wartime. It has even instituted certain preventive measures to help achieve this end. But when civilian casualties do occur, the government rarely accepts responsibility for them in any meaningful way.

Judging by past practice, the families of civilians killed in Iraq should not expect official apologies, or compensation, or justice. Nor should they imagine that the US government will expend significant effort investigating why and how their relatives died, or conducting a systematic assessment of how to prevent such deaths in the future.

THE US RECORD ON OFFICIAL APOLOGIES

Official apologies can be understood as the first step on a more extended scale of assuming responsibility for American errors or wrongs. Beyond apologies lies the possibility of compensation for the damage caused and, in some instances, sanctioning of the perpetrator. But the US government is rarely willing to take even this first step. Indeed, in past incidents involving civilian deaths, even extremely high numbers of deaths, the government has been notably unapologetic.

The bombing of Hiroshima and Nagasaki is the most glaring example. More than fifty years later, peace activists persist in their so far unheeded calls for an official apology and compensation. Nor has the government ever apologized for any of the atrocities committed by US forces in Vietnam, including the My Lai massacre, in which hundreds of innocent civilians were killed.

Just before he left office, President William J. Clinton did express regret about a massacre committed during the Korean War at the village of No Gun Ri, in which US troops fired on civilians who were hiding under a railroad bridge, killing a large but unknown number. 'I deeply regret that Korean civilians lost their lives at No Gun Ri,' Clinton said.

But the wording of Clinton's statement was telling. Expressions of regret, in international currency, are not entirely equivalent to apologies. While they indicate sorrow that an incident occurred, they lack the acceptance of responsibility implicit in a full apology. Unsurprisingly, South Korean groups have continued to press the US government to assume responsibility and provide compensation for No Gun Ri and other wartime incidents.

Besides the precise wording of an apology, the form in which it is made is also viewed as meaningful. Formal written apologies, preferably hand-delivered by a personal envoy of the head of state, carry much more weight than informal, verbal expressions of repentance. Squabbles over such differences, in addition to intense attention to wording, have been much in evidence during the acrimonious debate over Japanese apologies for crimes committed against Koreans and Chinese during World War Two.

SOME CIVILIANS COUNT MORE THAN OTHERS

Were one to judge by recent experience, one might conclude that, besides American deaths, the US government only registers Chinese deaths as truly significant. By a clear margin, the government's most openly apologetic response to civilian casualties was with the accidental bombing of the Chinese embassy in Belgrade, which occurred in May 1999 during the US-led war on Yugoslavia.

The embassy bombing, in which three Chinese civilians were killed, drew greater official attention than other far more deadly incidents. Although a total of about 500 civilians were killed during the conflict in Yugoslavia – indeed, 73 Kosovar Albanians died in a single incident in April 1999 – none of these deaths merited a reaction remotely comparable to that of the embassy bombing.

President Clinton personally apologized for the embassy bombing just days after it happened, and this time, for once, his wording was unequivocal: 'I want to say to the Chinese people and to the leaders of China, I apologize.' Members of Congress, too, immediately introduced a concurrent resolution expressing Congress's 'regret and apologies' for the bombing, and extending its 'deepest sympathies and condolences to the Chinese Government, citizens, and families of the bombing's victims.'

A US spy plane's collision with a Chinese plane, although it did not happen during military hostilities, provides a more recent example of US willingness to apologize when good relations with China are at risk. In April 2001, after a US aircraft collided with a Chinese fighter plane, resulting in the pilot's death, the US ambassador to China delivered a personal letter of apology to the Chinese authorities.

'Both President Bush and Secretary of State Powell have expressed their sincere regret over your missing pilot and aircraft,' the letter said. 'Please convey to the Chinese people and to the family of pilot Wang Wei that we are very sorry for their loss ... We are very sorry the entering of China's airspace and the landing did not have verbal clearance.'

No Chinese were killed during the US-led war in Afghanistan, but plenty of Afghans were. According to a survey carried out by Global Exchange, an international human rights group, at least 824 Afghan civilians were killed during the US-led bombing campaign between October 7, 2001, and the end of January 2002. (The researchers emphasized that their survey is far from comprehensive – it covered only ten of Afghanistan's thirty-two provinces – and that the actual number of deaths is higher.) One of the bloodiest single incidents of the war, in fact, may have occurred in mid-2002, after the study ended, and as US military operations in the country were winding down. On July 1, approximately forty-eight civilians, including a number of children, were killed in an air assault on a wedding party in the southern province of Kakarak. Nor have civilian deaths in Afghanistan come to an end. Most recently, in February 2003, Afghan authorities reported that at least seventeen civilians were killed in American bombing raids in the Baghran valley, a remote area of southern Afghanistan.

None of these incidents resulted in a full presidential apology, although President Bush did say that he called Afghan President Hamid Karzai on the telephone after the mistaken attack in July. His statement of remorse, if you can call it that, was studiously bland. 'Any time innocent life is lost,' Bush told Karzai, 'we're sad.' Deputy Defense Secretary Paul Wolfowitz's stab at apologizing was equally feeble. While stating that he regretted the loss of civilian life, he added that 'bad things happen in combat zones,' and the United States had 'no regrets about going after bad guys.'

COMPENSATION AND PROSECUTION

With apologies for the killing of civilians being scarce, it is unsurprising that compensation for such killings is even scarcer, and the criminal prosecution of the perpetrators is scarcer still.

The 1999 Chinese embassy bombing, always the exception, resulted in substantial US compensation both for the damage to the building and for the loss of life. But other than this incident, compensation has been extremely rare.

While it is believed that the CIA gave $1,000 cash to family members of Afghans killed in a mistaken attack that took place in January 2002, the war's other mistaken killings went uncompensated. Global Exchange, the organization that conducted the study of Afghan civilian deaths, has been pressing the US government to compensate Afghans in the amount of $10,000 per family, but so far its appeal has been unsuccessful.

Even the most negligent killings almost never lead to the successful criminal prosecution of responsible members of the military. A review of incidents that resulted in large numbers of civilian deaths shows that charges rarely reach the court-martial stage. When they do, moreover, the defendants are nearly always acquitted.

While civilian casualties may be an inescapable fact of war, it is apparently not one that the Pentagon has any real interest in examining. As former deputy assistant secretary of defense Sarah Sewall pointed out in an op-ed recently published in the *New York Times*, the Department of Defense has never undertaken a systematic evaluation of its record in preventing civilian casualties. Indeed, the military does not even officially tabulate the numbers of civilians killed in each war.

This studied official ignorance belies official expressions of concern. And the government's failure to take responsibility for the damage it wreaks on civilian lives is equally disappointing. Consider the words of an Afghan man who lost much of his family to American bombs. As he told the *Los Angeles Times* last year: 'We thought the Americans were good people. But they just drop their bombs and leave. They don't explain. They don't apologize. They don't even offer to pay for what they did.'

Joanne Mariner is a human rights lawyer based in New York. An earlier version of this article appeared in FindLaw's Writ.

April 7, 2003

EGO, CRUELTY AND LIES
by Diane Christian

CNN ran an elegiac piece on April 5th called 'The Road to Baghdad.' Among other stories it included one of US soldiers in an Iraqi town surrounded by a crowd yelling angrily at them. The soldiers watched uneasily and uncomprehendingly as people gestured and called out at them. The voiceover said the soldiers had been invited by a religious leader, but the crowd hadn't known this and just vented anger or anguish at their presence. The soldiers' response was to kneel down and to turn their weapons upside down. This quelled and calmed everyone. It took my breath away and made me cry.

The line from Isaiah that we can beat our swords into plowshares and our spears into pruning hooks is inscribed on the wall of the United Nations. The text goes on to predict that man can come to not learn war any more.

Can war make peace, as Saint Augustine's 'the purpose of war is peace' suggests? I presume the saint isn't cynical and just spinning or rationalizing. How could it be that fighting for peace isn't like fucking for virginity – i.e. the wrong tactic, as the Vietnam protesters chanted? Is war the required method to destroy a warmaker? Or is war the required pain that precedes the relief which comes when you stop banging your head against the wall? Or is it a mystery which can invoke its opposite – soldiers kneeling down and lowering their weapons? Christ and Gandhi and King preached peace and got assassinated as dangerous people. Everybody dies.

I search the news for bits of worry and self-consciousness – loving the soldier who fears his wife will think of him as a killer, applauding the officer who told the Marine to take down the American flag as we're not in Iraq to conquer but to liberate. In our wars pictures show soldiers fighting, suffering and handing out candy to kids, or sharing a smoke with a wounded enemy or carrying a wounded child. What you have to buy in a war scenario is that destruction is the necessary tool – like surgery. In this war we boast that we're even more surgical and precise in our targeting than in the 1991 Gulf War. We are destroying a regime of bad people, not the good people they oppress.

We see fireworks more than rubble and body parts. We see 24/7 coverage but we don't see much human damage or the dark side of destruction. 'Iraqi Freedom' may seem less sanitized than the wars where no photo of wounded or dead was permitted, but it is really even more sanitized because it claims to show more. The generals warn us that war isn't pretty, that war is cruel, that we regret all casualties. But they and the networks are anxious to protect us from the real scene. The Greek dramatists too insisted violence occur 'off-scene' – which is the literal meaning of 'obscene.' Ted Koppel quoted a Jack Nicholson movie general who sneered 'You can't stand to see it' and Ted opined we could and promised he would show us.

Nobody admits to feasting on the drama – to loving the blood and guts and thrill of vicarious danger. Our media priests and political leaders perform rituals pretending objectivity, detachment, humanity, national piety. That beautiful moment on the road to Baghdad is not war but peace, packaged into the story of war. Human history is a tragedy of ego and cruelty and lies. Only art approaches it. TV news is a soap – neither the real thing nor art, just entertainment.

Diane Christian is SUNY Distinguished Teaching Professor at University at Buffalo.

April 8, 2003

SAVING PRIVATE LYNCH: HOLLYWOOD AND WAR

by Doug Lummis

I have been hearing (I only have radio, no TV) over and over about the Heroic Rescue of Jessica Lynch. Bless her soul, I hope she gets well. But the reports raise doubts at various levels.

First, they say her arms and legs were broken. Hard to think of an accident that would do all that. And there were eight or nine dead GIs where she was. If they had been killed in the battle, the Iraqis would not have dragged them to the hospital. Maybe they were wounded, and all died of their wounds, but that sounds unlikely.

What seems likely is that those deaths, and Jessica's broken limbs, were the indirect result of the Heroic Rescue. It's common sense that one of the dangers in a rescue attempt like that is that when the captors see that rescue is coming, they kill the prisoners rather than have them taken away. If it turns out that the eight or nine died just when the rescue was taking place, that would be pretty strong evidence that it was the rescue that killed them.

Second, to what extent was this Heroic Rescue designed as a media event?

Nothing new in that: it has been pretty well proven that the assault on Mount Suribachi at Iwo Jima in World War Two (not just the flag-raising, but the whole assault) was largely a US Marine Corps media event. If it turns out to be true that the Heroic Rescue was also a media event, then the eight or nine dead and Ms Lynch's broken arms and legs will be something that the US planners will be hard put to explain (not that I absolve whoever did the killing and breaking).

Which leads to point three. One of my heroes, Allen Nelson, a Vietnam vet who turned pacifist and comes to Okinawa a lot, once told me: 'You know what surprised me the most the first time I went into combat? [long pause] There was no music.' For us moviegoers and TV viewers, war is something that is accompanied by music. It's the music that gives it its dignity. But on the battlefield, no music. But now on Fox and all the crap I get on the radio, the music has been restored. I get musical background to Bush's speeches, music between battle descriptions, music backing up Central Command briefings. This is a movie.

The advocates of the New American Century talk about the Roman Empire as a model, but I had been thinking, at least we don't do the Circus: battles to the death as entertainment. But now it has begun. Today I listened to (and I guess people with TVs watched) a live battle in which people were killed. You could see dead and dying bodies on real time. With music. After experiencing live (live-to-dead?) entertainment like this, can we hope that the viewers will be willing to go back to ordinary sitcoms?

Douglas Lummis is a political scientist living in Okinawa and the author of Radical Democracy. *Later on, Lummis's instincts were entirely confirmed. It turned out that the whole 'rescue' had been contrived as US PR: the hospital was not guarded; the hospital staff had tried to return Lynch; the behavior of the US troops in the unguarded hospital was violent.*

April 9, 2003

THE *NEW YORK TIMES* AND THE PEACE MOVEMENT
by Susan Davis

We need to remember that the antiwar movement has done something, and become something, remarkable. It's an international movement that has made it impossible for many otherwise supportive governments to join the coalition of the 'bribed and the bullied.' It brought much of the world to a halt on the day the bombing began, in huge demonstrations, strikes, school walkouts and civil disobedience. It's also time to recognize that the Bush administration has a great deal at stake in containing and isolating the domestic influence of the antiwar movement.

So let's take a look at one particular *New York Times* article. There it was, on Saturday March 29, below the fold on the first page of section B. It was titled 'Antiwar Movement Morphs from Wild-Eyed to Civil,' by Kate Zernike and Dean E. Murphy. This is not the worst article, not the best article, but it was a major piece of reporting, and one of the few by the mainstream media, which in general has frozen the antiwar movement out of serious coverage until recently. Here are five major points.

A first piece of conventional wisdom: the antiwar movement failed, because it failed to stop the war.

Second point: the antiwar movement is relatively recent, mobilized, at its earliest, after September 11, 2001. Therefore it is wider than it is deep.

Third pillar of wisdom: antiwar movements are protest movements − and limited to protest only, in the politest formulations. Protest is an entitlement in a democracy, as long as it doesn't threaten to change anything.

Fourth wisdom, encapsulated in the headline: the antiwar movement was wild-eyed, has been mainstreamed – a threat to good manners has been contained, because a sensible antiwar movement will try not to offend anyone. In order to appeal to the majority, you must not offend anyone.

Fifth wisdom: the antiwar movement is now being run from the top down (big sigh of relief), once again by responsible people. It's made up of mostly white peaceniks, guided by large organizations with public relations consultants, and it only connects tangentially with other so-called 'interest groups' like the religious, organized labor, and civil rights groups.

Now, I think it's a great error to consider the movement thus far a failure. We have done something remarkable. We have built an international movement that has made it much harder than it might have been for the Bush administration to act militarily. We built a prewar, antiwar movement before the local and national media took very much notice at all. And this was in spite of insistent mass media celebration – on CNN, MSNBC, Fox News, to name only television – that for fully six months made war seem inevitable. It is true that the attack on Iraq had been planned long before September 11, 2001, but it was never inevitable. Popular pressure from below delayed and delayed the attack, forced more and more spin-doctoring and manufactured evidence, and brow-beating and arm-twisting. As a result, the shifting and specious arguments for the war became more and more implausible, and the war's real, if mixed, rationale became more naked. The international antiwar resistance and mobilizations gave voice to skepticism and sentiment that already existed, and they fanned those sentiments. The resistance may very well have held back, and may still hold back, a further push into Iran.

The lack of cooperation from Turkey is an example. So are the resignations of Labour MPs and cabinet ministers in Great Britain. The premier of Indonesia, the largest Muslim country in the world, told George W. Bush that this adventure was a very, very bad idea, and George W. Bush had to listen. There are many more examples, all of them unprecedented, and largely unrecognized by the official voices that we have almost always to listen to.

Second: that the antiwar movement emerged in the last year, or at most two. It is true that following September 11, 2001, peace activists and citizens began to meet to discuss what might happen, and then to think through what a war in Afghanistan might mean in terms of future US policies, and the prospects for peace. Teach-ins, panels at universities, began immediately following September 11, and vigils as well. These were reinvigorated in the last year.

But there's been a long continuity of activism to draw on in the last decade, again largely under the radar of the mainstream media. The networks of independent media and Internet activism that the antiwar movement draws on grew out of the anti-globalization movements that became visible in Seattle. But they also drew on the knowledge and activism of the Anti-Nafta campaigns of the early 1990s, the movement for redress for the veterans of the first Gulf War, the American victims of which may number as many as 100,000 sick men, the anti-sweatshop movement, the living wage movement. These movements – and future historians will have to argue about their size and connections – have educated a generation of young people about the United States' political and economic relationship to the world. The last time this happened was with the Central American solidarity movement in the 1980s. And then there are the efforts of pacifists like Voices in the Wilderness – which have been part of a movement protesting the sanctions on Iraq for years. It's notable in the *New York Times* recent coverage of peace demonstrations that the name of Voices in the Wilderness cannot be mentioned. It's because their pacifist radicalism is deep and continuous. A base was there to draw on, and it usually spoke from deeply moral positions, rather than strategic or tactical positions.

Third point – and really my most important. Conventional wisdom would like the antiwar movement to be just protest, just disagreement, safely cordoned off. It's not just protest, as important as visible dissent is. One of the big successes of the antiwar movement is that it has been able to influence the media – in the face of unrelenting propaganda blitzes from the official sources, in the face of an enormous effort to make the war seem inevitable.

How has it done this? Certainly the Internet has been important – but without all the networks laid down, there would be nothing so powerfully informational to put on the Internet except for the same old stories. The Internet has absolutely been key, but so have the hundreds, maybe thousands of small groups meeting around the country to talk about the war and its meaning for the future of the United States. Talking about it, sharing information about it, digesting the news, and especially digesting the news from the foreign press which gives a much different perspective than the US press. In that way antiwar groups have been the media.

But also by writing position papers, flyering, cracking open the editorial pages of the local conglomerate chain media – forcing the local paper to cover them at the same time that they are working hard to produce real local media – organizing and faithfully attending demonstrations – these local activists have made the antiwar position news. They also worked hard to make the connections clear between the war and terrorism at home, with its repressive apparatus embodied in the USA Patriot Act, and the assault on Iraq. Taking up the space both physical, with demonstrations, and informational, with letter writing and editorial writing, the antiwar movement has become a movement for re-democratization of American society.

The fact that all over the country and here in Urbana we've been responded to by a corporate-sponsored pro-war campaign, orchestrated by radio station chains like clear channel and sponsored by Coca-Cola, means that we really forced ourselves into the picture. This is serious business.

More wisdom from the *New York Times*: the movement has become mainstream. It has broken with International Answer and its sectarian original organizers (who were not the movement's original organizers, let's make the distinction, but were organizers of mass demonstrations). The problem according to the *Times* – and certainly the leaders of Win Without War – was that the antiwar movement connected the impending attack on Iraq with supposedly unrelated domestic issues like the death penalty, the case of Mumia Abu Jamal and racism, and other international crises, such as the war under way in Palestine. In other words, the smaller, more radical and less generously funded antiwar groups insisted on connecting state violence, government authoritarianism and the Israeli war on the Palestinians, racism at home and abroad, with the assault on Iraq.

But more importantly, the rest of the world sees these issues as connected – they see the war on Iraq as a racist war, they continuously point out its connections to the United States' support for Israel, they see the connection between barbaric practices at home, such as the death penalty, and barbaric histories abroad.

This is what the pro-war party means when it says that the peace movement is 'anti-American': it means it is willing to consider the war in light of the broader picture of American relations abroad, many of which have been moral outrages. It is infuriating to many in the so-called mainstream that the heart of the antiwar movement recognizes Arab rage over the nuclear arming of Israel and US support for its policies toward Palestine. I think it is infuriating to the so-called political mainstream that American pacifists acknowledge and want to speak about the Israeli peace movement, and fears among the Israeli people aroused by this war. In the past, these were words that could not be spoken, and thoughts that could not be thought. But should not the antiwar movement in the United States continue to make these connections? Undoubtedly, given its origins and the work it has already done, it will make them, and perhaps pay the cost of being 'mainstream.'

Or perhaps the mainstream has moved just a little bit, just a little bit – and perhaps the antiwar movement has moved it. It is just possible that mobilization against this particular latest war is causing cracks in the American consciousness of foreign policy. It's very hard work, but some of the antiwar activists I know have simply refused to be intimidated by charges of anti-Semitism. That simple refusal, so hard, so painful, is so important. And so offensive.

Fifth point: that – big sigh of relief – it's being run from the top down by responsible people. They are using corporate-style public relations techniques to keep everybody on message. The *New York Times* writes: 'protest has become routine. It is no longer seen as an assault on the country's values.' Groups like the Sierra Club now find they can take an antiwar position. Well, that's a relief. Just a few months ago the Sierra Club was trying to expel local chapters for taking public antiwar positions. But this can happen because of the formulation linking antiwar sentiment to patriotism. Responsible people support the troops – they may be antiwar but they support the troops. Peace is patriotic. Carl Pope is patriotic.

While the patriotism of pacifists has always been an argument, it really got wheeled out in the big demonstrations after Christmas, and as groups like Win Without War, and MoveOn.org, which the *New York Times* especially approves of, stepped to the forefront to help organize the enormous national demonstrations of January and February and March. These were very useful and very threatening demonstrations. But in Win Without War's formulations, and I think arguably MoveOn.org's approach, the United States' policy towards Iraq before the war was fundamentally acceptable. That's a problem.

Groups like Voices in the Wilderness have worked for years to undermine the acceptability of so-called containment, which as Jeff Gunsel of Voices points out is really just another word for sanctions – but sanctions were becoming politically unacceptable. If you look today at MoveOn.org's call for letters to the editor about the management of postwar Iraq there isn't a single critical connection made – the argument is simply back to the status quo of European nations managing what will be Middle Eastern occupied territory.

There should be some limits on how responsible we want to be. There should be some limits, given the scale of mass death, the violation of the Nuremberg and Geneva conventions by our own country, the scale of impoverishment of an already brutalized country – some limits on how polite we want to be about this. If 'peace is patriotic' and 'support the troops' mean we will back off from these questions of illegality and atrocity – illegality and atrocities that are transparent to hundreds of millions of people around the world – then I strongly argue that we continue to have bad manners.

For after all, if we support the troops, do we really want our young men and women to have to say they were 'just following orders' as they move from one theater of war to what I am pretty certain will be the next?

Susan Davis teaches at the University of Illinois, Urbana-Champaign. She is the author of Spectacular Nature.

April 19, 2003

PATRIOT GORE: THE FATAL FLAWS IN THE PATRIOT MISSILE SYSTEM
by Jeffrey St. Clair

> Once the rockets are up
> Who cares where they come down?
> That's not my department
> Says Wernher von Braun.
>
> ('Wernher von Braun' by Tom Lehrer)

This time around it was going to be different. This time around the Patriot missile was going to live up to all the hype, unlike in the first installment of the Gulf War when the missiles nearly struck out against Iraqi Scuds, the softballs of the ballistic missile world.

There was a lot riding on the Patriot missile system's success. Not just the safety of American and British troops and journalists or Kuwaitis and Israelis, who feared they might be targets of Iraqi Scud missiles (assuming the regime had any left). The new and improved Patriot missile also was going to demonstrate the efficacy of the Bush administration's mad rush to deploy a revamped Ballistic Missile Defense System, the Star Wars of Reagan's fantasy. Billions in defense contracts were riding on the backs of those missile batteries.

As in the first Gulf War, the initial reports on the new Patriots were breathlessly glowing. As missile sirens went off in Kuwait, embedded reporters ritually donned their chemical gas masks, descended into bunkers, then emerged minutes later to announce that they'd been saved by the mighty Patriot missile.

The mobile missile batteries supposedly knocked down several Iraqi Scuds headed toward US Army positions and Kuwait City. Later, it turned out that the missiles weren't Scuds and they may have been brought down in the Kuwait desert under their own momentum, not by US missiles.

Then came the really bad news. On March 24, a Patriot missile battery near the Kuwait border locked onto a British Royal Air Force Tornado G-4 jet that was returning from a raid on Basra. Four Patriot missiles were fired and one hit the jet, destroying the plane and killing two British pilots. Two days later, the radar for another Patriot missile battery locked onto a US F-16. The pilot of the fighter jet located the radar dish and destroyed it. Then on April 2 a US Navy F/A-18 Hornet was shot down by another Patriot missile, killing the pilot.

'They're looking into a software problem,' said Navy Lt. Commander Charles Owens. 'They're going to check everything out. When they do find a fault, they'll put it out to the rest of the world.' But Pentagon watchers aren't holding their breath. Based on past experience, it's more likely that Pentagon brass will attempt to obscure the cause rather than reveal a fatal design flaw in a revered centerpiece in the Army's new arsenal of smart weapons.

Indeed, there's plenty of evidence that the Pentagon and the Patriot's contractors (Raytheon and Lockheed) have known for nearly a decade that the missile has difficulties discriminating incoming missiles from friendly aircraft. The target discrimination problem was first revealed during testing at Nellis Air Force Base in 1993. During that test a US aircraft simulating a return home from a mission was flying in a corridor reserved for friendly aircraft but still would have been shot down by the Patriot were it a combat situation.

Over the years, billions had been poured into the program with little sign of improvement in this fundamental and lethal defect.

Subsequent exercises and tests have revealed that the Patriot radar discrimination problems were not solved, according to Philip Coyle, former Director, Operational Test and Evaluation, the Pentagon's independent testing office. Coyle says the problems were identified in so-called Joint Air Defense Operations/Joint Engagement Zones exercises during the mid-1990s.

Despite this, the Pentagon pushed to increase production of the Patriot III in the months leading up to the invasion of Iraq. In November 2002, Lt. Gen. Ronald Kadish, the head of the Pentagon's Missile Defense Agency, told Congress that the Army needed to dramatically step up production of the new Patriots, not only for use in Iraq but also 'to counter threats in North Korea, Iran and Libya.'

'My recommendation is to buy PAC-3s as fast as we are able to buy them,' Kadish said. When asked about problems with the system, Kadish brushed them off, saying they were merely 'minor' and 'annoying.' Congress consented, ever anxious to peddle Pentagon pork, and boosted Patriot missile production by more than 10 per cent.

As usual with the Pentagon, cost is no object. But the Patriot is a very expensive system and it's getting costlier all the time. Raytheon and Lockheed originally promised to deliver the new system for $3.7 billion dollars. Now the cost has soared to $7.8 billion. Each Patriot missile unit costs about $170 million. In the first Gulf War, an average of four missiles were launched against a single incoming Scud.

The old PAC-2 is seriously flawed. But the new version of the Patriot has struggled through field testing, although this didn't deter the Pentagon's rush to increase production. Through the summer of 2002, the new Patriot missile had failed more than half of its field tests.

From the beginning there were signs of serious glitches in the software program that guides the missile. The program was two years behind schedule and the costs soared from $557 million to $1.1 billion for the software alone. And still it has never worked right. By 2001, the cost overruns for the system had topped $10 million a month.

You simply can't trust the Pentagon to be honest about the performance of its big ticket items. During the first Gulf War, the generals crowed about the success of the Patriot, saying that it hit more than 80 per cent of its targets. In fact, the missile scarcely hit any incoming missiles, as was revealed in a General Accounting Office investigation. The GAO audit concluded that the Patriot missiles hit less than 9 per cent of the Iraqi Scud missiles that were launched during the first Gulf conflict.

'The results of these studies are disturbing,' said Theodore Postol, the MIT scientist who studied the Patriot missile's kill rate in the first Gulf War. 'They suggest that the Patriot's intercept rate during the Gulf War was very low. The evidence from these preliminary studies indicates that the Patriot's intercept rate could be much lower than 10 per cent, perhaps even zero.' The Pentagon went after Postol with a vengeance, accusing him of using classified documents for his conclusions on the ineptitude of the Patriot system.

What's more disturbing is that the Pentagon knew all this and covered it up. So did the Patriot's prime contractor, Raytheon. In the immediate aftermath of the Gulf War, the US Army issued two assessments on the Patriot missile system's performance: one on Patriot Scud kills in Israel and another in Saudi Arabia. Initially, the Pentagon claimed a success rate of 80 per cent in Saudi Arabia and 50 per cent in Israel. A few months later, the Pentagon scaled those back to 70 per cent and 40 per cent. A year later, the Pentagon admitted that it had a high degree of confidence in only 'ten per cent' of the kills.

Why the slow comedown? American wars have served as live firearms shows. The hype on the Patriot, which the US media eagerly gobbled up, was designed to help market the missile system to other nations. In the immediate aftermath of the first Gulf War, more than a dozen nations placed orders for Patriot missile systems. The contracts were signed before the purchasers (including Turkey, South Korea, Kuwait and Saudi Arabia) learned of the Patriot's weak batting average.

There were lethal consequences to the Patriot's failures during the first Gulf War, which the Pentagon glossed over. On February 25, 1991, a Patriot missile battery in Dharhan, Saudi Arabia, missed an incoming Iraqi Scud. The Scud hit an army barrack housing US soldiers. It killed 28 people and injured more than 100 others.

The Patriot missile is based on 1970s technology and was originally designed for use as an anti-aircraft weapon, a role it reverted to with tragic consequences in the latest Gulf War. In the 1980s, the Patriot was modified to serve as an anti-ballistic missile system for use against short-range rocket attacks.

'The Pentagon has known for a decade that the Patriot cannot distinguish its targets from our own aircraft,' says Danielle Brian, Executive Director of the Project on Government Oversight, a Pentagon watchdog group. 'It is an outrage that they have not fixed this fundamental flaw, yet continue to buy it and sell it to our allies, and have the gall to promote this weapon in both Gulf Wars as a star when they've known it is a dud.'

April 22, 2003

WHAT IS HAPPENING IN THE UNITED STATES?
by Edward Said

In a scarcely reported speech given on the Senate floor on March 19, the day the war was launched against Iraq, Robert Byrd, Democrat of West Virginia and the most eloquent speaker in that chamber, asked: 'What is happening to this country? When did we become a nation which ignores and berates our friends? When did we decide to risk undermining international order by adopting a radical and doctrinaire approach to using our awesome military might? How can we abandon diplomacy when the turmoil in the world cries out for diplomacy?'

No one bothered to answer him, but as the vast American military machine now planted in Iraq begins to stir restlessly in other directions in the name of the American people, their love of freedom and their deep-seated values, these questions give urgency to the failure, if not the corruption of democracy we are living through.

Let's examine first what US Middle East policy has wrought since George W. Bush came to power almost three years ago in an election decided finally by the Supreme Court, not by the popular vote. Even before the atrocities of September 11, Bush's team had given Ariel Sharon's government a free hand to colonize the West Bank and Gaza, to kill, detain and expel people at will, to demolish their homes, expropriate their land, imprison them by curfew and hundreds of military blockades, make life for them generally speaking impossible; after 9/11, Sharon simply hitched his wagon to 'the war on terrorism' and intensified his unilateral depredations against a defenseless civilian population, now under occupation for thirty-six years, despite literally tens of UN Security Council resolutions enjoining Israel to withdraw and otherwise desist from its war crimes and human rights abuses. Bush called Sharon a man of peace last June, and kept the $5 billion subsidy coming without even the vaguest hint that it was at risk because of Israel's lawless brutality. On October 7, 2001 Bush launched the invasion of Afghanistan, which opened with concentrated high-altitude bombing (increasingly an 'anti-terrorist' military tactic, bearing in its effects and structure a strong resemblance to ordinary, garden-variety terrorism), and by December had installed in that devastated country a client regime with no effective power beyond a few streets in Kabul. There has been no significant US effort at reconstruction, and it would seem the country has returned to its former abjection, albeit with a noticeable return of elements of the Taliban, as well as a thriving drug-based economy.

Since the summer of 2002, the Bush administration has conducted an all-fronts campaign against the despotic government of Iraq and, having unsuccessfully tried to push the Security Council into compliance, began its war along with the United Kingdom against the country. I would say that from about last November on, dissent disappeared from a mainstream media swollen with a surfeit of ex-generals and ex-intelligence agents sprinkled with recent terrorism and security experts drawn from the Washington right-wing think tanks. Anyone who spoke up and actually managed to appear was labeled anti-American by failed academics who mounted websites to list 'enemy' scholars who didn't toe the line. Emails of the few visible public figures who struggled to say something were swamped, their lives threatened, their ideas trashed and mocked by media newsreaders who had just become the self-appointed, all-too-embedded sentinels of America's war.

An overwhelming torrent of crude as well as sophisticated material appeared everywhere equating the tyranny of Saddam

Hussein not only with evil, but with every known crime: much of this in part was factually correct but it eliminated from mention the extraordinarily important role played by the US and Europe in fostering the man's rise, fueling his ruinous wars, and maintaining his power. No less a personage than the egregious Donald Rumsfeld visited Saddam in the early Eighties as a way of assuring him of US approval for his catastrophic war against Iran. The role of the various US corporations who supplied Iraq with nuclear, chemical and biological material for the weapons that we supposedly went to war for was simply erased from the public record.

All this and more was deliberately obscured by both government and media in manufacturing the case for the further destruction of Iraq which has been taking place for the past month. The demonization of the country and its strutting leader turned it into a simulacrum of a formidable quasi-metaphysical threat whereas – and this bears repeating – its demoralized and basically useless armed forces were a threat to no one at all. What was formidable about Iraq was its rich culture, its complex society, its long-suffering people: these were all made invisible, the better to smash the country as if it were only a den of thieves and murderers. Either without proof or with fraudulent information, Saddam was accused of harboring weapons of mass destruction that were a direct threat to the US 7,000 miles away. He was identical with the whole of Iraq, a desert place 'out there' (to this day most Americans have no idea where Iraq is, what its history consists of, and what besides Saddam it contains) destined for the exercise of US power unleashed illegally as a way of cowing the entire world in its Captain Ahab- like quest for reshaping reality and imparting democracy to everyone. At home the Patriot and Terrorist Acts have given the government an unseemly grip over civil life. A dispiritingly quiescent population for the most part accepts the bilge, passed off as fact, about imminent security threats, with the result that preventive detention, illegal eavesdropping and a menacing sense of a heavily policed public space have made even the university a cold, hard place to be for anyone who tries to think and speak independently.

The appalling consequences of the US and British intervention in Iraq are only just beginning to unfold, first with the coldly calculated destruction of its modern infrastructure, then with the looting and burning of one of the world's richest civilizations, and finally the totally cynical American attempt to engage a band of motley 'exiles' plus various large corporations in the supposed rebuilding of the country and the appropriation not only of its oil but also its modern destiny. In his reaction to the dreadful scenes of looting and burning which in the end are the occupying power's responsibility, Rumsfeld managed to put himself in a class beyond even Hulagu. 'Freedom is untidy,' he said on one occasion, and 'Stuff happens' on another. Remorse or sorrow were nowhere in evidence.

General Jay Garner, handpicked for the job (and soon fired), seems like a person straight out of the TV serial *Dallas*. The Pentagon's favorite exile, Ahmad Chalabi, for example, has intimated openly that he plans to sign a peace treaty with Israel, hardly an Iraqi idea. Bechtel has already been awarded a huge contract. This too in the name of the American people. The whole business smacks of nothing so much as Israel's 1982 invasion of Lebanon.

This is an almost total failure in democracy, ours as Americans, not Iraq's. Seventy per cent of the American people are supposed to be for all this, but nothing is more manipulative and fraudulent than polls of random numbers of Americans who are asked whether they 'support our President and troops in time of war.' As Senator Byrd said in his speech, 'there is a pervasive sense of rush and risk and too many questions unanswered. A pall has fallen over the

Senate Chamber. We avoid our solemn duty to debate the one topic on the minds of all Americans, even while scores of our sons and daughters faithfully do their duty in Iraq.' Who is going to ask questions now that that Middle Western farm boy General Tommy Franks sits triumphantly with his staff around one of Saddam's tables in a Baghdad palace?

I am convinced that in nearly every way, this was a rigged, and neither a necessary nor a popular war. The deeply reactionary Washington 'research' institutions that spawned Wolfowitz, Perle, Abrams, Feith and the rest provide an unhealthy intellectual and moral atmosphere. Policy papers circulate without real peer review, adopted by a government requiring what seems to be rational (even moral) justification for a dubious, basically illicit policy of global domination. Hence, the doctrine of military preemption, which was never voted on either by the people of this country or by their half-asleep representatives. How can citizens stand up against the blandishments offered the government by companies like Halliburton, Boeing and Lockheed? And as for planning and charting a strategic course for what in effect is by far the most lavishly endowed military establishment in history, one that is fully capable of dragging us into unending conflicts, that task is left to the various ideologically based pressure groups such as the fundamentalist Christian leaders like Franklin Graham who have been unleashed with their bibles on destitute Iraqis, the wealthy private foundations, and such lobbies as AIPAC, the American-Israel Public Affairs Committee, along with its associated think tanks and research centers.

What seems so monumentally criminal is that good, useful words like 'democracy' and 'freedom' have been hijacked, pressed into service as a mask for pillage, muscling in on territory, and the settling of scores. The American program for the Arab world is the same as Israel's. Along with Syria, Iraq theoretically represents the only serious long-term military threat to Israel, and therefore it had to be put out of commission for decades. What does it mean to liberate and democratize a country when no one asked you to do it, and when in the process you occupy it militarily and, at the same time, fail miserably to preserve public law and order? The mix of resentment and relief at Saddam's disappearance that most Iraqis feel has brought with it little understanding or compassion either from the US or from the other Arab states, who have stood by idly quarreling over minor points of procedure while Baghdad burned. What a travesty of strategic planning when you assume that 'natives' will welcome your presence after you've bombed and quarantined them for thirteen years. The truly preposterous mindset about American beneficence, and with it that patronizing Puritanism about what is right and wrong, has infiltrated the minutest levels of the media. In a story about a seventy-year-old Baghdad widow who ran a cultural center from her house – wrecked in the US raids – and is now beside herself with rage, *New York Times* reporter Dexter Filkins implicitly chastises her for having had 'a comfortable life under Saddam Hussein,' and then piously disapproves of her tirade against the Americans – 'and this from a graduate of London University.'

Americans have been cheated, Iraqis have suffered impossibly, and Bush looks like the moral equivalent of a cowboy sheriff who has just led his righteous posse to a victorious showdown against an evil enemy. On matters of the gravest importance to millions of people, constitutional principles have been violated and the electorate lied to unconscionably. We are the ones who must have our democracy back. Enough of smoke and mirrors and smooth-talking hustlers.

Edward Said, who died on September 25, 2003, authored Orientalism, Out of Place: A Memoir, Freud and the Non-European, *and many other books.*

May 3, 2003

THE CONTINUING DANGER
OF CLUSTER BOMBS
by Joanne Mariner

Human rights groups criticize cluster munitions for the threat they pose to civilians; the Pentagon defends them for their effectiveness. With the Iraq war, the debate over cluster bomb use has a new test case.

The US military used cluster munitions in 1991, during the Persian Gulf War; in 1999, during the Kosovo conflict; and in 2001 and 2002 in Afghanistan. The resulting civilian casualties led human rights groups to urge the Pentagon not to deploy the weapon in or near populated areas during the war in Iraq.

Recent statements by the chairman of the Joint Chiefs of Staff suggest that the Pentagon has taken heed of this advice. At a press conference in Washington last Friday, General Richard B. Myers said that US and British forces had dropped 'nearly 1,500 cluster bombs of varying types' during the Iraq War, but that only 26 of these bombs had hit targets within 1,500 feet of civilian neighborhoods. The result, he noted with satisfaction, was 'only one recorded case of collateral damage' caused by cluster munitions. (This means, in non-military-speak, that only one civilian was killed or injured.)

It would be heartening to think that the Pentagon is finally getting the message. Although twenty-six cluster bombs aimed at or near civilian areas are twenty-six too many, they obviously represent a tiny proportion of the total ordnance used in Iraq. Unfortunately, Myers's figures are highly disingenuous. They only cover air-dropped cluster munitions, not the surface-launched type that are believed to have caused many more civilian casualties in

Iraq. Not only that, but unexploded cluster bomblets, lying in wait for future victims, are likely to increase the toll of civilian deaths and injuries.

WHAT CLUSTER BOMBS ARE

Cluster bombs are large weapons that contain dozens and often hundreds of smaller submunitions. They come in over 200 models and can be delivered from the air or the ground, releasing 'bomblets' or 'grenades' respectively.

Because of the wide dispersal pattern of their bomblets, cluster munitions can destroy broad, relatively 'soft' targets, such as airfields and surface-to-air missile sites. They are also effective against targets that move or do not have a precise location, such as enemy troops or vehicles.

THE DANGERS OF CLUSTER BOMB USE

It is precisely the qualities that make cluster bombs militarily desirable that make them so dangerous to civilians. From the humanitarian perspective, the weapons have two main problems: they are difficult to target accurately, and they leave large numbers of unexploded bomblets, or duds.

Cluster bombs cannot be precisely targeted. Once a cluster casing opens, it releases hundreds of unguided bomblets that disperse over a wide area. The wide dispersal pattern of these submunitions makes it very difficult to avoid civilians if they are in the area in which the bombs are dropped.

Cluster bombs also produce problematic after-effects because many of the bomblets do not explode on impact as intended. While all weapons have a failure rate, cluster bombs are more dangerous because they release such large numbers of bomblets. As a result, every cluster bomb leaves some unexploded ordnance.

This high dud rate puts civilians at great risk. Unexploded bomblets become like landmines: they lie in wait, killing civilians who visit the battlefield days or weeks after an attack is over. Some people consider cluster bomblet duds even worse than landmines because of their extreme volatility.

Sadly, children are particularly vulnerable to unexploded bomblets because of their curiosity and failure to understand danger. On Sunday, the *Los Angeles Times* reported the case of Nabil Khalil, age fourteen, hospitalized in Kirkuk after playing with a cluster bomblet that he found in an abandoned Iraqi army camp. He lost one hand, suffered severe face injuries and can barely open his eyes.

It is because of these dangers that human rights groups contend that cluster bombs should never be deployed in civilian areas. While the Pentagon has offered figures indicating low use of air-dropped cluster bombs in Iraqi cities, it has not provided similar information regarding ground-based cluster munitions.

According to Human Rights Watch, the US Army did, in fact, use ground-based cluster munitions in populated areas of Baghdad, as well as in other Iraqi cities. Its researchers believe that these weapons caused many more civilian casualties than did air-based cluster bombs.

Media reports have confirmed these claims. Several journalists have provided eyewitness accounts of cluster munitions use against populated areas in the southern part of Baghdad. *Newsday* reported on April 15 that two children were killed, and one seriously injured, when a cluster munition they were playing with exploded.

At Friday's press conference, discussing cluster bomb use, General Myers talked about the 'tough choices' that the military faces in making targeting decisions. But some choices should not just be tough; they should be excluded.

The record shows that the military should not use cluster bombs of any type in populated areas. Moreover, given the weapon's terrible impact on civilians, the Pentagon should reconsider whether the cluster bomb is necessary to its arsenal.

Joanne Mariner is a human rights attorney and regular CounterPunch *contributor.*

May 10, 2003

LABOR IN THE DAWN OF EMPIRE
by JoAnn Wypijewski

EDITORS' NOTE: *This last May Day CounterPuncher JoAnn Wypijewski spoke about those heroes of the US labor movement who denounced their country's first imperial lunges, in the Spanish–American war and in the Philippines. It was a powerful address, warmly received, given as part of the Fifth Annual Hudson Mohawk May Day Festival at the First Unitarian Society, Schenectady, NY; sponsored by the Troy Area Labor Council (AFL-CIO), the New York Labor History Association, the Solidarity Committee of the Capital District and Eighth Step. – AC/JSC*

Workers, Comrades, Friends,

We gather here to celebrate May Day – Workers' Day, 8-Hour-Day Day, Revolutionary Labor Day, Haymarket Riot Day, give or take a few days.

Some might say 'terror day' but terror cuts two ways.

We commemorate May Day, Workers' Day, but in another, less-remembered sense, May 1st might also be called Empire Day.

For on this day in 1886, labor had declared itself dedicated to effect the eight-hour day. And on this day in 1898, American warships commenced the Battle of Manila Bay, which would be the culminating act of the Spanish-American War, and thus the inauguration of America as an overseas imperial power.

Separated by twelve years, those two events are nonetheless on a continuum – as we, this day, with the fresh memory of the bombardment of Iraq, its culture looted, its cities devastated, its children crying out, gagged with rags to keep from howling as their ruined limbs are amputated without anaesthetic or clean water – just as we are on a continuum. Call it the war at home and the war abroad. Call it capitalism and imperialism. We have seen this before. We are in it, deep in it.

We are being seduced, even by some of our allies, to think that what we are seeing unfold today – the cries of terror, the call to arms, the assaults on workers, the false consciousness, the scoundrel's patriotism – is something new.

Of course, its features are new, its details, simply because history moves. We are in new times. But it is good to remember that history is not something frozen in the past. It is revived and revised, made and remade in the present. And if the details of what is unfolding today are new, the outline is familiar.

So while we are concentrated here today on the matter of the working class in the midst of war, at home, abroad, I thought it necessary for us to remember the Battle of Manila Bay as well:

- to remember the Philippines and its people, slaughtered fighting for their independence in the aftermath of that famous battle.

- to remember a war that in many ways resembled the one just prosecuted in Iraq – prosecuted in most elemental form by the working class against the working class, for the rich.

- and to consider its meanings for workers, for people of conscience, for anyone keen to the lessons of the past.

The wonderful Czech writer Milan Kundera once said: 'The struggle of people against power is the struggle of memory against forgetting.' So let us remember curious things. In 1886, the bomb that was rolled into Chicago's Haymarket Square during a labor rally may have been the work of anarchists – or it may have been the work of police or agents provocateurs.

Louis Lingg, the only one of the seven men later prosecuted for the bombing who may have actually done it, told the court upon sentencing: 'I despise you! I despise your "order", your laws, your force-propped authority. Hang me for it!'

Before they could hang him, his sweetheart smuggled a tiny percussion cap into his cell. He bit down on it, and blew his head off. But he never claimed the bombing as his deed.

To this day, we don't know exactly who was responsible for it. But we do know that in its wake came a crackdown on labor: came the blacklist, came a generation-long setback for the eight-hour movement, came fear and, among too many, resignation.

And we also know that elsewhere in the country at about that same time, the counselors to power were propounding theories of expansion. The histories of the period are full of the propaganda of intellectuals: urging America to build a great Navy – to claim dominion over the Pacific – to gain a foothold for trade (i.e., theft) in China – to find a solution to the problem of America's 'surplus manufactures.'

Before the election of 1896, William McKinley cried: 'We need foreign markets for our surplus products!'

Like his capitalist braintrust, he never considered that the solution to the surplus might be found in those who created it: in other words, in raising the wages of American workers, in limiting their work hours and employing the jobless, in eliminating child labor and general misery; in short, in transforming a system that made the American working class a band of near-beggars.

There was a simple solution, a Robin Hood solution: take from the rich and give to the poor. Bye-bye surplus.

But markets were all anyone in power could think about. While the workers toiled and starved, their masters spoke of markets, which is a more polite way of saying: take from the poor, from the poorest, create a bigger band of beggars and near-beggars, and give to the rich.

Westward expansion had created markets, but now the frontier was closed. While workers in the industrial cities had been agitating for better conditions, taking rifle practice in the woods, reading dangerous tracts on revolution and dynamite, the cavalry had been subduing the last of the Indians. Four years after the Haymarket explosion came the massacre at Wounded Knee, and with it the official closing of the frontier. That was 1890.

Westward expansion continued on, across the waters, its racist presumptions going international too.

In 1893, white American planters backed by American guns overthrew the sovereign kingdom of Hawai'i. The USS *Boston* supplied the guns, and after Queen Lili'uokalani was led away in chains and the American flag was raised atop her palace, US troops began training exercises in Honolulu, rapelling off the walls of Kawaiaha'o Church, preparing for their next mission.

The USS *Boston* would go on to Manila Bay. But it took another mysterious explosion to set that war in motion.

As with the Haymarket bomb, to this day we do not know precisely who was responsible for the explosion that led to the

Spanish-American War, sinking the USS *Maine* and with it 268 seamen in Havana harbor in February 1898.

Terror! Outrage! screamed the yellow press.

Meanwhile, the journal of the International Association of Machinists pointed out that on America's own soil 'a carnival of carnage takes place every day, month and year in the realm of industry; the thousands of useful lives that are annually sacrificed to the Moloch of greed, the blood tribute paid by labor to capitalism, brings forth no shout for vengeance and reparation.'

Before the first spark flew – a year before – Teddy Roosevelt, then Assistant Secretary of the Navy, wrote to a friend: 'in strictest confidence, I should welcome almost any war, for I think the country needs one.'

Like George Bush today, he had a particularly narrow definition of 'the country,' for in fact much of the organized working class opposed the gunboat drive for markets early on.

They opposed America's coup against the Hawaiian sovereign.

They opposed annexation of Hawai'i.

And before war was declared on Spain, most of them opposed it, not believing President McKinley's high-sounding talk of democracy and liberty for the Cubans, the Filipinos and the others under Spanish rule.

After the sinking of the *Maine*, a fellow named Bolton Hall, treasurer of the American Longshore Union, wrote what he called 'A Peace Appeal to Labor.'

'If there is war,' it declared, 'you will furnish the corpses and the taxes, and others will get the glory. Speculators will make money out of it – that is, out of you. You will have to pay the bill, and the only satisfaction you will get is the privilege of hating your Spanish fellow-workmen, who are really your brothers, and who have had as little to do with the wrongs of Cuba as you have.'

Replace 'Spanish' and 'Cuba' in that declaration with 'Iraqi' and 'Iraq,' and it is as apt today as it was more than a century ago.

Before war began, Samuel Gompers and the American Federation of Labor cautiously opposed intervention. But once it began, Gompers, infected by false patriotism, shifted course and declared America's cause against the Spanish 'glorious and righteous.' As it happened, that righteous cause was also against the people of Cuba and the Philippines, who'd been fighting for their independence.

John Sweeney's turnaround this year on Iraq — first cautiously opposing unilateral intervention but then, as soon as it was on, falling in line — was not as dramatic, but a similar politics of no politics was at work.

They didn't chant 'Support our troops' in 1898. Rather, tens of thousands of working men, caught up by war fever, rushed to enlist. Others gestured approvingly at the booty.

The mineworkers hoped the spike in coal prices would reflect in their wages.

The typographers cheered that the establishment of English schools in Spain's former territories would help the printing trade.

Glassmakers looked forward to a surge in demand for bottles and so for their craft.

Railroad unions said more goods moving meant more work for them.

'Where shall we turn for consumers of our surplus?' Albert Beveridge thundered on the Senate floor. 'Geography answers the question.'

Remarkably, or maybe not, some unions parroted the same opinion. Thus was American labor made complicit in American imperialism, a complicity that bedevils unions and the working class as a whole to this day.

McKinley's men called the Spanish-American encounter 'a splendid little war.' Admiral Dewey out in the Pacific had predicted it would last five days. It lasted three months. This, remember, was over a hundred years ago.

More than a quarter-million American soldiers were mustered for the fight in the Caribbean and the Pacific combined. Today, with respect to Iraq, we hear of US overwhelming force, of war as a low-casualty or even, for Americans, a no-casualty enterprise. It's worth contemplating that in the Spanish-American War, only 379 American soldiers died as a result of combat. Five thousand more, it also ought to be remembered, died of diseases or other causes, such as rotten, contaminated meat, sold to the government by the Armour Company of Chicago for a nice profit. Thus were the injuries of war and the injuries of capital twinned.

In the 'pacification' of the Philippines that took place afterwards and lasted until 1904, hundreds of thousands of Filipinos – 'rebels' or 'terrorists' in the argot of the day – were exterminated. In 1899, before the worst of the slaughter, in debate on the Senate floor (something we have not seen in the current period) one Senator Tillman of South Carolina asked whether it had ever previously happened that a colony at war for its freedom with one nation had ever been sold in the meantime to another nation (here the US) that was also at war with the colonizer.

'I think,' said Henry Cabot Lodge in reply, 'the situation is unique in the fact that the people whom we liberated down there have turned against us.'

To which Tillman replied: 'Well, the question of liberation is one which will present two points of view.' He couldn't know the half of it.

That era's 'smart bombs' were 500-pound shells, which Admiral Dewey shot into Filipino trenches. In some places, the Filipinos fought back with bow and arrow. Along the Pasig River dead Filipinos were piled up like sandbags. Americans used their bodies for fortifications.

One US soldier from Washington State wrote home: 'Our fighting blood was up, and we all wanted to kill "niggers". This shooting human beings beats rabbit hunting all to pieces.'

Back home in these years, there was a frenzy of lynching, and though called upon to intervene, McKinley cared no more about stopping it than stopping the 'nigger-killing' that his white troops abroad boasted of. And yet, African-American soldiers were deeply involved in the fight as well.

One famous regiment was responsible for winning all of the major battles in Cuba that Teddy Roosevelt, with his own embedded reporters and photographers, made sure to be credited with. When those black soldiers returned home, they were shunned and spit upon, despised and sometimes killed.

This particular regiment had been Buffalo Soldiers before they went to Cuba, mustered against the Indians. Their next deployment after Cuba was to Colorado – to put down strikes and radical rebellion by the Western Federation of Miners; to terrorize the militant mining towns and guard the infamous bullpens. For the working classes, these were wars of all against all.

When liberation struggles in Cuba and the Philippines were finally suppressed, American capitalists ravaged the land and the resources. The dupes of the working class saw their benefit as well. During the war, employment in the US did rise. Wages did rise too, albeit meagerly. But prices rose more. Over the course of the war, the purchasing power of workers' wages dropped 20 per cent.

Worse than that, labor was divided and compromised. A vast segment made its peace with barbarism. It made its pact with expansionism, colonialism, capitalist exploitation of the worst sort.

Throughout the land there were rebellious workers. And those who'd joined their voices to the Anti-Imperialist League would fight on against foreign adventures and brutality up into World War One. Their children and children's children, and children's children's children fight on to this day.

But 'the war at home' – the essential complement of every war abroad – struck equally at those workers who praised the bloodletting and those who damned it.

One hundred years later, no cowed or cowardly support for George Bush's war will save American workers from the blows of the war at home. That war began precisely at the moment Bush declared 'You're with us or against us,' and it will continue on as part of the administration's strategy of endless war – or what, in a McKinleyite formulation, the National Security Council described as its mission: to impose 'democracy, development, free markets and free trade to every corner of the world.'

It will continue on unless we stop it. And we must stop it.

Do not imagine that my advertings to the nineteenth century are simply the product of my own quirky historical interests. They are that, of course. But in the councils of power, the enemies of the working class are also reviewing history for its nourishing lessons. Grover Norquist, part of the Bush team's activist light artillery from his redoubt at Americans for Tax Reform, was recently asked just what is the fundamental goal of the right in the current period.

'The McKinley era,' he replied, 'absent the protectionism. You're looking at the history of the country for the first 120 years, up until Teddy Roosevelt, when the socialists took over. The income tax, the death tax, regulation – all that' presumably must go.

That is where the enemies of labor would have us on this May Day of 2003: peering backward at the abyss of the nineteenth century.

History, as I have said, is no frozen, finished thing. The legacy of America's first overseas imperial adventure takes a very live form in the Filipino laborers lining up for jobs with Bechtel, Brown & Root, the union-busting Stevedore Services of America and others in the reconstruction of Iraq.

Their own economy pillaged over 100 years, they are the Philippines' chief export, and the remittances they send home the country's number one source of income. Before the first contracts were awarded, the *New York Times* reported that whichever companies were named, they are likely to use Filipino labor, which is skilled, plentiful, reliable and, above all, cheap.

Their desperation is our shame, and a warning both to the newly 'liberated' Iraqis and to the American working class. There are no winners on our side in the war program: workers of the world are being pitted in ferocious competition to see who comes out last.

For workers, there is always a war at home and a war abroad, and it is not enough – it will never be enough – to oppose one without the other.

JoAnn Wypijewski can be reached at jwyp@thenation.com

May 17, 2003

THE DIXIE CHICKS CROSS THE ROAD
by Dave Marsh and Lee Ballinger

Last year, Natalie Maines of the Dixie Chicks contemptuously dismissed Toby Keith's popular pro-war song 'Courtesy of the Red, White, and Blue,' saying it was 'ignorant and it makes country music sound ignorant.' No boycott was called. In fact, not a word was said.

So there's no reason to interpret the hostile response that followed Maines's antiwar comments as the spontaneous reaction of an out-raged country audience. In fact, the attack on the Dixie Chicks was a political maneuver no less calculated than the Watergate break-in.

According to a story from americannewsreel.com sent to *Rock and Rap Confidential* by former Reprise president Howie Klein, 'Phone calls originating from Republican Party headquarters in Washington went out to country stations, urging them to remove the Chicks from their playlists. The "alternative concert" [to the Dixie Chicks' tour opener] is actually the work of the South Carolina Republican Party and party officials are helping promote the concert. We received a call from 'Gallagher's Army,' urging us to support the alternative concert. Caller ID backtraced the call to South Carolina GOP headquarters.'

Chain radio stations were quick to dump the Chicks because their parent companies (Clear Channel, Viacom, *et al.*) have pressing business in the nation's capital and they want help from the Republican Party.

The Dixie Chicks' Top of the World tour was set to begin in Greenville, South Carolina, on May 1. The state legislature had passed a resolution condemning the group. Lipton Tea, their corporate tour sponsor, scrapped most of its endorsement deal with the Chicks, saying that it's 'wrong' to be for peace. In the wake of the many death threats against the three young women in the group, bomb dogs searched the Bi-Lo Center in Greenville before the show.

Lon Helton, country music editor of *Radio & Records*, claimed that country fans are all right-wing, saying: 'Country music is for people who live in between the Hudson and the Hollywood sign and they have a different view.' If all country fans opposed Natalie

Maines's plea for peace, that raised the question: Would anyone show up at the Dixie Chicks' shows? Would the group back away from its beliefs in a desperate attempt to save its career?

Before the concert in Greenville, the arena sound system played 'Everybody Wants to Save the World,' 'Our Lips Are Sealed' by the Go-Gos, 'Band on the Run' by Wings, and Tammy Wynette's 'Your Good Girl's Gonna Go Bad.' There were only a few empty seats and the crowd was doing the wave even before the show began. As soon as it did, there was what the *LA Times*'s Geoff Boucher described as 'a landslide of fan love.'

After the third song, Natalie Maines, clad in a tank-top emblazoned with 'Dare to Be Free,' offered the crowd a chance to boo. 'If there were any boos, they couldn't be heard over the huge applause,' reported the *Greenville News*. Nor was there any booing during the performance of Patty Griffin's 'Truth No. 2' ('You don't like the sound of the truth coming out of my mouth') when a video was shown onstage that highlighted the civil rights movement, Gandhi, Malcolm X, and women's rights, along with footage of people stomping on records by the Beatles, Sinead O'Connor, and the Dixie Chicks.

The Chicks got the same enthusiastic response everywhere they went on the first Southern leg of their tour. Sometimes there would be one protester standing outside with a pro-Bush sign, sometimes none. The reception given the Dixie Chicks below the Mason-Dixon line doesn't change the reality that there is a powerful and dangerous streak of jingoism in America, one that has its strongest roots in the South. But the Dixie Chicks have proven that there are two sides to that story. Even more than their music and their courage, that may turn out to be their greatest gift of all.

Rock and Rap Confidential, *edited by Dave Marsh and Lee Ballinger, is the nation's best newsletter on music and politics.*

May 29, 2003

WEAPONS OF MASS DESTRUCTION: WHO SAID WHAT WHEN

by Jeffrey St. Clair

'Every day Saddam remains in power with chemical weapons, biological weapons, and the development of nuclear weapons is a day of danger for the United States.' – *Sen. Joseph Lieberman, D-CT, September 4, 2002*

'Simply stated, there is no doubt that Saddam Hussein now has weapons of mass destruction.' – *Dick Cheney, August 26, 2002*

'If we wait for the danger to become clear, it could be too late.' – *Sen. Joseph Biden, D-Del., September 4, 2002*

'Right now, Iraq is expanding and improving facilities that were used for the production of biological weapons.' – *George W. Bush, September 12, 2002*

'If he declares he has none, then we will know that Saddam Hussein is once again misleading the world.' – *Ari Fleischer, December 2, 2002*

'We know for a fact that there are weapons there.' – *Ari Fleischer, January 9, 2003*

'Our intelligence officials estimate that Saddam Hussein had the materials to produce as much as 500 tons of sarin, mustard and VX nerve agent.' – *George W. Bush, January 28, 2003*

'We know that Saddam Hussein is determined to keep his weapons of mass destruction, is determined to make more.' – *Colin Powell, February 5, 2003*

'Iraq both poses a continuing threat to the national security of the United States and international peace and security in the Persian Gulf region and remains in material and unacceptable breach of its international obligations by, among other things, continuing to possess and develop a significant chemical and biological weapons capability, actively seeking a nuclear weapons capability, and supporting and harboring terrorist organizations.' – *Sen. Hillary Clinton, D-NY, February 5, 2003*

'We have sources that tell us that Saddam Hussein recently authorized Iraqi field commanders to use chemical weapons – the very weapons the dictator tells us he does not have.' – *George W. Bush, February 8, 2003*

'So has the strategic decision been made to disarm Iraq of its weapons of mass destruction by the leadership in Baghdad? I think our judgment has to be clearly not.' – *Colin Powell, March 8, 2003*

'Intelligence gathered by this and other governments leaves no doubt that the Iraq regime continues to possess and conceal some of the most lethal weapons ever devised.' – *George W. Bush, March 18, 2003*

'We are asked to accept Saddam decided to destroy those weapons. I say that such a claim is palpably absurd.' – *Tony Blair, March 18, 2003*

'Well, there is no question that we have evidence and information that Iraq has weapons of mass destruction, biological and chemical particularly ... all this will be made clear in the course of the operation, for whatever duration it takes.' – *Ari Fleischer, March 21, 2003*

'There is no doubt that the regime of Saddam Hussein possesses weapons of mass destruction. As this operation continues, those weapons will be identified, found, along with the people who have produced them and who guard them.' – *Gen. Tommy Franks, March 22, 2003*

'I have no doubt we're going to find big stores of weapons of mass destruction.' – *Kenneth Adelman, Defense Policy Board, March 23, 2003*

'One of our top objectives is to find and destroy the WMD. There are a number of sites.' – *Pentagon spokeswoman Victoria Clark, March 22, 2003*

'We know where they are. They are in the area around Tikrit and Baghdad.' – *Donald Rumsfeld, March 30, 2003*

'Saddam's removal is necessary to eradicate the threat from his weapons of mass destruction.' – *Jack Straw, 2 April, 2003*

'Obviously the administration intends to publicize all the weapons of mass destruction US forces find – and there will be plenty.' – *Neocon 'scholar' Robert Kagan, April 9, 2003*

'I think you have always heard, and you continue to hear from officials, a measure of high confidence that, indeed, the weapons of mass destruction will be found.' – *Ari Fleischer, April 10, 2003*

'We are learning more as we interrogate or have discussions with Iraqi scientists and people within the Iraqi structure, that perhaps he destroyed some, perhaps he dispersed some. And so we will find them.' – *George W. Bush, April 24, 2003*

'Before people crow about the absence of weapons of mass destruction, I suggest they wait a bit.' – *Tony Blair, 28 April, 2003*

'There are people who in large measure have information that we need ... so that we can track down the weapons of mass destruction in that country.' – *Donald Rumsfeld, April 25, 2003*

'We'll find them. It'll be a matter of time to do so.' – *George W. Bush, May 3, 2003*

'I am confident that we will find evidence that makes it clear he had weapons of mass destruction.' – *Colin Powell, May 4, 2003*

'I never believed that we'd just tumble over weapons of mass destruction in that country.' – *Donald Rumsfeld, May 4, 2003*

'I'm not surprised if we begin to uncover the weapons program of Saddam Hussein – because he had a weapons program.' – *George W. Bush, May 6, 2003*

'US officials never expected that we were going to open garages and find weapons of mass destruction.' – *Condoleezza Rice, May 12, 2003*

'I just don't know whether it was all destroyed years ago – I mean, there's no question that there were chemical weapons years ago – whether they were destroyed right before the war, [or] whether they're still hidden.' – *Maj. Gen. David Petraeus, Commander 101st Airborne, May 13, 2003*

'Before the war, there's no doubt in my mind that Saddam Hussein had weapons of mass destruction, biological and chemical. I expected them to be found. I still expect them to be found.' – *Gen. Michael Hagee, Commandant of the Marine Corps, May 21, 2003*

'Given time, given the number of prisoners now that we're interrogating, I'm confident that we're going to find weapons of mass destruction. – *Gen. Richard Myers, Chairman Joint Chiefs of Staff, May 26, 2003'*

'They may have had time to destroy them, and I don't know the answer.' – *Donald Rumsfeld, May 27, 2003*

'For bureaucratic reasons, we settled on one issue, weapons of mass destruction [as justification for invading Iraq], because it was the one reason everyone could agree on.' – *Paul Wolfowitz, May 28, 2003*

June 1, 2003

THE RAT IN THE GRAIN: DAN AMSTUTZ AND THE LOOTING OF IRAQI AGRICULTURE
by Jeffrey St. Clair

The war on Iraq couldn't have come at a more dire time for Iraq's beleaguered farmers. Spring is harvest time in the barley and wheat fields of the Tigris river valley and planting time in the vast vegetable plantations of southern Iraq.

The war is over, but the situation in the fields of Iraq continues to rapidly deteriorate. The banks, which provide credit and cash, have been looted, irrigation systems destroyed, road travel restricted, markets closed, warehouses and grain silos pillaged.

To harvest the grain before it rots in the fields Iraqi farmers need more than 8 million gallons of diesel fuel to power Iraq's corroding armada of combines and harvesters. But most of the fuel depots were incinerated by US bombing strikes. There's no easy way to get the fuel that remains to the farmers who need it most and no desire to do so by the US forces of occupation.

Even if the crops can be harvested, there's no clear way for the grain to get stored, marketed, sold and distributed to hungry Iraqi families. Under the Hussein regime, the crops were bought by the Baghdad government at a fixed price and then distributed through a rationing system. This system, inefficient as it was, is gone. But nothing has taken its place. Iraqi farmers are still owed $75 million for this year's crop, with little sign that the money will ever arrive. There's speculation throughout the country that one intent of the current policy is to force many farmers off their farms and into the cities so that their lands can be taken over by favorites of Ahmed Chalabi and his US protectors. The post-Saddam Iraq will almost certainly witness a land redistribution program: more farmland going into fewer and fewer hands.

Grain farmers aren't alone. As in the first Gulf War, US bombing raids targeted cattle feed lots, poultry farms, fertilizer warehouses, pumping stations, irrigation systems and pesticide factories (the closest thing the US has come to finding Weapons of Mass Destruction in the country) – the very infrastructure of Iraqi agriculture. It will take years to restore these operations.

Many fields in southern Iraq lie fallow, as vegetable farmers have been unable to secure seeds to grow the usual melons, tomatoes, onions, cucumbers and beans – all mainstays of the Iraqi diet.

'We expect failures,' said Abdul Aziz Nejefi, a barley farmer from Mosul, in a dispatch from the *Guardian*. 'We never had this situation before. There is no government.'

Meanwhile, millions of Iraqis face starvation this summer. A UN staff report from late May paints a bleak portrait. It notes that Iraq's poultry industry has effectively been decimated. Millions of chickens perished during the war. Millions of others face starvation, since nearly all of the chicken feed stored in government warehouses has been looted. Chicken and eggs are staples of the Iraqi diet, accounting for more than half of the animal protein consumed by the population.

Many other farm animals, including sheep and goats, could be ravaged by disease, since the nation's stockpiles of veterinary medicines and vaccines have been almost totally destroyed or looted.

Some 60 per cent of Iraq's 24 million people depend totally for their food on the food ration system that was established after the first Gulf War. Each week, these Iraqis could count on a 'food basket' consisting of wheat flour, rice, vegetable oil, lentils, beans, milk, sugar and salt. That system is now in shambles and is scorned by US policymakers. And promised grain imports have yet to materialize.

'Before there is unwarranted military technological triumphalism, let those setting out to manage the peace think mouths,' says Tim Land, professor of food policy at City University in London. 'Grumbling stomachs are bad politics as well as disastrous for the public health. There has to be a food democracy after decades of food totalitarianism.'

Into this dire circumstance strides Daniel Amstutz, the Bush administration's choice to oversee the reconstruction of Iraq's agricultural system. Now an international trade lobbyist in DC with a fat roster of big ag clients, Amstutz once served as a top executive at Cargill, the food giant which controls much of the world trade in grain. During Amstutz's tenure at Cargill, the grain company went on a torrid expansion campaign. It is now the largest privately held corporation in the US and controls about 94 per cent of the soybean market and more than 50 per cent of the corn market in the Upper Midwest. It also has its hands on the export market, controlling 40 per cent of all US corn exports, a third of all soybean exports and at least 20 per cent of wheat exports.

Al Krebs, who edits the *Agribusiness Examiner*, a vital publication on US farm policy, unearthed a 1982 questionnaire on food, politics and morality that vividly illustrates the Cargill philosophy. The Joseph Project, a public policy research group sponsored by the Senate of Catholic Priests of the Archdiocese of Minneapolis-St. Paul, asked Cargill executives to explain the company's attitude toward hunger and famine issues. The executives responded as follows:

The assumption that there are moral priorities that are offended in serving world or domestic markets as economically and efficiently as possible rests on a confusion about economic facts. It is also a highly objectionable characterization of business's role. Before one makes moral judgments and advocates economic actions, one should understand the economic issues that are involved.

The business of making moral judgments is both hazardous and potentially irresponsible unless one is fully satisfied that all the facts and causal relationships have been explored ... We are not in a position – given time and other constraints – to provide all the relevant background. Nor are we anxious to make moral judgments – or moral defenses – of our own.

In 2000, the biggest food companies in the world, Cargill, Archer Daniels Midland, Cenex Harvest States Co-op, DuPont and Louis Dreyfus, got together to form Pradium Inc., a kind of secret, internal grain market that offered real-time, cash commodity exchanges for grains, oilseeds and agricultural by-products as well as global information services. It also offered ways to fix grain prices on a global scale. Amstutz served as Pradium's chairman.

Amstutz is no stranger to government, either. During the first Bush administration he served as Undersecretary of Agriculture for International Affairs and Commodity programs. He was also the chief US negotiator on agricultural issues for the Uruguay Round of GATT talks, which led to the WTO.

'Daniel Amstutz, an ex-Cargill executive, is there to push the agribusiness agenda, not a democratic agenda,' says George Naylor, president of the National Family Farm Coalition. 'He will excel in telling the world that his policy is good for farmers, consumers and the environment when just the opposite is true.'

The small farmers of the grain belt of the Midwest have a particular loathing for Amstutz. During his stint in the first Bush administration, Amstutz devised the notorious Freedom to Farm Bill, which eliminated tariffs and slashed federal farm price supports – all in an effort to lower grain prices for the benefit of Amstutz's cronies in the big agricultural conglomerates. As a result, thousands of American farmers lost their farms and monopolists like Cargill reaped the benefits.

The contours of Amstutz's plan for Iraq are familiar: a combination of free-market shock therapy and predation by multinational corporations. Gliding over a decade of UN sanctions that have starved the nation and a war that ravaged the nation's infrastructure, Amstutz announced that the real problem facing Iraqi agriculture is, naturally, government subsidies. 'Iraqi farmers have had little incentive to increase production because of price controls that have kept food very inexpensive,' Amstutz announced. 'With a transition to a market economy, we can see health returning to agriculture and incentives to employ good farming practices and modern techniques.'

The more likely scenario is that Amstutz will use the destitute condition of Iraq's farmlands as a lucrative opportunity to dump cheap grain from American companies like Cargill, all of it paid for by Iraqi oil. If this scenario plays out, it will spell disaster for Iraq's struggling farmers. Prior to the 1991 Gulf War, Iraq imported more than 1 million metric tonnes per year of American wheat. Since then, however, no direct sales of American agricultural products have occurred. Amstutz is anxious to begin flooding Iraq with Cargill grain.

Moreover, Iraq owes the US Department of Agriculture's Commodity Credit Corp. $2 billion on loans that facilitated pre-1991 ag sales and nearly $2 billion in interest on the loans. Amstutz will certainly demand that those loans be recouped through oil sales.

'Someone needs to warn the Iraqi people that other Third World countries can already attest that the dependence Amstutz will create surely means that Iraq's sovereignty will be greatly compromised,' says Naylor. And Naylor argues that cash-strapped American farmers won't see any benefits, either. 'Amstutz perpetuates the more exports lie because his agribusiness cronies are encouraging overproduction all over the world, thus being able to sell more genetically modified seeds and chemicals and buying ever cheaper farm commodities.'

Even as millions of Iraqis face starvation under the stern hand of their food proconsul, Amstutz's appointment has excited little commentary in the US. His most virulent critic has been Kevin Watkins, Oxfam's policy director in London. Watkins warns that Amstutz is little more than a carpetbagger seeking to advance the interests of the same food titans that his lobbying outfit in DC represents: Cargill, DuPont, Cenex and Archer Daniels Midland. 'This guy is uniquely well-placed to advance the commercial interests of American grain companies and bust open the Iraqi market, but singularly ill-equipped to lead a reconstruction effort in a war-torn country,' Watkins warns. 'Putting Dan Amstutz in charge of agricultural reconstruction in Iraq is like putting Saddam Hussein in the chair of a human rights commission.'

Amstutz was recently spotted in Iowa, pitching his agricultural reconstruction plan to Iowa feedlot owners. He told the farmers that they stood to profit handsomely from his plan to bring to Iraq modern feedlots, those foul-smelling operations that pack thousands of cattle and hogs into tightly confined pens. 'They are meat eaters,' he brayed. 'Iraq is not a vegetarian society.'

Iowa doesn't have many cattle or sheep operations. Most of the people in his audience raised hogs. And unless Amstutz has joined in a partnership with Franklin Graham to Christianize Iraq, there won't be a big market for pork products in Baghdad.

June 12, 2003

DECEIVED INTO WAR
by Ray McGovern, former CIA analyst

When FOX TV asked me to present my views Sunday on the ongoing quest for weapons of mass destruction in Iraq, the first thing the anchor asked was why I should care about the phantom WMDs when the vast majority of Americans don't.

I responded, somewhat indecorously, that this was largely the fault of FOX News and other media that have kept Americans malnourished on small issues like why our country launched a 'pre-emptive' war. I was dyspeptic on Sunday after watching Condoleezza Rice and Colin Powell blow still more smoke at these key issues and disparage those with altogether legitimate questions.

Powell said it was 'nonsense' to brand as 'bogus' the intelligence adduced to justify making war on Iraq. But, sadly, 'bogus' is precisely the correct word to apply to the key piece of 'evidence' used to deceive our representatives and senators into voting to give President Bush permission to launch an unprovoked war on Iraq.

However strong a word, 'bogus' pales in comparison with the seven-letter F-word to which Powell and Rice showed themselves allergic: F for forgery. Yes, forgery. Had FOX and other news outlets adequately reported on what both Powell had already conceded was a forgery, the American people might have a better appreciation as to why they should care.

I refer to the bogus story that Iraq was attempting to acquire uranium from Niger to develop nuclear weapons. Those who followed developments at the UN have known since February that that story was based on a crude forgery. What is little known is that the Bush administration knew it was bogus a full year earlier. (Those who find themselves wondering why Powell and Rice have conceded the point need only to remember that the UN now has the forged documents.)

To his credit, early last year Vice-President Dick Cheney sent to Niger a former US ambassador in Africa to investigate the story. The latter brought back word that the documents were not authentic. But this did not prevent senior administration officials from using them in the critical run-up to Congress's vote to give the president the authority to make war.

Indeed, President Bush included the forged 'evidence' in his state-of-the-union address on January 28 – something Dr Rice, when asked about it by George Stephanopoulos on Sunday, was at a loss to explain satisfactorily. Now 'senior administration officials' are telling gullible reporters that Cheney was never informed of the outcome of the investigation he ordered. I'm not making this up.

Recent press reports of a Defense Intelligence Agency study of Sept. 2002 that found 'no definitive, reliable information' that Iraq was producing or stockpiling chemical or biological weapons has helped me connect the dots, so to speak.

Last fall's full-court press to get Congress to vote for war required proof that Iraq posed a clear and present danger. As Bush's strategists reviewed the bidding, it became painfully clear that allegations of a confirmed chemical and biological threat would run too great a risk of being undermined by uncooperative analysts in the DIA.

At that point the White House decided to present evidence raising the specter of nuclear weapons in the hands of Saddam Hussein and play up the danger of a 'mushroom cloud.' Former UN nuclear inspector David Albright said on Sunday that he was 'deeply troubled by the selective use of information to basically scare people. People are scared by nuclear weapons. And it's a button.'

But where was the evidence? It is now clear that the only thing available at that time was the so-called argument from aluminum tubes. There had been reports of Iraq trying to procure them from abroad, and those eager to please the White House offered instant 'analysis' that the tubes were for Iraq's 'nuclear program.' Thus, Dr Rice on September 8, 2002 told Wolf Blitzer that 'Saddam Hussein is actively pursuing a nuclear weapon. We do know that there have been shipments into Iraq of aluminum tubes that really are only suited to nuclear weapons programs.'

But when the engineers and scientists at US nuclear labs were consulted, their virtually unanimous conclusion was that the tubes were not suitable for a nuclear application. So that line of argument turned out to be as weak as the chemical and biological weapons evidence about which DIA analysts were so suspicious.

What was left? Someone remembered the forged correspondence between Iraq and Niger, decided that it could be used to win the vote in Congress, to win the war in Iraq, and in the afterglow of victory, no one would care that the evidence was bogus.

It worked.

Small wonder that Rep. Henry Waxman (D, CA), in a March 17 letter to the president, expressed outrage at having been deceived into voting for war, since 'the evidence cited regarding Iraq's efforts to obtain nuclear weapons is a hoax.'

Ray McGovern, a CIA analyst from 1964 to 1990, regularly reported to the vice-president and senior policy-makers on the President's Daily Brief from 1981 to 1985. He is now on the Steering Group of Veteran Intelligence Professionals for Sanity. His day job is co-director of the Servant Leadership School, an inner-city outreach ministry in Washington DC.

June 27, 2003

CHENEY, FORGERY AND THE CIA
by Ray McGovern, former CIA analyst

As though this were normal! I mean the repeated visits Vice-President Dick Cheney made to the CIA before the war in Iraq. The visits were, in fact, unprecedented. During my twenty-seven-year career at the Central Intelligence Agency, no vice-president ever came to us for a working visit.

During the Eighties, it was my privilege to brief Vice-President George H. W. Bush and other very senior policy-makers every other morning. I went either to the vice-president's office or (on weekends) to his home. I am sure it never occurred to him to come to CIA headquarters.

The morning briefings gave us an excellent window on what was uppermost in the minds of those senior officials and helped us refine our tasks of collection and analysis. Thus, there was never any need for policy-makers to visit us. And the very thought of a vice-president dropping by to help us with our analysis is extraordinary. We preferred to do that work without the pressure that inevitably comes from policy-makers at the table.

Cheney got into the operational side of intelligence as well. Reports in late 2001 that Iraq had tried to acquire uranium from Niger stirred such intense interest that his office let it be known he wanted them checked out. So, with the CIA as facilitator, a retired US ambassador was dispatched to Niger in February 2002 to investigate. He found nothing to substantiate the report and lots to call it into question. There the matter rested – until last summer, after the Bush administration made the decision for war in Iraq.

Cheney, in a speech on August 26, 2002, claimed that Saddam Hussein had 'resumed his effort to acquire nuclear weapons.'

At the time, CIA analysts were involved in a fierce argument with the Pentagon on this very point. Most of the nuclear engineers at the CIA, and virtually all scientists at US government laboratories and the International Atomic Energy Agency, found no reliable evidence that Iraq had restarted its nuclear weapons program. But the vice-president had spoken. Sad to say, those in charge of the draft National Intelligence Estimate took their cue and stated, falsely, that 'most analysts assess Iraq is reconstituting its nuclear weapons program.'

Smoke was blown about aluminum tubes sought by Iraq that, it turns out, were intended for conventional weapons programs. The rest amounted to things like Hussein's frequent meetings with nuclear scientists and Iraq's foot-dragging in providing information to UN inspectors.

Not much heed was paid to the fact that Hussein's son-in-law, who supervised Iraq's nuclear program before he defected in 1995, had told interrogators that Iraq's nuclear capability – save the blueprints – had been destroyed in 1991 at his order. (Documents given to the United States this week confirm that. The Iraqi scientists who provided them added that, even though the blueprints would have given Iraq a head start, no order was given to restart the program; and even had such an order been given, Iraq would still have been years away from producing a nuclear weapon.)

In sum, the evidence presented in last September's intelligence estimate fell far short of what was required to support Cheney's claim that Iraq was on the road to a nuclear weapon. Something scarier had to be produced, and quickly, if Congress was to be persuaded to authorize war. And so the decision was made to dust off the uranium-from-Niger canard.

The White House calculated – correctly – that before anyone would make an issue of the fact that this key piece of 'intelligence' was based on a forgery, Congress would vote Yes. The war could then be waged and won. In recent weeks, administration officials have begun spreading the word that Cheney was never told the Iraq–Niger story was based on a forgery. I asked a senior official who recently served at the National Security Council if he thought that was possible. He pointed out that rigorous NSC procedures call for a very specific response to all vice-presidential questions and added that 'the fact that Cheney's office had originally asked that the Iraq–Niger report be checked out makes it inconceivable that his office would not have been informed of the results.'

Did the president himself know that the information used to secure congressional approval for war was based on a forgery? We don't know. But which would be worse – that he knew or that he didn't?

August 1, 2003

A CONFIDENCE GAME ON IRAQ: WAR PIMPS
by Jeffrey St. Clair

The war on Iraq won't be remembered for how it was waged so much as for how it was sold. It was a propaganda war, a war of perception management, where loaded phrases such as 'weapons of mass destruction' and 'rogue state' were hurled like precision weapons at the target audience: us.

To understand the Iraq war you don't need to consult generals, but reformed spin doctors or, even better, two of the most seasoned investigators into the dark arts of political propaganda, John Stauber and Sheldon Rampton.

Stauber and Rampton run PR Watch, the Madison, Wisconsin-based group that keeps tabs on the nefarious schemes of the global PR industry to sugarcoat useless, costly and dangerous products. They have also written three of the most important non-fiction books of the last decade. In 1995, they published *Toxic Sludge Is Good For You*, a detailed exposé of how the PR industry plots and executes campaigns to greenwash corporate malfeasance. This was followed by the prescient and disturbing *Mad Cow USA*. Last year they produced *Trust Us We're Experts*, a grim and exacting account of the way scientists-for-hire are deployed to rationalize the risks of dangerous products and smear opponents as know-nothings and worrywarts.

Now comes their exquisitely timed *Weapons of Mass Deception: The Uses of Propaganda in Bush's War on Iraq*. Here Stauber and Rampton give us an immediate history, a real-time deconstruction of the mechanics of the Bush war machine. This lushly documented book is a chilling catalog of lies and deceptions, which shows the press contretemps over the Niger yellowcake forgeries to be but a minor distraction given the outlandish frauds pullulating daily from the White House and the Pentagon. The history Rampton and Stauber recounts is every bit as ground-breaking as Chomsky and Herman's *Manufacturing Consent* and *War Without Mercy*, John Dower's riveting account of the vile uses of propaganda against Japan during World War Two. *Weapons of Mass Deception* shreds the lies, and the motives behind them, as they were being told and describes the techniques of the cover-up as they were being spun. Stauber and Rampton cut through the accumulated media fog to reveal how the war on Saddam was conceived and how the media battle plan developed and deployed. They identify the key players behind the scenes who stage-managed the countdown to war and follow their paper trails back through the murky corridors of Washington where politics, corporate spin and psy-ops spooks cohabit.

Most of this book was written well before the invasion of Iraq. Yet the story it relates is only now being nibbled at by the mainstream press, which had done so much to promote the vaporous deceptions of the Bush administration. Stauber and Rampton expose the gaping holes in the administration's war brief and shine an unforgiving light on the neocon ministers, such as Paul Wolfowitz, Douglas Feith and Richard Perle, who concocted the war in the sebaceous quadrants of the White House and the Pentagon, over the objections of the senior analysts at the CIA and State Department.

The two journalists also trace in comic detail the picaresque journey of Tony Blair's plagiarized dossier on Iraq, from a grad student's website to a cut-and-paste job in the prime minister's bombastic speech to the House of Commons. Blair, stubborn and verbose, paid a price for his grandiose puffery. Bush, who looted whole passages from Blair's speech for his own clumsy presentations, has skated freely through the tempest. Why?

Stauber and Rampton offer the best explanation to date. Unlike Blair, the Bush team never wanted to present a legal case for war. They had no interest in making any of their allegations about Iraq hold up to a standard of proof. The real effort was aimed at amping up the mood for war by using the psychology of fear.

Facts were never important to the Bush team. They were disposable nuggets that could be discarded at will and replaced by whatever new rationale played favorably with their polls and focus groups. The war was about weapons of mass destruction one week, Al Qaeda the next. When neither allegation could be substantiated on the ground, the fall-back position became the mass graves (many from the Iran/Iraq war supported by the US) proving that Saddam was an evil thug who deserved to be toppled. The motto of the Bush PR machine was: Move on. Don't explain. Say anything to conceal the perfidy behind the real motives for war. Never look back. Accuse questioners of harboring unpatriotic sensibilities. Eventually, even the cagey Wolfowitz admitted that the official case for war was made mainly to make the invasion palatable, not to justify it.

The Bush claque of neocon hawks viewed the Iraq war as a product and, just like a new pair of Nikes, it required a roll-out campaign to soften up the consumers. Stauber and Rampton demonstrate in convincing and step-by-step detail how the same techniques (and often the same PR gurus) that have been used to hawk cigarettes, SUVs and nuclear waste dumps were deployed to retail the Iraq war.

To peddle the invasion, Donald Rumsfeld and Colin Powell and company recruited public relations gurus into top-level jobs at the Pentagon and the State Department. These spinmeisters soon had more say over how the rationale for war on Iraq should be presented than intelligence agencies and career diplomats. If the intelligence didn't fit the script, it was either shaded, retooled or junked.

Take Charlotte Beers, who Powell tapped as Undersecretary of State in the post-9/11 world. Beers wasn't a diplomat. She wasn't even a politician. She was the grand diva of spin, known on the business and gossip pages as 'the queen of Madison Avenue.' On the strength of two advertising campaigns, one for Uncle Ben's Rice and another for Head and Shoulders' dandruff shampoo, Beers rocketed to the top of the heap in the PR world, heading two giant PR houses, Ogilvy & Mather and J. Walter Thompson. At the State Department, Beers, who had met Powell in 1995 when they both served on the board of Gulf Airstream, worked at, in Powell's words, 'the branding of US foreign policy.' She extracted more than $500 million from Congress for her Brand America campaign, which largely focused on beaming US propaganda into the Muslim world, much of it directed at teens.

'Public diplomacy is a vital new arm in what will combat terrorism over time,' said Beers. 'All of a sudden we are in this position of redefining who America is, not only for ourselves, but for the outside world.' Note the rapt attention Beers pays to the manipulation of perception, as opposed, say, to alterations of US policy.

Old-fashioned diplomacy involves direct communication between representatives of nations, a conversational give and take, often fraught with deception (see April Glaspie), but an exchange nonetheless. Public diplomacy, as defined by Beers, is something else entirely. It's a one-way street, a unilateral broadcast of American propaganda directly to the public, domestic and international – a kind of informational carpet bombing.

The themes of her campaigns were as simplistic and flimsy as a Bush press conference. The American incursions into Afghanistan and Iraq were all about bringing the balm of 'freedom' to oppressed peoples. Hence, the title of the US war: Operation Iraqi Freedom, where cruise missiles were depicted as instruments of liberation.

Bush himself distilled the Beers equation to its bizarre essence: 'This war is about peace.'

Beers quietly resigned her post a few weeks before the first volley of Tomahawk missiles battered Baghdad. From her point of view, the war itself was already won, the fireworks of Shock and Awe were all after-play.

Over at the Pentagon, Donald Rumsfeld drafted Victoria 'Torie' Clarke as his director of public affairs. Clarke knew the ropes inside the Beltway. Prior to becoming Rumsfeld's mouthpiece she had commanded one of the world's great parlors for powerbrokers: Hill and Knowlton's DC office.

Almost immediately upon taking up her new gig Clarke convened regular meetings with a select group of Washington's top private PR specialists and lobbyists to develop a marketing plan for the Pentagon's forthcoming terror wars. The group was filled with heavy hitters and was strikingly bipartisan in composition. She called it the Rumsfeld Group and it included PR executive Sheila Tate, columnist Rich Galen, and Republican political consultant Charlie Black.

The braintrust also boasted top Democratic fixer Tommy Boggs, brother of NPR's Cokie Roberts and son of the late Congressman Hale Boggs of Arkansas. At the very time Boggs was conferring with top Pentagon brass on how to frame the war on terror, he was also working feverishly for the royal family of Saudi Arabia. In 2002 alone, the Saudis paid his Qorvis PR firm $20.2 million to protect its interests in Washington. In the wake of hostile press coverage following the exposure of Saudi links to the 9/11 hijackers, the royal family needed all the well-placed help it could buy. They seem to have gotten their money's worth. Boggs's felicitous influence-peddling may help to explain why the damning references to Saudi funding of Al Qaeda were edited out of the recent congressional report on the investigation into intelligence failures and 9/11.

According to the trade publication *PR Week*, the Rumsfeld Group sent 'messaging advice' to the Pentagon. The group told Clarke and Rumsfeld that in order to get the American public to buy into the war on terrorism they needed to suggest a link to nation states, not just nebulous groups such as Al Qaeda. In other words, there needed to be a fixed target for the military campaigns, some distant place to drop cruise missiles and cluster bombs. They suggested the notion (already embedded in Rumsfeld's mind) of playing up the notion of so-called rogue states as the real masters of terrorism. Thus was born the Axis of Evil, which, of course, wasn't an 'axis' at all, since two of the states, Iran and Iraq, hated each other, and neither had anything at all to do with the third, North Korea.

Tens of millions in federal money were poured into private public relations and media firms working to craft and broadcast the Bush diktat that Saddam had to be taken out before the Iraqi dictator blew up the world by dropping chemical and nuclear bombs from long-range drones. Many of these PR executives and image consultants were old friends of the high priests in the Bush inner sanctum. Indeed they were veterans, like Cheney and Powell, of the previous war against Iraq, another engagement that was more spin than combat.

At the top of the list was John Rendon, head of the DC firm the Rendon Group. Rendon is one of Washington's heaviest hitters, a Beltway fixer who never let political affiliation stand in the way of an assignment. Rendon served as a media consultant for both Michael Dukakis and Jimmy Carter, as well as Reagan and George H. W. Bush. Whenever the Pentagon wanted to go to war, he offered his services at a price. During Desert Storm Rendon pulled in $100,000 a month from the Kuwaiti royal family. He followed this up with a $23 million contract from the CIA to produce anti-Saddam propaganda in the region.

As part of this CIA project, Rendon created and named the Iraqi National Congress and tapped his friend Ahmad Chalabi, the shady financier, to head the organization. Shortly after 9/11, the Pentagon handed the Rendon Group another big assignment: public relations for the US bombing of Afghanistan. Rendon was also deeply involved in the planning and public relations for the pre-emptive war on Iraq, though both Rendon and the Pentagon refuse to disclose the details of the group's work there.

But it's not hard to detect the manipulative hand of Rendon behind many of the Iraq War's signature events, including the toppling of the Saddam statue (by US troops and Chalabi associates) and videotape of jubilant Iraqis waving American flags as the Third Infantry rolled by them. Rendon had pulled off the same stunt in the first Gulf War, handing out American flags to Kuwaitis and herding the media to the orchestrated demonstration. 'Where do you think they got those American flags?' clucked Rendon in 1991. 'That was my assignment.'

The Rendon Group may also have played a role in pushing the phony intelligence that has now come back to haunt the Bush administration. In December of 2002, Robert Dreyfuss reported that the inner circle of the Bush White House preferred the intelligence coming from Chalabi and his associates to that being proffered by analysts at the CIA. So Rendon and his circle represented a new kind of off-the-shelf psy-ops, the privatization of official propaganda. 'I am not a national security strategist or a military tactician,' said Rendon. 'I am a politician, and a person who uses communication to meet public policy or corporate policy objectives. In fact, I am an information warrior and a perception manager.'

What exactly, pray tell, is perception management? Well, the Pentagon defines it this way: 'actions to convey and/or deny selected information and indicators to foreign audiences to influence their emotions, motives and objective reasoning.' In other words, lying about the intentions of the US government. In a rare display of public frankness, the Pentagon actually let slip its plan (developed by Rendon) to establish a high-level den inside the Department of Defense for perception management. They called it the Office of Strategic Influence, and among its many missions was to plant false stories in the press.

Nothing stirs the corporate media into outbursts of pious outrage like an official government memo bragging about how the media is manipulated for political objectives. So the *New York Times* and *Washington Post* threw indignant fits about the Office of Strategic Influence, the Pentagon shut down the operation and the press gloated with satisfaction on its victory. Yet Rumsfeld told the Pentagon press corps that while he was killing the office, the same devious work would continue. 'You can have the corpse,' said Rumsfeld. 'You can have the name. But I'm going to keep doing every single thing that needs to be done. And I have.'

At a diplomatic level, despite the hired guns and the planted stories, this image war was lost. It failed to convince even America's most fervent allies and dependent client states that Iraq posed much of a threat. It failed to win the blessing of the UN and even NATO, a wholly-owned subsidiary of Washington. At the end of the day, the vaunted coalition of the willing consisted of Britain, Spain, Italy, Australia, and a cohort of former Soviet bloc nations. Even so the citizens of the nations that threw in their lot with the US overwhelmingly opposed the war.

Domestically, it was a different story. A population traumatized by terror threats and its shattered economy became easy prey for the saturation bombing of the Bush message that Iraq was a terrorist state linked to Al Qaeda that was only minutes away from launching attacks on America with weapons of mass destruction.

Americans were the victims of an elaborate con job, pelted with a daily barrage of threat inflation, distortions, deceptions and lies. Not about tactics or strategy or war plans, but about justifications for war. The lies were aimed not at Saddam's regime, but at the American people. By the start of the war, 66 per cent of Americans thought Saddam Hussein was behind 9/11 and 79 per cent thought he was close to having a nuclear weapon.

Of course, the closest Saddam came to possessing a nuke was a rusting gas centrifuge buried for thirteen years in the garden of Mahdi Obeidi, a retired Iraqi scientist. Iraq didn't have any weaponized chemical or biological weapons. In fact, it didn't even possess any Scud missiles, despite erroneous reports fed by Pentagon PR flacks alleging that it had fired Scuds into Kuwait.

This charade wouldn't have worked without a gullible or a complicit press corps. Victoria Clarke, who developed the Pentagon plan for embedded reports, put it succinctly a few weeks before the war began: 'Media coverage of any future operation will to a large extent shape public perception.'

During the Vietnam War, TV images of maimed GIs and napalmed villages suburbanized opposition to the war and helped hasten the US withdrawal. The Bush gang meant to turn the Vietnam phenomenon on its head by using TV as a force to propel the US into a war that no one really wanted.

What the Pentagon sought was a new kind of living-room war, where instead of photos of mangled soldiers and dead Iraqi kids, they could control the images Americans viewed and to a large extent the content of the stories. By embedding reporters inside selected divisions, Clarke believed the Pentagon could count on the reporters to build relationships with the troops and to feel dependent on them for their own safety. It worked, naturally. One reporter for a national network quavered on camera that the US army functioned as 'our protectors.' The late David Bloom of NBC confessed on the air that he was willing to do 'anything and everything they can ask of us.'

When the Pentagon needed a heroic story, the press obliged. Jessica Lynch became the war's first instant celebrity. Here was a neo-Gothic tale of a steely young woman wounded in a fierce battle, captured and tortured by ruthless enemies and dramatically saved from certain death by a team of selfless rescuers, knights in Kevlar and nightvision goggles. Of course, nearly every detail of her heroic adventure proved to be as fictive and maudlin as any made-for-TV-movie. But the ordeal of Private Lynch, which dominated the news for more than a week, served its purpose: to distract attention from a stalled campaign that was beginning to look a lot riskier than the American public had been hoodwinked into believing.

The Lynch story was fed to the eager press by a Pentagon operation called Combat Camera, the army network of photographers, videographers and editors that sends 800 photos and 25 video clips a day to the media. The editors at Combat Camera carefully culled the footage to present the Pentagon's montage of the war, eliding such unsettling images as collateral damage, cluster bombs, dead children and US soldiers, napalm strikes and disgruntled troops.

'A lot of our imagery will have a big impact on world opinion,' predicted Lt. Jane Larogue, director of Combat Camera in Iraq. She was right. But as the hot war turned into an even hotter occupation, the Pentagon, despite airy rhetoric from occupation supremo Paul Bremer about installing democratic institutions such as a free press, moved to tighten its monopoly on the flow of images out of Iraq. First, it tried to shut down Al Jazeera, the Arab news channel. Then the Pentagon intimated that it would like to see all foreign TV news crews banished from Baghdad.

Few newspapers fanned the hysteria about the threat posed by Saddam's weapons of mass destruction as sedulously as did the *Washington Post*. In the months leading up to the war, the *Post*'s pro-war op-eds outnumbered the antiwar columns by a 3 to 1 margin.

Back in 1988, the *Post* felt much differently about Saddam and his weapons of mass destruction. When reports trickled out about the gassing of Iranian troops, the *Washington Post* editorial page shrugged off the massacres, calling the mass poisonings 'a quirk of war.'

The Bush team displayed a similar amnesia. When Iraq used chemical weapons in grisly attacks on Iran, the US government not only didn't object, it encouraged Saddam. Anything to punish Iran was the message coming from the White House. Donald Rumsfeld himself was sent as President Ronald Reagan's personal envoy to Baghdad to convey the bold message that an Iraqi defeat would be viewed as a 'strategic setback for the United States.' This sleazy alliance was sealed with a handshake caught on videotape. When CNN reporter Jamie McIntyre replayed the footage for Rumsfeld in the spring of 2003, the secretary of defense snapped: 'Where'd you get that? Iraqi television?'

The current crop of Iraq hawks also saw Saddam much differently then. Take the writer Laura Mylroie, sometime colleague of the *New York Times*'s Judy Miller, who persists in peddling the ludicrous conspiracy that Iraq was behind the 1993 bombing of the World Trade Center. How times have changed. In 1987, Mylroie felt downright cuddly toward Saddam. She penned an article for the *New Republic* titled 'Back Iraq: Time for a US Tilt in the Mideast,' arguing that the US should publicly embrace Saddam's secular regime as a bulwark against the Islamic fundamentalists in Iran. The co-author of this mesmerizing weave of wonkery was none other than the minor demon himself, Daniel Pipes, perhaps the nation's most bellicose Islamophobe. 'The American weapons that Iraq could make good use of include remotely scatterable and anti-personnel mines and counterartillery radar,' wrote Mylroie and Pipes. 'The United States might also consider upgrading intelligence it is supplying Baghdad.'

In the roll-out for the war, Mylroie seemed to be everywhere hawking the invasion of Iraq. She would often appear on two or three different networks in the same day. How did the reporter manage this feat? She had help in the form of Eleana Benador, the media placement guru who runs Benador Associates. Born in Peru, Benador parlayed her skills as a linguist into a lucrative career as media relations whiz for the Washington foreign policy elite. She also oversees the Middle East Forum, a fanatically pro-Zionist white paper mill. Her clients include some of the nation's most fervid hawks, including Michael Ledeen, Charles Krauthammer, Al Haig, Max Boot, Daniel Pipes, Richard Perle and Judy Miller. During the Iraq War, Benador's assignment was to embed this squadron of pro-war zealots into the national media, on talk shows and op-ed pages.

Benador not only got them the gigs, she also crafted the message and made sure they all stayed on the same theme. 'There are some things, you just have to state them in a different way, in a slightly different way,' said Benador. 'If not people get scared.' Scared of the intentions of their own government.

It could have been different. All of the holes in the Bush administration's gossamer case for war detailed by Stauber and Rampton (and other independent journalists) were right there for the mainstream press to unearth and expose. Instead, the US press, just like the oil companies, cravenly sought to commercialize the Iraq War and profit from the invasions. They didn't want to deal with uncomfortable facts or present voices of dissent.

Nothing sums up this unctuous approach more brazenly than MSNBC's firing of liberal talk show host Phil Donahue on the eve of the war. The network replaced the Donahue show with a running segment called *Countdown: Iraq*, featuring the usual nightly coterie of retired generals, security flacks and other cheerleaders for invasion. The network's executives blamed the cancellation on sagging ratings. In fact, during its run Donahue's show attracted more viewers than any other program on the network. The real reason for the pre-emptive strike on Donahue was spelled out in an internal memo from anxious executives at NBC. Donahue, the memo said, offered 'a difficult face for MSNBC in a time of war. He seems to delight in presenting guests who are antiwar, anti-Bush and skeptical of the administration's motives.'

The memo warned that Donahue's show risked tarring NBC as an unpatriotic network, 'a home for a liberal antiwar agenda at the same time that our competitors are waving the flag at every opportunity.' So, with scarcely a second thought, the honchos at MSNBC gave Donahue the boot and hoisted the battle flag.

It's war that sells.

There's a helluva caveat, of course. Once you buy it, the merchants of war accept no returns.

August 18, 2003

JUDY MILLER'S WAR
by Alexander Cockburn

Lay all Judith Miller's *New York Times* stories end to end, from late 2001 to June 2003, and you get a desolate picture of a reporter with an agenda, both manipulating and being manipulated by US government officials, Iraqi exiles and defectors, an entire Noah's Ark of scam artists.

And while Miller, either under her own single byline or with NYT colleagues, was touting the bioterror threat, her book *Germs*, co-authored with *Times*-men Steven Engelberg and William Broad, was in the bookstores and climbing the bestseller lists. The same day that Miller opened an envelope of white powder (which turned out to be harmless) at her desk at the *New York Times*, her book was number 6 on the *New York Times* bestseller list. The following week (October 21, 2001), it reached number 2. By October 28 – at the height of her scare-mongering campaign – it was up to number 1. If we were cynical ... We don't have full 20/20 hindsight yet, but we do know for certain that all the sensational disclosures in Miller's major stories between late 2001 and early summer 2003, promoted disingenuous lies. There were no secret biolabs under Saddam's palaces, no nuclear factories across Iraq secretly working full-tilt. A huge percentage of what Miller wrote was garbage, garbage that powered the Bush administration's propaganda drive towards invasion.

What does that make Miller? She was a witting cheerleader for war. She knew what she was doing.

And what does Miller's performance make the *New York Times*? Didn't any senior editors, or even the boss, A. O. Sulzberger, ask themselves whether it was appropriate to have a trio of *Times* reporters touting their book *Germs* on TV and radio, while simultaneously running stories in the paper headlining the risks of biowar and thus creating just the sort of public alarm beneficial to the sales of their book? Isn't that the sort of conflict of interest prosecutors have been hounding Wall Street punters for?

The knives are certainly out for Miller. Leaked internal email traffic disclosed her self-confessed reliance on Ahmad Chalabi, a leading Iraqi exile with every motive to produce imaginative defectors eager to testify about Saddam's biowar, chemical and nuclear arsenal. In late June Howard Kurtz of the *Washington Post* ran a long story about Miller's ability in recent months to make the US Army jump, merely by threatening to go straight to Rumsfeld.

It was funny, but again, the conflicts of interest put the *New York Times* in a terrible light. Here was Miller, with a contract to write a new book on the post-invasion search for 'weapons of mass destruction,' lodged in the army unit charged with that search, fiercely insisting that the unit prolong its futile hunt, while simultaneously working hand in glove with Chalabi. Journalists have to do some complex dance steps to get good stories, but a few red flags should have gone up on that one.

A brisk, selective timeline:

December 20, 2001. Headline: 'Iraqi Tells of Renovations at Sites For Chemical and Nuclear Arms.' Miller rolls out a new Iraqi defector, in the ripe tradition of her favorite, Khidir Hamza, the utter fraud who called himself Saddam's Bombmaker.

Story:

An Iraqi defector who described himself as a civil engineer said he personally worked on renovations of secret facilities for biological, chemical and nuclear weapons in underground wells, private villas and under the Saddam Hussein Hospital in Baghdad as recently as a year ago.

The defector, Adnan Ihsan Saeed al-Haideri, gave details of the projects he said he worked on for President Saddam Hussein's government in an extensive interview last week in Bangkok. The interview with Mr. Saeed was arranged by the Iraqi National Congress, the main Iraqi opposition group, which seeks the overthrow of Mr. Hussein.

If verified, Mr. Saeed's allegations would provide ammunition to officials within the Bush administration who have been arguing that Mr Hussein should be driven from power partly because of his unwillingness to stop making weapons of mass destruction.

Notice the sedate phrase 'if verified.' It never was verified. But the story served its purpose.

September 7, 2002. Headline: 'US says Hussein intensifies quest for A-bomb parts.' This one was by Miller and Michael Gordon, promoting the aluminum tube nonsense: 'In the last 14 months, Iraq has sought to buy thousands of specially designed aluminum tubes, which American officials believe were intended as components of centrifuges to enrich uranium.' All lies of course. Miller and Gordon emphasize 'Mr. Hussein's dogged insistence on pursuing his nuclear ambitions, along with what defectors described in interviews as Iraq's push to improve and expand Baghdad's chemical and biological arsenals.'

Another of Miller's defectors takes a bow:

Speaking on the condition that neither he nor the country in which he was interviewed be identified, Ahmed al-Shemri, his pseudonym, said Iraq had continued developing, producing and storing chemical agents at many mobile and fixed secret sites throughout the country, many of them underground.

'All of Iraq is one large storage facility,' said Mr. Shemri. Asked about his allegations, American officials said they believed these reports were accurate.

A final bit of brazen chicanery from Gordon and Miller:

Iraq denied the existence of a germ warfare program entirely until 1995, when United Nations inspectors forced Baghdad to acknowledge it had such an effort. Then, after insisting that it had never weaponized bacteria or filled warheads, it again belatedly acknowledged having done so after Hussein Kamel, Mr. Hussein's brother-in-law, defected to Jordan with evidence about the scale of the germ warfare program.

What Gordon and Miller leave out (or lacked the enterprise or desire to find out) is that Hussein Kamel told UN inspectors that he had destroyed all Iraq's WMDs, on Saddam Hussein's orders. *September 13, 2002.* Headline: 'White House Lists Iraq Steps To Build Banned Weapons.' Miller and Gordon again, taking at face value the administration's claims that it was 'the intelligence agencies' unanimous view that the type of [aluminum] tubes that Iraq has been seeking are used to make such centrifuges.'

If nothing else this shows what rotten reporters Miller and Gordon are, because it now turns out that the intelligence analysts across Washington were deeply divided on precisely this issue.

September 18, 2002. Headline: 'Verification Is Difficult at Best, Say the Experts, and Maybe Impossible.' This is Miller helping the War Party lay down a pre-emptive barrage against the UN inspectors: 'verifying Iraq's assertions that it has abandoned weapons of mass destruction, or finding evidence that it has not done so, may not be feasible, according to officials and former weapons inspectors.'

A cameo appearance by Khidir Hamza reporting his supposed knowledge that 'Iraq was now at the "pilot plant" stage of nuclear production and within two to three years of mass producing centrifuges to enrich uranium for a bomb.'

December 3, 2002. A Miller Special, murky with unidentified informants: 'CIA Hunts Iraq Tie to Soviet Smallpox.'

Classic Miller: 'The CIA is investigating an informant's accusation that Iraq obtained a particularly virulent strain of smallpox from a Russian scientist who worked in a smallpox lab in Moscow during Soviet times.'

January 24, 2003. 'Defectors Bolster US Case Against Iraq, Officials Say.'

Another Miller onslaught on the UN inspectors:

> Former Iraqi scientists, military officers and contractors have provided American intelligence agencies with a portrait of Saddam Hussein's secret programs to develop and conceal chemical, biological and nuclear weapons that is starkly at odds with the findings so far of the United Nations weapons inspectors.

Al-Haideri is still in play:

> Intelligence officials said that some of the most valuable information has come from Adnan Ihsan Saeed al-Haideri, a contractor who fled Iraq in the summer of 2001. He later told American officials that chemical and biological weapons laboratories were hidden beneath hospitals and inside presidential palaces. Mr. Haideri was relocated anonymously to a small town in Virginia.

We'll leave al-Haideri in well-earned retirement and Miller heading towards her supreme triumph of April 20, 2003, relaying the allegations of chemical and bio-weapon dumps made by an unnamed Iraqi scientist she'd never met.

August 2, 2003

MEET THE REAL WMD FABRICATOR:
A SWEDE CALLED ROLF EKEUS
by Alexander Cockburn

Week after week Bush and his people have been getting pounded by newly emboldened Democrats and liberal pundits for having exaggerated the threat posed by Saddam Hussein and his still-elusive weapons of mass destruction. One day CIA director George Tenet is hung out to dry; the next it's the turn of Paul Wolfowitz's platoon of mad Straussians. The other side of the Atlantic, the same sort of thing has been happening to Tony Blair.

They deserve the pounding, but if we're to be fair there's an even more deserving target, a man of impeccable liberal credentials, well respected in the sort of confabs attended by New Labour and espousers of the Third Way. I give you Rolf Ekeus, former Swedish ambassador to the United States and, before that, the executive chairman of the United Nations Special Commission (UNSCOM) on Iraq from 1991 to 1997. These days he's chairman of the Stockholm International Peace Research Institute, a noted dovecote of the olive-branch set.

In the wake of the first Iraq war it was UNSCOM chief Ekeus, exuding disinterested integrity as only a Swede can, who insisted that Saddam Hussein was surely pressing forward with the manufacture of weapons of mass destruction. It was Ekeus who played a pivotal role in justifying the continued imposition of sanctions, on the grounds that these sanctions were essential as a means of applying pressure to the tyrant in Baghdad.

In 1996 Ramsey Clark, former US Attorney General, and a leading critic of the indiscriminate cruelty of these sanctions, wrote an open letter to Ekeus beginning thus:

Dear Mr. Ekeus, How many children are you willing to let die while you search for 'items' you 'are convinced still exist in' Iraq? Every two months for the past half year, and on earlier occasions, you or your office have made some statement several weeks before the Security Council considers sanctions against Iraq which you know will be used to cause their continuation ... This cruel and endless hoax of new disclosures every two months must stop. The direct consequence of your statements which are used to justify continuation of the sanctions against Iraq is the deaths of hundreds of thousands of innocent and helpless infants, children and elderly and chronically ill human beings.

Despite many such furious denunciations, till the day he handed over his job as UNSCOM chief to the more obviously suspect and disheveled Australian Richard Butler, Ekeus continued in the manner stigmatized by Clark and others. US Ambassador to the UN Madeleine Albright notoriously said to Lesley Stahl of CBS, of the lethal sanctions which killed over half a million Iraqi children, 'We think the price is worth it,' but Ekeus was the one who furnished the UN's diplomatic cover for that repulsive calculus.

It's fortunate for Ekeus's reputation among the genteel liberal crowd that public awareness of what he really knew about Saddam's chemical, biological and nuclear weapons is still slight. In fact Ekeus was perfectly well aware from the mid-1990s on that Saddam Hussein had no such weapons of mass destruction. They had all been destroyed years earlier, after the first Gulf War. Ekeus learned this on the night of August 22, 1995, in Amman, from the lips of General Hussein Kamel, who had just defected from Iraq, along with some of his senior military aides. Kamel was Saddam's son-in-law and had been in overall charge of all programs for chemical, biological and nuclear weapons and delivery systems.

That night, in three hours of detailed questioning from Ekeus and two technical experts, Kamel was categorical. The UN inspection teams had done a good job. When Saddam was finally persuaded that failure to dispose of the relevant weapons systems would have very serious consequences, he issued the order and Kamel carried it out. As he told Ekeus that night, 'All weapons, biological, chemical, missile, nuclear, were destroyed.' (The UNSCOM record of the session can be viewed at http://www.fair.org/press-releases/kamel.pdf). In similar debriefings that August, Kamel said the same thing to teams from the CIA and MI6. His military aides provided a wealth of corroborative details. Then, the following year, Kamel was lured back to Iraq and at once executed.

Did Ekeus immediately proclaim victory, and suggest that sanctions could be abated? As we have seen, he did not. In fact he urged that they be intensified. The years rolled by and Iraqi children by the thousand wasted and died. The war party thumped the drum over Saddam's WMDs, and Kamel's debriefings stayed under lock and key. Finally, John Barry of *Newsweek* unearthed details of those sessions in Amman and in February this year *Newsweek* ran his story, though not with the play it deserved. I gather that when Barry confronted Ekeus with details of the suppressed briefing, Ekeus was stricken. Barry's sensational disclosure was mostly ignored.

And Ekeus's rationale for suppressing the disclosures of Kamel and his aides? He claims that the plan was to bluff Saddam and his scientists into further disclosures. Try to figure that out.

For playing the game the way the US desired it to be played, Ekeus got his rewards: a pleasing welcome in Washington when he arrived there as Swedish ambassador, respectful audiences along the world's diplomatic circuits. To this day he zealously burnishes his 'credibility' with long, tendentious articles arguing that Bush and Blair had it right. He betrays no sign of being troubled by his horrible role. He will never be forced to squirm in hearings by Democratic senators suddenly as brave as lions. He won't have to wade through raw sewage to enter the main hospital in Baghdad and watch children die, or ride in a Humvee and wait for someone to drop a hand-grenade off a bridge and blow his head off.

Today he grazes peacefully in the tranquil pastures of the Stockholm Peace Research Institute. But if we're going to heap recriminations on Bush and Blair and the propagandists who fashioned their lies, don't forget Ekeus. He played a worse role than most of them, under the blue flag of the UN.

September 1, 2003

HANDMAID IN BABYLON: ANNAN, VIEIRA DE MELLO AND THE UN'S DECLINE AND FALL
by Alexander Cockburn

'One has to be careful,' said UN Secretary-General Kofi Annan in late August, 'not to confuse the UN with the US.' If the Secretary-General had taken his own advice, then maybe his Brazilian subordinate, Sergio Vieira de Mello, might not have been so summarily blown to pieces in Baghdad two days earlier. As things are, the UN still craves the handmaid role the US desperately needs in Iraq as political cover.

Whichever group sent that truck bomb on its way decided that Vieira and his boss were so brazen in moving the UN to play a figleaf role in the US occupation of Iraq that spectacular action was necessary to draw attention to the process. So the UN man handpicked by the White House paid with his life.

To get a sense of how swift has been the conversion of the UN into after-sales service provider for the world's prime power, just go back to 1996, when the United States finally decided that Annan's predecessor as UN Secretary-General, Boutros Boutros-Ghali, had to go.

In a pleasing foreshadowing of Annan's plaintive remark cited above, Boutros-Ghali told Clinton's top foreign policy executives: 'Please allow me from time to time to differ publicly from US policy.' But unlike Annan he did so, harshly contrasting Western concern for Bosnia, whose conflict he described as 'a war of the rich,' with its indifference to the genocide in Rwanda and to horrifying conditions throughout the Third World. Then, in April 1996, he went altogether too far, when he insisted on publishing the findings of the UN inquiry which implicated Israel in the killing of some hundred civilians who had taken refuge in a United Nations camp in Kanaa in south Lebanon.

In a minority of one on the Security Council, the US insisted on exercising its veto of a second term for Boutros-Ghali. James Rubin, erstwhile State Department spokesman, wrote his epitaph in the *Financial Times*: Boutros-Ghali was 'unable to understand the importance of cooperation with the world's first power.' It took another foreign policy operative of the Clinton era to identify Annan's appeal to Washington. Richard Holbrooke later recalled that in 1995 there was a 'dual-key' arrangement, whereby both Boutros-Ghali and the NATO commander had to jointly approve bombing. Boutros-Ghali had vetoed all but the most limited pinprick bombing of the Serbs, for fear of appearing to take sides. But when Boutros-Ghali was traveling, Annan was left in charge of the UN key. 'When Kofi turned it,' Holbrooke told Philip Gourevich of the *New Yorker*, 'he became Secretary-General in waiting.' There was of course a further, very terrible service rendered by Annan, in which, in deference to the American desire to keep Sarajevo in the limelight, he suppressed the warnings of the Canadian General Roméo Dallaire that appalling massacres were about to start in Rwanda.

Of course even in the UN's braver days, there were always the realities of power to be acknowledged, but UN secretaries-general such as Dag Hammarskjöld and U Thant were men of stature. These days UN functionaries such as Annan and the late Vieira know full well that their careers depend on American patronage. Vieira was a bureaucrat, never an elected politician, instrumental in establishing the UN protectorate system in Kosovo. Then he was the beneficiary of an elaborate and instructive maneuver, in which the US was eager to rid itself of the inconvenient Jose Mauricio Bustani, another Brazilian, from his post as head of the Organization for the Prohibition of Chemical Weapons, the Chemical Weapons Convention's implementing organization. Bustani was no US cat's-paw but adamant in maintaining his organization's independence, and admired round the world for his energy in seeking to rid the world of chemical weapons.

When UNSCOM withdrew from Iraq in 1998, hopelessly compromised and riddled with spies, Bustani's OPCW was allowed in to continue verification of destruction of WMDs. The US feared Bustani would persuade Saddam Hussein to sign the Chemical Weapons Convention and accept inspections from Bustani's organization, thus allowing the possibility of credible estimates of Iraq's arsenal that might prove inconvenient to the US. Brazil was informed that if it supported the ouster of Bustani, it would be rewarded with US backing for Vieira's elevation to the post of UN High Commissioner for Human Rights, replacing another object of US disfavor, Mary Robinson.

Vieira was duly appointed. Then, earlier this year, the imperial finger crooked an urgent summons for him to come to Washington for inspection by Condoleezza Rice. Vieira made all the right noises. Desperate for UN cover in Iraq, the Bush White House pressured Annan to appoint Vieira as UN Special Envoy to Iraq.

Vieira installed himself in Baghdad where, in cooperation with the US proconsul Paul Bremer, his priority was to put together a puppet Governing Council of Iraqis, serving at the pleasure of the Coalition Provisional Authority. The council was replete with such notorious fraudsters as Ahmad Chalabi. It was formed on July 13. Nine days later Vieira was at the UN in New York, proclaiming with a straight face that 'we now have a formal body of senior and distinguished Iraqi counterparts, with credibility and authority, with whom we can chart the way forward. We now enter a new stage that succeeds the disorienting power vacuum that followed the fall of the previous regime.'

Though it did not formally recognize the Governing Council, the UN Security Council eagerly commended this achievement. The *Financial Times* editorialized on August 19: 'America's friends, such as India, Turkey Pakistan and even France, which opposed the war, should stand ready to help. But they need UN cover.' In Baghdad, the next day, in the form of the truck bomb, came an answer. Two days later, Kofi Annan counseled on the dangers of confusing the UN with the US.

If he meant what he said, Annan should obviously resign forthwith as the man who has done more than any figure alive to equate the two. But who would imagine Africa's Waldheim being capable of that?

November 7, 2003

BUSH'S IRAQ MESS: GETTING WORSE BY THE DAY
by Patrick Cockburn

BAGHDAD: A plume of dust and smoke rose, the morning of November 3, from a field just outside Fallujah, west of Baghdad, where a giant American Chinook helicopter, crippled by a missile, had crashed and burned, killing at least 18 and wounding another 20 of the soldiers and crew on board. It was the worst single military disaster for the US in Iraq since the war to overthrow Saddam Hussein started in March. It means that the US forces in Iraq may in future have to rely less on helicopters and use the roads – which in this part of Iraq are almost equally hazardous.

The destruction of the helicopter should underline the speed with which the war in Iraq is intensifying: 16 US soldiers were killed in September, 33 in October and a further 16 in just the first two days of November. It is also spreading further north, to the cities of Mosul and Kirkuk. But even as I was driving to Fallujah, just before the helicopter was brought down, I heard on the radio President Bush repeat his old mantra that 'the Iraqi people understand that there are a handful of people who do not want to live in freedom.'

It is an extraordinarily active handful. I heard from a shopkeeper in the centre of Fallujah that a Chinook helicopter had been shot down on the other side of the Euphrates river, which flows through the town. It was only three or four miles away, but on the way we drove past the remains of a US truck which had been blown up two hours earlier by a bomb or rocket-propelled grenade. On the other side of a bridge over the river was a minibus taxi punctured by shrapnel, its interior sodden with blood. Locals claimed it had been hit by a US missile, which killed one passenger and wounded nine others.

But the White House and the Pentagon seem unable to take on board how swiftly the US political and military position in Iraq is deteriorating. Even after half a dozen rockets hit the al-Rashid Hotel, narrowly missing Paul Wolfowitz, the US Deputy Secretary of Defense and one of the architects of the war in Iraq, US generals in Baghdad were still contending to incredulous journalists that overall security in Iraq was improving.

In his blindness to military reality Mr Bush sounds more and more like the much-derided former Iraqi Information Minister, 'Comical Ali,' still claiming glorious victories as the US army entered Baghdad. Every attack is interpreted as evidence that the 'remnants' of Saddam's regime are becoming 'desperate' at the great progress being made by the US in Iraq.

Two arguments are often produced to downplay the seriousness of the resistance. One is the 'remnants' theory: a small group of Saddam loyalists have created all this turmoil. This is a bit surprising, since the lesson of the war was that Saddam Hussein had few supporters prepared to fight for him.

In fact the 'remnants' of the old regime have become greater in number since the end of the war. The US occupation authority has been the main recruiting sergeant. It has behaved as if Saddam Hussein were a popular leader with a mass following. It has dissolved the Iraqi army, leaving 400,000 trained soldiers without a job, and sacked Ba'ath party members. A friend, long in opposition to Saddam, told me: 'Two of my brothers were murdered by Saddam, I fled abroad, but now they are going to fire four of my relatives because they were forced to join the Ba'ath party to keep their jobs.'

Another comforting method of downplaying the resistance is to say it is all taking place in the 'Sunni triangle.' The word 'triangle' somehow implies that the area is finite and small. In fact the Sunni

Arabs of Iraq live in an area almost the size of England. Ghassan Atiyah, a distinguished Iraqi historian and political activist, believes that 'if the Sunni Arabs feel they are being made second-class citizens they will permanently destabilize Iraq, just as the Kurds used to do.'

Bush's solution to all this is to get Iraqis to fight the resistance. The US-run Coalition Provisional Authority, isolated in its fortified headquarters in Baghdad, says it plans to deploy a force of 222,000 police, military, civil defense and other security organizations by next September.

This sounds impressive. But only 35,000 of these will be troops of the new American-trained Iraqi army. There are many police on the streets of Baghdad, and they have successfully reduced crime. But in interviews they always make clear that they see their job as protecting ordinary Iraqis from criminals. They very reasonably have no desire to be pushed into a paramilitary role, for which they are neither trained nor equipped. They do not want to be portrayed as collaborators, particularly in areas where the resistance is strongest and the Americans would need them most. In Fallujah, perhaps the most militant town in Iraq, the police openly say they will not patrol or man checkpoints with US troops. As I was leaving the police station in the town last week, I heard an unseen policeman in a sentry box crooning a patriotic song filled with praise of Saddam Hussein.

The US could have avoided many of its present problems if it had given greater legitimacy to the occupation at an early stage. It can only recruit an effective Iraqi security force, capable of fighting guerrillas, if there is a legitimate Iraqi provisional government. Iraqis simply will not fight if they are asked to join a force which is viewed as an adjunct to an American army. They see no reason why they should be cannon fodder for a foreign regime. The US could have legitimized the political reconstruction of Iraq in the eyes of Iraqis if it had placed the process under the auspices of the UN. Instead it repeatedly rebuffed the idea. Now, as the last UN foreign staff leave the country, it is probably too late.

At the turn of the month Paul Bremer, the head of the CPA, pledged to hand over more power to Iraqis. But there is no sign in Baghdad that this is more than window-dressing. The US-appointed Governing Council is mostly made up of exiles and nonentities. Only its Kurdish members have a demonstrable constituency in Iraq. It has little authority. Ministers privately complain that US officials in Baghdad simply bypass them and take all the important decisions themselves. Because the US has sought to monopolize power in Iraq, it has few real allies aside from the Kurds, the smallest of Iraq's three communities. The Sunni Arabs are mostly hostile, and the Shias increasingly so. The only way out for the US – though it is getting very late in the day – is to hold elections to create an Iraqi authority, effectively a provisional government, which Iraqis know they have chosen themselves. A general election would be difficult to organize at short notice. But even a body of delegates chosen by local leaders in each governorate would have some claim to speak for Iraq.

The US toyed with the idea of local elections in midsummer. But it was frightened off by a fear that the new body would be dominated by Shia clerics or their supporters. The Shia, at least 55 per cent of the population, are eager to show their electoral strength.

The failure to create an elected and legitimate Iraqi provisional government, even if it is an interim administration, will make it impossible for the US to set up a security force that will not be seen as collaborators by most Iraqis. Fallujah, where hatred of the Americans is almost palpable, is not yet a typical Iraqi town, even in Sunni areas, but it may soon become so.

Patrick Cockburn, a reporter with The Independent, *is the co-author of* Saddam Hussein: An American Obsession.

REPRISE

THE THIRTEEN YEARS' WAR
by Alexander Cockburn and Jeffrey St. Clair

ONE

The 'war,' officially designated by the US government as such and inaugurated with the 'decapitation' strike of March 19, 2003, was really only a change of tempo in the overall war on Iraq, commenced with the sanctions imposed by the UN and by a separate US blockade in August of 1990, stretching through the first 'hot' attack of January 16, 1991 on through the next twelve years. 1990–2003: a long war, and a terrible one for the Iraqi people.

On April 3, 1991, the UN Security Council approved Resolution 687, the so-called mother of all resolutions, setting up the sanctions committee, dominated by the United States.

It is vital to understand that the first 'hot' Gulf War was waged as much against the people of Iraq as against the Republican Guard. The US and its allies destroyed Iraq's water, sewage and water-purification systems and its electrical grid. Nearly every bridge across the Tigris and Euphrates was demolished. They struck twenty-eight hospitals and destroyed thirty-eight schools. They hit all eight of Iraq's large hydropower dams. They attacked grain storage silos and irrigation systems.

Farmlands near Basra were inundated with saltwater as a result of allied attacks. More than 95 per cent of Iraq's poultry farms were destroyed, as were 3.5 million sheep and more than 2 million cows. The US and its allies bombed textile plants, cement factories and oil refineries, pipelines and storage facilities, all of which contributed to an environmental and economic nightmare that continued nearly unabated over the twelve years.

When confronted by the press with reports of Iraqi women carting home buckets of filthy water from the Tigris river, itself contaminated with raw sewage from the bombed treatment plants, an American general shrugged his shoulders and said: 'People say, "You didn't recognize that the bombing was going to have an effect on water and sewage". Well, what were we trying to do with sanctions: help out the Iraqi people? What we were doing with the attacks on the infrastructure was to accelerate the effect of the sanctions.'

After this first 'hot' war in early 1991, with Iraq's civilian and military infrastructure in ruins, the sanctions returned, as an invisible army of what we could call 'external occupation,' with a vise grip: the intent was to keep Iraq from rebuilding not only its army but the foundations of its economy and society.

Despite the efforts of outfits such as Voices in the Wilderness, embargoes don't draw the same attention as salvoes of cruise missiles or showers of cluster bombs. But they're infinitely more deadly, and the perpetrators and executives deserve to end up on trial as war criminals as richly as any targeting officer in the Pentagon.

By 1998, UN officials working Baghdad were arguing that the root cause of child mortality and other health problems was no longer simply lack of food and medicine but lack of clean water (freely available in all parts of Iraq prior to the Gulf War) and of electrical power, now running at only 30 per cent of the pre-bombing level, with consequences for hospitals and water-pumping systems that can be all too readily imagined.

Many of the contracts vetoed at the insistence of the US by the Sanctions Committee were integral to the repair of water and sewage systems. By some estimates, the bombings from the Gulf War inflicted nearly $200 billion worth of damage to the civilian infrastructure of Iraq. 'Basically, anything with chemicals or even pumps is liable to get thrown out,' one UN official revealed.

The sanctions, then, served as a pretext to bring this hidden war home to the Iraqi people, to 'soften them up' from the inside, as one Pentagon official put it. The same trend was apparent in the power supply sector, where around 25 per cent of the contracts were vetoed. This meant not only were homes without power, but also hospitals, schools, the infrastructure of everyday life.

But even this doesn't tell the whole story. UN officials referred to the 'complementarity issue,' meaning that items approved for purchase would be useless without other items that had been vetoed. For example (as *CounterPunch* reported at the time) the Iraqi Ministry of Health ordered $25 million worth of dentist chairs. This order was approved by the sanctions committee, except for the compressors, without which the chairs were useless and consequently gathered dust in a Baghdad warehouse.

These vetoes served as a constant harassment, even over petty issues. In February 2000 the US moved to prevent Iraq from importing 15 bulls from France. The excuse was that the animals, ordered with the blessing of the UN's humanitarian office in Baghdad to try to restock the Iraqi beef industry, would require certain vaccines which (who knows?) might be diverted into a program to make biological weapons of mass destruction.

For sheer sadistic bloody-mindedness, however, the interdiction of the bulls pales beside an initiative of the British government, which banned the export of vaccines for tetanus, diphtheria and yellow fever on the grounds that they too might find their way into the hands of Saddam's biological weaponeers. It has been the self-exculpatory mantra of US and British officials that 'food and medicine are exempt from sanctions.' As the vaccine ban shows, this, like so many other pronouncements on Iraq, turns out to be a lie.

Indeed, the sanctions policy was always marked by acts of captious cruelty. Since 1991, the US and Britain slapped their veto on requests by Iraq for infant food, ping-pong balls, NCR computers for children's hospitals for blood analysis, heaters, insecticide, syringes, bicycles, nail polish and lipstick, tennis balls, children's clothes, pencil sharpeners and school notebooks, cotton balls and swabs, hospital and ambulance radios and pagers, and shroud material.

TWO

But the prolonged onslaught on the Iraqi people by the sanctions did not mean that direct military attack stopped in March of 1991. Indeed, though it received scant attention in the press, Iraq was hit with bombs or missiles an average of every three days since the ceasefire that purportedly signaled the end of the first Gulf War. Its feeble air defense system was shattered and its radars were jammed and bombed; its air force was grounded, the runways of its airports were repeatedly cratered; its navy, primitive to begin with, was destroyed. The nation's northern and southern territories were occupied by hostile forces, armed, funded and overseen by the CIA.

Every bit of new construction in the country was scrutinized for any possible military function by satellite cameras capable of zooming down to a square meter. Truck and tank convoys were zealously monitored. Troop locations were pinpointed. Bunkers were mapped, the coordinates programmed into the targeting software for bunker-busting bombs.

Iraq after the Gulf War wasn't a rogue state. It was a captive state. This daily military harassment was the normal state of play, but there were also more robust displays of power. In June of 1993, Bill Clinton okayed a cruise missile strike on Baghdad, supposedly in response to an alleged and certainly bungled bid by Iraqi agents to assassinate George Bush the first on his triumphal tour of Kuwait.

Twenty-three cruise missiles were launched on Baghdad from two aircraft carriers in the Persian Gulf. With deadly imprecision, eight of the missiles hit a residential suburb of Baghdad, killing dozens of civilians, including one of Iraq's leading artists, Leila al-Attar.

Then in December of 1998 another raid on Baghdad was launched, this one timed to divert attention from the House of Representatives' vote on the question of Clinton's impeachment. This time more than 100 missiles rained down on Baghdad, Mosul, Tikrit and Basra, killing hundreds. Clinton's chief pollster, Stan Greenberg, imparted the welcome news that the bombings had caused Clinton's poll numbers to jump by 11 points. When in doubt, bomb Iraq.

The message was not lost on Bush. In late February of 2001, less than a month into office, Bush let fly with two dozen cruise missiles on Baghdad, a strike that Donald Rumsfeld described as an 'act of protective retaliation.' And alongside these attacks the CIA was busy sponsoring assassination bids and, with sometimes comical inefficiency, trying to mount coups against Saddam Hussein.

After five years of sanctions Iraq was in desperate straits. The hospitals filled with dying children, while medicines necessary to save them were banned by the US officials in New York supervising the operations of the sanctions committee. Half a million children had died in the time span. The mortality rates were soaring with terrifying speed. The infant mortality rate had gone from 47 per 1,000 in 1989 to 108 per 1,000 in 1996. For kids under five the increase in the rate was even worse, from 56 per 1,000 in 1989 to 131 per 1,000 in 1996. By 1996 the death count was running at 5,000 children a month, to which Madeleine Albright made the infamous comment, 'we think the price is worth it.'

THREE

One might think this carefully planned and deadly onslaught on a civilian population, year after year, surely was retribution enough for Saddam's invasion of Kuwait. But what allowed the ultra-hawks in Washington to press for another hot war on Iraq was Saddam's personal survival as Iraqi dictator. Though the aims of the war party were much broader, the brazen survival of Saddam was always the pretext.

On July 8, 1996 the Institute for Advanced Strategic and Political Studies sent a strategy memo to Israel's new prime minister, Benjamin Netanyahu. Grandly titled 'A Clean Break: A New Strategy for Securing the Realm' (the realm in this instance being Israel), the memorandum had among its sponsors several notorious Washington characters, some of them accused more than once down the years of being agents of influence for Israel, including Richard Perle and Douglas Feith.

Among the recommendations for Natenyahu were these:

roll-back some of [Israel's] most dangerous threats. This implies clean break from the slogan 'comprehensive peace' to a traditional concept of strategy based on balance of power ...

Change the nature of [Israel's] relations with the Palestinians, including upholding the right of hot pursuit for self-defense into all Palestinian areas ...

Israel can shape its strategic environment, in cooperation with Turkey and Jordan, by weakening, containing, and even rolling back Syria. This effort can focus on removing Saddam Hussein from power in Iraq – an important Israeli strategic objective in its own right – as a means of foiling Syria's regional ambitions.

Within a few short months this strategy paper for Netanyahu was being recycled through the agency of a Washington bucket shop called the Project for a New American Century, which was convened by William Kristol with infusions of cash from the right-wing Bradley Foundation. The PNAC became a roosting spot for a retinue of DC neocons, headlined by Donald Rumsfeld, Dick Cheney and Paul Wolfowitz.

On the eve of Clinton's 1998 State of the Union address, Rumsfeld and Wolfowitz sent Clinton a letter on PNAC stationery urging the president to radically overhaul US policy toward Iraq. Instead of the slow squeeze of sanctions, Rumsfeld and Wolfowitz declared that it was time for Saddam to be forcibly evicted and Iraq reconstructed along lines favorable to US and Israeli interests. The UN be damned. 'We are writing you because we are convinced that current American policy toward Iraq is not succeeding, and that we may soon face a threat in the Middle East more serious than any we have known since the end of the Cold War,' the letter blared.

> In your upcoming State of the Union Address, you have an opportunity to chart a clear and determined course for meeting this threat. We urge you to seize that opportunity, and to enunciate a new strategy that would secure the interests of the US and our friends and allies around the world. That strategy should aim, above all, at the removal of Saddam Hussein's regime from power … American policy cannot continue to be crippled by a misguided insistence on unanimity in the UN Security Council.

In all likelihood, the strategy outlined in the letter was aimed not at Clinton, the lame duck, but at Gore, who Wolfowitz, Rumsfeld *et al.* believed might be more receptive to this rhetoric.

They had reason for hope. One of the PNAC's members was James Woolsey, former CIA head and long-time Gore advisor on intelligence and military matters. And it worked. As the campaign season rolled into action Gore began to distance himself from Clinton on Iraq. He embraced the corrupt Ahmad Chalabi and his Iraqi National Congress, indicted the Bush family for being soft on Saddam and called for regime topple.

Had Gore been elected he likely would have stepped up the tempo of military strikes on Iraq within weeks of taking office.

FOUR

After seizing power, the Bush crowd didn't have wait long to draw Iraqi blood. Less than a month after taking office, cruise missiles pummeled Baghdad, killing dozens of civilians. Then, came the attacks of 9/11. Just hours into that day of disaster, Rumsfeld convened a meeting in the war room. He commanded his aides to get 'best info fast. Judge whether good enough hit S.H.' – meaning Saddam Hussein – 'at same time. Not only U.B.L.' – the initials used to identify Osama bin Laden. 'Go massive.' Notes taken by these aides quote him as saying: 'Sweep it all up. Things related and not.' The notes were uncovered by David Martin of CBS News.

The preparations for overthrowing Saddam began that day, under the pretense that Saddam was somehow connected to bin Laden's Wahhabite kamikazes. Rumsfeld knew then that the connection was illusory, and despite lots of bluster and digging it didn't became any more substantial over the next year and a half.

In the months that preceded the second 'hot' war, started on March 19, 2003, many a theory was advanced for the prime motive of the war party. Was it the plan of the pro-Israel neocon hawks? Was it all about oil and (a subvariant) because Saddam was insisting on being paid for his oil in euros? Was it, in the wake of 9/11, a peremptory message about US power (this is the current White House favorite)? Was it essentially a subject change from the domestic economic slump?

The answer is the essentially unconspiratorial one that it was a mix. Bush's initial policy in his first fumbling months in office was far from the chest-pounding stance of implacable American might that it became after 9/11 changed the rule book. 9/11 is what gave the neocons their chance, and allowed them to push forward and eventually trump the instincts of a hefty chunk of the political and corporate elites.

For many in these elites, the survival of Saddam Hussein was a small blip on the radar screen. For a résumé of what preoccupied these elites, here's a useful account from Jeffrey Garten, who was Clinton's first undersecretary of commerce for international trade, writing in *Business Week*:

The biggest issues the Administration faced were not military in nature but competition with Japan and Europe, financial crises in Latin America and Asia, negotiations over the North American Trade Agreement, and the establishment of the World Trade Organization and China's entrance into it. In Washington's eyes, the policies of the IMF, the World Bank, and the WTO were bigger issues than the future of NATO. The opening of Japan's markets was more critical than its military posture in Asia. The rating that Standard & Poor's gave to Indonesia was of greater significance than sending our military advisers there. We pushed deregulation and privatization. We mounted massive trade missions to help US companies win big contracts in emerging markets. Strengthening economic globalization became the organizing principle for most of our foreign policy. And American corporations were de facto partners all along the way.

That's a fair account of how the agenda looks, from the imperial battlements. Run the show as best you can, but don't rock the boat more than you have to. Acting too blatantly as prime world gangster, dissing the Security Council, roiling the Arab world, prompting popular upheavals in Turkey, all counted as boat-rocking on a dangerous scale.

By the end of half a year's national debate on the utility of attacking Iraq, business leaders were still chewing their fingernails and trembling at the economic numbers; the *New York Times* was against war and George Jr had lost the support of his father, who issued a distinct rebuke during a question-and-answer session at Tufts in mid-spring. George Senior's closest associates, James Baker and Brent Scowcroft, similarly expressed disagreement.

But against this opposition, domestic political factors proved paramount and overwhelming. The post-9/11 climate offers the American right its greatest chance since the first days of the Reagan administration, maybe even since the early 1950s, to set in blood and stone its core agenda: untrammeled exercise of power overseas, and at home roll-back of all liberal gains since the start of the New Deal. And not just that, but an opportunity too to make a lasting dent in the purchase on Jewish support and money held since Truman by the Democratic Party.

FIVE

These are the prizes, and so it was never in doubt, since the morning hours of 9/11, that the Bush regime would attack Iraq and bring home the head of … no, not Saddam, who may now be putting up his Vargas drawings in some motel in Minsk. What the Bush regime needed, and got, was not the head, but the image of the head, wrapped in the US flag. That came with the images of Iraqis – actually a small knot of Chalabi's supporters plus some journalists – cheering US troops in the Baghdad square in front of the Palestine Hotel on April 9 as they hauled down Saddam's statue in one small portion of that square, itself sealed off by three US tanks. (Online CounterPunchers can go to www.counterpunch.org/statue.html and see for themselves.) As for the looting, it's entirely in character for US planners to have had plans for the 'attrition of Iraqi national self-esteem,' but also we wouldn't discount local initiative, probably with inside help, in looting the archeological museum and the national library.

The non-discovery of the weapons of mass destruction has become a huge embarrassment for both Bush and Blair. The Sunday's British *Independent* (April 20, 2003) carried the following huge frontpage banner headlines: 'SO WHERE ARE THEY, MR BLAIR? NOT ONE ILLEGAL WARHEAD. NOT ONE DRUM OF CHEMICALS. NOT ONE INCRIMINATING DOCUMENT. NOT ONE SHRED OF EVIDENCE THAT IRAQ HAS WEAPONS OF MASS DESTRUCTION IN MORE THAN A MONTH OF WAR AND OCCUPATION.'

CounterPunch tends to agree with the assessment of the Russian commentator 'Venik,' who remarked when the 'hot war' was over (at last temporarily, and excluding summary and ongoing shootings of Iraqis) that, as in the initial US engagement in Afghanistan, the prime US weapon of mass destruction was the dollar.

We have read many highly detailed accounts of how, in the first week of April, the impending siege of Baghdad turned into a cakewalk, and though we don't believe most of those details, we do agree that there were some big pay-offs and US guarantees of assisted flight. Indeed here at *CounterPunch* we wonder whether some of those billion-dollar stashes found by US troops in Baghdad were not US pay-off money that speeded the departure of the Republican Guard's commanders, duly followed by the defection of the prudent troops.

Iraq's thirteen years' war is not over. That's obvious enough, and we expect many long years of travail and struggle lie ahead for those millions of people in the cradle of civilization. We will report on them to the best of our ability. CounterPunchers should not neglect, in pondering those thirteen years, the fact that US officials spent years knowingly making decisions that spelled certain death to hundreds of thousands of the poorest Iraqi civilians, the bulk of them children.

January 14, 2004

AND SOME FINAL THOUGHTS
by Alexander Cockburn

First, I think the left needs to get a lot more hard-eyed about what the actual function of the UN is.

Nikita Khrushchev wrote in his incomparable memoirs that Soviet admirals, like admirals everywhere, loved battleships, because they could get piped aboard in great style amid the respectful hurrahs of their crews. It's the same with the UN, now more than ever reduced to the servile function of after-sales service provider for the United States, on permanent call as the mop-up brigade. It would be a great step forward if several big Third World nations were soon to quit the United Nations, declaring that it has no political function beyond ratifying the world's present distasteful political arrangements.

The trouble is that national political elites in pretty much every UN-member country – now 191 in all – yearn to live in high style for at least a few years, and in some cases for decades, on the Upper

East side of Manhattan and to cut a dash in the General Assembly. They have a deep material stake in continuing membership, even though in the case of small, poor countries the prodigious outlays on a UN delegation could be far better used in some decent domestic application, funding orphanages or local crafts back home.

Barely a day goes by without some Democrat piously demanding 'an increased role' for the UN in whatever misadventure for which the US requires political cover. Howard Dean built his candidacy on clarion calls for the UN's supposedly legitimizing assistance in Iraq. Despite the political history of the Nineties many leftists still have a tendency to invoke the UN as a countervailing power. When all other argument fails they fall back on the International Criminal Court, an outfit that should by all rights should have the same credibility as a beneficial institution as the World Bank or Interpol.

On the issue of the UN I can boast a record of matchless consistency. As a toddler I tried to bar my father's exit from the nursery of our London flat when he told me he was leaving for several weeks to attend, as diplomatic correspondent of the *Daily Worker*, the founding conference of the UN in San Francisco. Despite my denunciation of all such absence-prompting conferences (and in my infancy there were many), he did go.

He wrote later in his autobiography, *Crossing the Line*, that

The journey of our special train across the Middle West ... was at times almost intolerably moving. Our heavily laden special had some sort of notice prominently displayed on its sides indicating it was taking people to the foundation meeting of the United Nations ... From towns and lonely villages all across the plains and prairies, people would come out to line the tracks, standing there with the flags still flying half-mast for Roosevelt on the buildings behind them, and their eyes fixed on this train with extraordinary intensity, as though it were part of the technical apparatus for the performance of a miracle … On several occasions I saw a man or woman solemnly touch the train, the way a person might touch a talisman.

It was understandable that an organization aspiring to represent All Mankind and to espouse Peace should have excited fervent hopes in the wake of terrible war, but the fix was in from the start, as Peter Gowan reminds us in a spirited essay in *New Left Review* for November/December 2003. The Rooseveltian vision was for an impotent General Assembly with decision-making authority vested in a Security Council without, in Gowan's words, 'the slightest claim to rest on any representative principle other than brute force,' and of course dominated by the United States and its vassals. FDR did see a cosmopolitan role for the UN; not so Truman and Acheson who followed Nelson Rockefeller's body-blow to the nascent UN when, as assistant secretary of state for Latin American Affairs, the latter brokered the Chapultepec Pact in Mexico City in 1945, formalizing US dominance in the region through the soon-to-be familiar regional military-security alliance set up by Dean Acheson in the next period.

These days the UN has the same restraining role on the world's prime imperial power as did the Roman Senate in the fourth century AD, when there were still actual senators spending busy lives bustling from one cocktail party to another, intriguing to have their sons elected quaestor and so forth, deliberating with great self-importance and sending the Emperor pompous resolutions on the burning issues of the day.

For a modern evocation of what those senatorial resolutions must have been like, read the unanimous Security Council resolution on October 15, 2003, hailing the US-created 'Governing Council of Iraq,' and trolling out UN-speak to the effect that the Security

Council '*welcomes* the positive response of the international community to the establishment of the broadly representative council'; '*supports* the Governing Council's efforts to mobilize the people of Iraq'; '*requests* that the United States on behalf of the multinational force report to the Security Council on the efforts and progress of this force.' Signed by France, Russia, China, UK, US, Germany, Spain, Bulgaria, Chile, Mexico, Guinea, Cameroon, Angola, Pakistan and Syria. As Gowan remarks, this brazen twaddle evokes 'the seating of Pol Pot's representatives in the UN for fourteen years after his regime was overthrown by the DRV.'

Another way of assaying the UN's role in Iraq is to remember that it made a profit out of its own blockade and the consequent starvation of hundreds of thousands of Iraqi babies in the 1990s. As a fee for its part in administering the oil-for-food program, the UN helped itself to 2 per cent off the top. (On more than one account members of the UN-approved Governing Council, whose most conspicuous emblem is the bank-looter Ahmad Chalabi, are demanding a far heftier skim in the present looting of Iraq's national assets.)

Two months before the October resolution, the US's chosen instrument for selling the Governing Council, UN Special Envoy Vieira de Mello, was blown up in his office in Baghdad by persons with a realistic assessment of the function of the UN. Please, my friends, no more earnest calls for 'a UN role,' at least not until the body is radically reconstituted along genuinely democratic lines. As far as Iraq is concerned, all occupying forces should leave, with all contracts concerning Iraq's national assets and resources written across the last nine months repudiated, declared null and void, illegal under international covenant.

And finally, there is the matter of imperial motive. So why did the US want to invade Iraq in 2003 and finish off Saddam? There are as many rationales as there were murderers on Christie's Orient Express. In the end my mind goes back to something my friend the political scientist Doug Lummis wrote from his home in another outpost of the Empire, in Okinawa at the time of the first onslaught on Iraq at the start of the Nineties.

Iraq, Lummis wrote, had been in the Eighties a model of an oil producing country thrusting its way out of the Third World, with its oil nationalized, a good health system, and an efficient bureaucracy cowed from corrupt practices by a brutal regime. The fundamental intent of the prime imperial power was to thrust Iraq back, deep and ever deeper into Third World indigence, and of course to reappropriate Iraq's oil.

In the fall of 2003 I was in London and for a weekend enjoyed the hospitality of the first-class journalist Richard Gott, also of his wife Vivienne. At one point our conversation turned to this question of motive, and I was interested to hear Gott make the same point as Lummis, only about the attack of 2003. I asked him why he thought this, and Gott recalled a visit he'd made to Baghdad in the very early spring of 2003.

This was a time when the natural and political inclination of most opponents of the impending war was to stress the fearful toll of the sanctions imposed from 1990 onwards. Gott had a rather different observation, in part because of his experience in Latin America. Baghdad, he said, looked a lot more prosperous than Havana. 'It was clear today,' Gott wrote after his visit, 'from the quantity of goods in the shops, and the heavy traffic jams in the urban motorways, that the sanctions menace has been effectively defeated. Iraq is awakening from a long and depressing sleep, and its economy is clearly beginning to function once more. No wonder it is in the firing line.'

Eyes other than Gott's no doubt observed the same signs of

economic recovery. Iraq was rising from the ashes, and so, it had to be thrust down once more. The only 'recovery' permitted would be on Uncle Sam's terms. Or so Uncle Sam, in his arrogance, supposed.

Then, in January 2004, former US Treasury Secretary Paul O'Neill disclosed that George Bush had come into office planning to overthrow Saddam Hussein. MSNBC promptly polled its audience with the question, Did O'Neill betray Bush?

Was that really the big question? The White House had a sharper nose for the real meat of Leslie Stahl's *60 Minutes* interview with O'Neill and Ron Suskind, the reporter who based much of his exposé of the Bush White House, *The Price of Loyalty*, on 19,000 government documents O'Neill provided him.

What bothered the White House is one particular National Security Council document shown in the *60 Minutes* interview, clearly drafted in the early weeks of the new administration, which showed plans for the post-invasion dispersal of Iraq's oil assets among the world's great powers, starting with the major oil companies.

For the brief moment it was on the TV screen one could see that this bit of paper, stamped Secret, was undoubtedly one of the most explosive documents in the history of imperial conspiracy. Here, dead center in the camera's lense, was the refutation of every single rationalization for the attack on Iraq ever offered by George W. Bush and his co-conspirators, including Tony Blair.

That NSC document told *60 Minutes'* vast audience the attack on Iraq was not about national security in the wake of 9/11. It was not about weapons of mass destruction. It was not about Saddam Hussein's possible ties to Osama bin Laden. It was about stealing Iraq's oil, same way the British stole it three quarters of a century earlier. The major oil companies drew up the map, handed it to their man George, helped him (through such trusties as James Baker) steal the 2000 election, and then told him to get on with the attack.

O'Neill said that the Treasury Department's lawyers okayed release of the document to him. The White House, which took 78 days to launch an investigation into the outing of Valerie Plame as a CIA officer, clearly regarded the disclosure of what Big Oil wanted as truly reprehensible, as opposed to endangering the life of Ms Plame.

Forget about O'Neill 'betraying' Bush. How about Bush lying to the American people? It's obvious from that document that Bush, on the campaign trail in 2000, was as intent on regime change in Iraq as was Clinton in his second term and as Gore was publicly declaring himself to be.

Here's Bush in debate with Gore October 3, 2000:

If we don't stop extending our troops all around the world in nation-building missions, then we're going to have a serious problem coming down the road. I'm going to prevent that.

The second quote is from a joint press conference with Tony Blair on January 31, 2003. Bush's reply:

Actually, prior to September 11, we were discussing smart sanctions. We were trying to fashion a sanction regime that would make it more likely to be able to contain somebody like Saddam Hussein. After September 11, the doctrine of containment just doesn't hold any water. The strategic vision of our country shifted dramatically because we now recognize that oceans no longer protect us, that we're vulnerable to attack. And the worst form of attack could come from somebody acquiring weapons of mass destruction and using them on the American people. I now realize the stakes. I realize the world has changed. My most important obligation is to protect the American people from further harm, and I will do that.

In his cabinet meetings before 9/11 Bush may, in O'Neill's words, have been like a blind man in a room full of deaf people. But, as O'Neill also says, in those early strategy meetings Bush did say the plan from the start was to attack Iraq, using any pretext. Bush's language about 'smart sanctions' from the press conference at the start of last year was as brazen and far more momentous a lie as any of those that earned Bill Clinton the Republicans' impeachment charges.

INDEX